Detroit Monographs in Musicology

* * *

Explorations in Ethnomusicology:
Essays
in Honor of
David P. McAllester

edited by

Charlotte J. Frisbie

DETROIT MONOGRAPHS IN MUSICOLOGY   NUMBER 9
INFORMATION COORDINATORS   1986   DETROIT

Permission to reproduce material copyrighted in the United States
is gratefully acknowledged by the following contributors for the materials specified:

MARK SLOBIN
    Dakubu (1979:110), by permission of Mouton, The Hague.
    Baumann (1981:1, 9, 12), by permission of Gerd Baumann.
LEANNE HINTON
    McAllester (1979:182), by permission of *Ethnomusicology.*
    Bright (1963:26), by permission of *Ethnomusicology.*
    Herndon (1980:107), by permission of Norwood Editions, Norwood, Pa.
    Haefer (1981:134), by permission of J. Richard Haefer.
ADRIENNE L. KAEPPLER
    Freedman (1980:86), by permission of *Visual Communication.*
    Sapir (in Mandelbaum 1949:546), by permission of the University of California Press, Berkeley.
    Feld (1981), by permission of Steven Feld.
ASHENAFI KEBEDE
    McAllester (1979:181), by permission of *Ethnomusicology.*
    Materials from Kebede, *Roots of Black Music,* by permission of Spectrum Books/Prentice-Hall,
        Englewood Cliffs, New Jersey.
MARTIN HATCH
    Shiraishi (1981:103), by permission of *Indonesia.*
CHARLOTTE J. FRISBIE
    Hill (1940:24), by permission of *Plateau.*
JOANN W. KEALIINOHOMOKU
    Arnet (1974:10), Brasch (1977:55-56, 60), and Henry (1975:7), by permission of the American Indian
        Historical Society; Theisz (1965: n.p.), by permission of *Powwow Trails* through William K. Powers.
STEVEN FELD
    Diamond (1972:293-94), by permission of Jared M. Diamond.

Permission to reproduce photographs is gratefully acknowledged by Charles Capwell to the
Harvard University Archives and by David P. McAllester to Francis Cancian and William P. Malm.

Printed and bound in the United States of America
Published by
Information Coordinators, Inc.
1435-37 Randolph Street
Detroit, Michigan 48226

Editing by J. Bunker Clark
Book design by Nicholas Jakubiak
Photocomposition by Elaine Gorzelski, Kristin Gorzelski

Library of Congress Cataloging in Publication Data

    Explorations in ethnomusicology.

    (Detroit monographs in musicology ; no. 9)
    Bibliography: p.
    Includes indexes.
    1. McAllester, David Park, 1916-   . 2. Ethno-
musicology.   I. McAllester, David Park, 1916-
II. Frisbie, Charlotte Johnson.   III. Series.
ML3799.E9   1986   780'.01   86-21291
ISBN 0-89990-030-5

We shall not cease from exploration

And the end of all our exploring

Will be to arrive where we started

And know the place for the first time.

— T. S. Eliot

CONTENTS

ILLUSTRATIONS

MUSICAL EXAMPLES

ACKNOWLEDGEMENTS

A volume of collected essays depends on the interest, dedication, and cooperation of a number of people during all phases of preparation and production. In this particular instance, Susan W. McAllester deserves special thanks for her initial and continuing interest in the project, her moral support, and her willingness to supply lists of her husband's former and present students and colleagues, which were used to augment the editor's own lists. William O. Beeman contributed significantly to early discussions about the type of volume most appropriate for the honoree; while his original intention was to share in the editorial labors, his own 1981-82 schedule made that impossible.

Thanks are also due to the forty individuals who initially responded, indicating an interest in participating in the project, and the twenty-seven who produced abstracts of their potential essays. These abstracts were presented to David P. McAllester by Richard K. Winslow at the opening of the Wesleyan University celebration, "Navajo Art," held in McAllester's honor from January 27 through March 31, 1982. Special thanks go to Judith Gray, then a Ph.D. candidate at Wesleyan, for all of her work on that celebration, and to Richard K. Winslow for making the presentation, announcing the forthcoming volume, and for so doing with his usual finesse.

Conflicting academic and/or administrative commitments, research schedules, and other temporal demands regretfully necessitated the withdrawal of eleven authors who had originally planned to contribute essays to this volume. They included: William O. Beeman, Paul Berliner, Robert Black, John Blacking, Robert E. Brown, J. Richard Haefer, Jon B. Higgins, Norma McLeod, Carol E. Robertson, and Gen'ichi Tsuge. The untimely death, on June 28, 1982, of Joseph B. Casagrande who was coauthoring an essay with David K. Stigberg resulted in that essay being completed with the help of Norman Whitten, who has also had extensive field experience with the Salasaca. The editor expresses her thanks to Louis B. Casagrande of the Science Museum of Minnesota, and to Bruno Nettl, David Stigberg, and Norman Whitten of the University of Illinois, for help in resolving this particular situation.

Thanks are also due to Adrienne Kaeppler, Bill and Marla Powers, Bonnie Wade, Marcia Herndon, Susan McAllester, Bruno Nettl, Ted Frisbie, Mark Slobin, and Barbara Tedlock for suggestions made during discussions of potential publishers, and to Marcia, Bruno, Barbara, and Ted for their suggestions about other aspects of the volume's mechanics. To all individual authors, the editor wishes to express gratitude for their willingness to produce manuscripts within the allotted temporal framework and to expedite editorial queries efficiently, despite their own summer 1982 schedules. These individuals also deserve special

ACKNOWLEDGEMENTS

thanks for their *patience* during the unavoidable four-year gap between authorship and publication, and for their acceptance of the fact that "annual revisions" were disallowed, despite the temporal lag.

Recognition is also deserved by Susan W. McAllester, for assistance with preparing the illustrations for David's autobiography and Cynthia Brooks, former secretary of the Anthropology Department, Southern Illinois University at Edwardsville, for typing the original abstracts for presentation to McAllester. The rest of the department deserves thanks for 1981-82 postal and telephone support of the editorial labors, and Suzanne Jacobitti, former Dean of the School of Social Sciences, appreciation for assistance with photocopying. The Graduate School's Research and Projects office is also thanked for 1985-86 support of photocopying and proofreading assistance, as are Elizabeth Frisbie, Laura Buehler, and Jennifer Frisbie, for their help with this latter phase of production. Sincere appreciation is also expressed to J. Bunker Clark for his "in-house" editorial skills, relevant queries, and watchful eyes. In Detroit, the volume's production would not have been possible without the technical expertise and professional assistance of Elaine Gorzelski, Nicholas Jakubiak, and Kristin Gorzelski.

Finally, special thanks to the honoree, David P. McAllester, for preparing an autobiography/bibliography for this volume in the summer of 1982 and updating it at the end of December 1985, and for being the challenging teacher and supportive colleague that he has been through the years. A large number of individuals in anthropology and ethnomusicology have benefited from his wide-ranging interests, original thoughts, persistent queries, thorough research work, and his willingness to serve and contribute professionally to anthropology, ethnomusicology, and public education throughout the years. His career continues to be an active, exemplary one, and his productivity, humaneness, and inquisitiveness, a model for us all.

INTRODUCTION

While numerous definitions of ethnomusicology exist, chief among them is the study of music *in* culture, or the simultaneous consideration of musical and cultural phenomena. Those interested in the connections between music and anthropology have learned that the relationships are numerous, multifaceted, and comprehensible through exploratory devices which vary methodologically, topically, and theoretically. The present collection of essays is a tribute to a humanist who continues to be a leader in such explorations through his own work and his encouragement of that of students. Originally designed to honor his 1982 "partial retirement," the collection is emerging in 1986, the year of his "full retirement" from Wesleyan University. It seems fitting that a collection of essays in honor of David P. McAllester reflect not only some of the issues that have already occupied much of his own attention—such as music as part of culture, ethnomusicology of Native Americans, music and social change, linguistics and translation, and musicians as culture-bearing human beings—but also some of the topics currently receiving increased discussion in anthropology and its related disciplines, yet, as in the case of ethnoaesthetics, foreshadowed in some of his own earlier work.

The essays that follow could have been ordered in several different ways since many of them defy single thematic or topical classification. The headings which have been chosen are meant to reflect the main intent of the essays and to provide yet another sample of the diverse explorations which occupy the research efforts of ethnomusicologists interested in the relationships between music and anthropology.

In "Method, Theory, and History," Mark Slobin, Leanne Hinton, and Adrienne Kaeppler examine specific linguistic issues while advancing the discussion of the general applicability of linguistic methodology to the study of music as an integral part of culture. Bruno Nettl gives much needed attention to the effect that ethnomusicology's Western European roots have had on its methodological and theoretical development.

Another area of continuing importance in anthropological and ethnomusicological research is that of cultural change. In "The Question of Change," Charles Capwell examines social changes in the roles of the Bauls while Ashenafi Kebede discusses innovations and other examples of change in African music that are reflective of international developments. Martin Hatch moves the discussion to Java in his consideration of the effect of social and political change on the functions of music.

Interest in the people who make the music and in the ways in which they affect and are affected by their cultural systems continues to be strong. In "Musicians in Culture," both

Charlotte Frisbie and Bonnie Wade, using ethnohistorical data, augment the still minimal literature on relationships among music, musicians, and politics. Joann Kealiinohomoku provides a long-needed essay that examines Native American and outsiders' perceptions and misconceptions about "would-be Indians."

The importance of the perceptions and understandings that culture-bearers have of their own music, music-makers, and instruments has been receiving increased attention for over a decade in anthropology, ethnomusicology, folklore, choreology, and other disciplines. In "Symbol and Meaning," Marcia Herndon and William Powers use two different Native American groups to show how perception of the situation and contextual information significantly affect meaning. Steven Feld's essay shifts the setting to Papua New Guinea for an in-depth analysis of the symbolic meanings of the sound of the Kaluli drum.

The diversity of ethnomusicological interests is further exemplified in "The Art and the Arts." In the first essay in this section, the late Joseph Casagrande and David Stigberg, using ethnographic data and musical analysis techniques, document the Salasacan tradition of music-making with cherry leaves, thereby substantially augmenting existing information about this performance practice in highland Ecuador and identifying some of the many challenges that await future inquiry. Ruth Stone and Barbara Tedlock move the discussion from the art to the arts by focusing on ethnoaesthetics. Using information from two different world areas, they indicate the possibilities that await those willing first to learn to understand native definitions of aesthetics in one of the arts, and then to open the inquiry to all sensory domains in a culture.

The volume ends with an autobiographical sketch and current bibliography of the honoree. The former, which he volunteered to prepare, is based on journals kept through the years. Since David McAllester is one of the founding fathers of the Society for Ethnomusicology, this essay is, in itself, an addition to the "history" of the discipline.

It is hoped that these essays, which express opinions of individual authors, will collectively serve both to reflect some of the directions of current research in ethnomusicology, and to stimulate additional work, further refinement, and an active, ongoing interest in these and other issues in the future. A commitment to active exploration, yet exploration which is humane, sensitive, and tempered by time for contemplation and reflection, is indeed one of the many facets of David P. McAllester's imprint on anthropology and music.

CHARLOTTE J. FRISBIE

Southern Illinois University at Edwardsville
February 1986

PART I

METHOD, THEORY, AND HISTORY

Multilingualism in Folk Music Cultures

Mark Slobin
Wesleyan University

A great many of the world's folksongs have been, and still are, sung by multilingual singers. This simple fact has not received the attention it deserves in our work on language and music. Most studies, often for very good reasons, tend to assume a monolingual singer. For example, a scholar seeking to define a distinctive ethnic or "national" style may look for songs in a single language, ignoring "influences" from neighboring peoples. The more abstract theorists who align linguistic and musicological theory, reasonably enough, proceed with one language at a time.

The present brief contribution[1] attempts only to outline the scope of multilingualism in folk music cultures and to suggest in a preliminary way the inherent research potential of this approach. I will point out some avenues of exploration and introduce examples from world areas where beginning research has started to yield interesting insights. My working hypothesis is that, for folksingers, multilingualism can provide the material for personal and cultural strategies not available to monolinguals.

It seems to me that there are two basic viewpoints from which to examine multilingualism in folk music cultures in an introductory way. One might approach the question holistically. This would mean investigating multilingualism as a general phenomenon within an entire music culture, or coexisting, co-territorial music cultures. It would include the study of the historical determinants and cultural underpinnings affecting musical choices.

The other way to address the issue is from the standpoint of individuals. Looking at singers whose repertory includes items in more than one language, what can we say about this factor in their singing lives? Here we may have to look beyond cultural formants to biographical and psychological aspects. In the balance of the present essay, I would like to sketch briefly the basics of both avenues to multilingual folk musics, beginning with the holistic viewpoint.

Let us begin at the far end of the multilingualism continuum. In some regions where ethnic groups and languages are tightly bundled over a long period of time, a kind of cultural knot is tied. Though the individual strands can be identified, at the point of juncture a Gordian merging occurs which only an Alexandrian scholar tries to cut. Linguists refer to such a situation as *Sprachbund*. In my work on northern Afghanistan (Slobin 1976), I describe such

---

[1] The present essay is a slightly amplified version of a paper delivered at the International Symposium on Music and the Language Mode of the International Folk Music Council, Kolobrzeg, Poland, May 1981.

a situation among the co-territorial Uzbeks and Tajiks. Two languages, the former Turkic and the latter Iranian, along with associated musics, had coexisted for nearly five hundred years. This resulted in a pattern of convergence, more marked in some districts than others. In certain areas, the Uzbek language was heavily Tajikized, and vice versa. Musically, I found teahouse musicians performing for a mixed ethnic audience, purveying a consensus music involving improvised quatrains that often showed the effects of bilingualism. Performers from a crossroads town at the juncture of the two ethnic/language/musical style areas specialized in this eclecticism and some were themselves considered ethnically ambiguous. Here the inter-ethnic contact situation had settled into a complex series of adjustments of which the multi-musical element was just one symptom: in Afghan Turkestan there was no way to discuss either Uzbek or Tajik music in complete isolation.

A more radical *Sprachbund* situation exists in an area of Eastern Europe described by the Soviet musicologist V. I. Elatov (1977). At the intersection of the Russian, Belorussian, and Ukrainian music areas, there is a triangular area Elatov calls the GBCh (Gomel'-Briansk-Chernigov) Region. Members of the three local ethnic groups have formed a fused musico-linguistic cultural unit, a sort of *Musik-und-Sprachbund*:

> Over the course of the whole history of their existence, first at the level of
> individual peoples, and then as independent nations, the Russians, Ukrainians,
> and Belorussians on the territory of the GBCh Region have shown an enviable
> unit in the formation of a common folksong repertoire and in the working out
> of specific stylistic musical norms [Elatov 1977:6].

First, Elatov demonstrates the marked linguistic convergence of the three local languages. Then he points to a jointly-held repertory and approach to folksinging. What his data indicate is an absence of distinctively ethnic songs, so that the GBCh Region stands out, in a sense, due to its grayness rather than to its color. It seems the population has chosen to retain archaic song styles which antedate the more recent, strongly ethnic repertories of the surrounding regions.

My concern here is not with such extreme cases of fusion, but it is well worth citing these examples to indicate one type of choice available in a multilingual region: convergence. We often tend to view convergence as a result of the intensive acculturation so prominent in recent times as a result of "westernization" and "modernization," those bogeymen who force cultures to surrender older values along the road to world musical standardization. What I am suggesting through the Afghan and GBCh Region examples is that patterns of ethnic accommodation are quite old and can result in a mutually agreed-upon cultural truce where the existence of multilingualism is a key factor in compromise.

The main body of multilingual songs probably occurs outside fusion situations, as part of everyday patterns of inter-ethnic contact. A number of my examples come from Eastern Europe, as this is a region where scholarship has long been cognizant of the importance of musical meeting grounds. In 1932 the Ukrainian researcher Filaret Kolessa pointed to the extraordinary uniformity of certain genres, as well as specific songs, among the Ukrainians, Slovaks, Czechs, and Poles of the Carpathian region, which covers a large territory. He focused specifically on one group, the Lemki, as being the epicenter of this phenomenon. Kolessa (1932) raised the possibility that the transhumant mountain Lemki acted as a channel for the dissemination of folksongs across a wide stretch of space, even influencing the Hungarians adjacent to the Carpathians. Of particular interest is the variety of common traits Kolessa found in his corpus of songs. All the ethnic groups apparently shared certain basic topics in their balladry and lyrical songs. Furthermore, within these particular genres there was a whole series of direct translations from one language to another. Kolessa pointed out the commonality of the Western Slavic languages, which fosters musical closeness, and pinpointed specific similarities in the metrics of the song types. He therefore suggested a specific cross-ethnic Carpathian folksong cycle.

The details of this situation are not germane here. What emerges from Kolessa's work is that a high degree of multilingualism correlates with very concrete and specific aspects of the folksong repertory in a given region. It was not possible, in 1932, for Kolessa to examine ethnic folksongs as isolated products of monolingual singers. One had to think of folksingers as people who use their knowledge of more than one language creatively, to enrich individual and group repertories and to build a common regional stock of songs. We do not find the convergence pattern of the GBCh Region here; translation, not fusion of languages, is the norm. What we do see is the spreading out into the music culture of ideas from neighboring groups, evident in the sharing of specific topics of song texts. This suggests that multilingualism works through stimulus diffusion, influencing parallelism of choices based on multiple models, not just in point diffusion, where specific song texts are adapted across language lines.

Of course, the ethnomusicologist will want to know why multilingualism produces particular results in specific instances. This can only be answered on a case-by-case basis, and we have remarkably few published examples to draw on in order to build hypotheses. From the functionalist's point of view, there must be a good solid reason for the sorts of influences we are citing here. Perhaps there is political domination by one group, or there are ritual reasons for the incorporation of outside text items. I believe that a whole range of rather complex, often shifting reasons might be found. Let us look at two recent studies, both from African data, that attempt to delineate the specifics of multilingualism.

The African scholar Dakubu (1979) has written a short study appropriately entitled "Other People's Words." It seems that speakers of the Ga language in Ghana incorporate both English words and phrases plus items from the neighboring Akan languages into certain songs. Dakubu concludes by speculating on the motivation for this phenomenon:

> Ultimately, Akan and English words occur in Ga songs because these are the languages of powerful states whose cultures exerted what might have been an overwhelming influence on Ga culture and the Ga language for a long time, and still do. This fact seems to rest rather lightly on the singers of Ga songs. They seem far more interested in what they can do with this additional material than in what it may ever have done to them [Dakubu 1979:110].

In other words, Dakubu suggests that beyond historical preconditions may lie another reason for the multilingualism of Ga songs: a folk aesthetic which regards the total pool of words, from whatever sources, as raw material for the shaping of songs. Dakubu begs the question a bit by leaving open the specifics of that aesthetic, not making entirely clear why particular items from given languages are chosen and how they fit into an overall pattern.

A rather more comprehensive study comes from the Sudan, where Gerd Baumann (1981) has attempted an analysis of multilingualism in the songs of the Miri, a people of the Nuba Mountain region. He arrives at two conclusions; the first supports Dakubu's tilt towards an aesthetic interest in multilingual borrowing, while the second reaches for another level of analysis:

> 1) songs show patterns of absorption of, and resistance to, linguistic change which follow genre-specific considerations of musical aesthetics, rather than linguistic convenience;

> 2) the specific combination of music and language in certain songs is understood
> as establishing a new discourse which is perhaps best to be called "myth"
> [Baumann 1981:1].

The Miri, a numerically small people, are exposed to modern life styles tied to the Arabic language. They sing songs in both languages. Conveniently for analysis, those in Miri are inseparable from the Miri ethnic way of life, while those in Arabic speak to the newer model the Miri observe among Arab speakers:

> In a Miri language song, to change but a personal name, a location, or a date,
> will affect the contents, as it is about known people, real things, and specific
> events. By contrast, an Arabic language song can, and very many do, replace
> one personal name by another, and one thing by another. . . . If Miri language
> songs can be compared to films, Arabic language songs are like photographic
> stills: they describe not a process of doing, but a state of being; their characters
> are not actors, but models, their things not real, but props; their words not
> things, but symbols [Baumann 1981:9].

So for Baumann, the use of language is synonymous with a cultural pattern of ambivalence, an interest in two parallel but opposed life styles: the traditional Miri way and that of the "dream world of Arab-style comfort," of "The Good Life" (ibid.). This is what he means by "myth," so he concludes that:

> If language and music do indeed, in specific combination and at specific
> historical junctures, establish the discourse of myth, then it becomes all the more
> necessary to view music as an active force which, of its own momentum, reacts
> WITH, rather than TO, the language mode [Baumann 1981:12].

I am not sure Baumann's definition of "myth" as part of a musical/cultural process is as yet focused. The idea that language and music must be seen as two equal, dynamic systems, is one which has been accepted for some time. What is salient, however, about his argument for our purposes is the suggestion that situations of multiple languages and musics can offer some really fruitful, otherwise unavailable examples of the specific ways in which these two systems interact. In the Miri case, opposed song styles as a paradigm of a cultural dichotomy present us with a very different use of multilingualism than the inter-ethnic accommodation pattern of Eastern Europe and northern Afghanistan cited earlier.

Having briefly surveyed multilingualism as a holistic phenomenon embracing entire music cultures, I would like now to turn to the question of the individual multilingual folksinger. We might think of such musicians as people who build a personal repertory from a pool of songs in more than one language. This leads to a linguistic stratification of the individual's song world, a fact I find to be of more than passing interest. It is at the micro-level of such highly personal choices that one can gain valuable insights into the processes that shape the music culture as a whole. I will take my examples from Jewish materials, both in the Mediterranean area and in Eastern Europe. The Jews offer a particularly rich case to examine: multilingualism has been built into their varied regional cultures for two thousand years. Internally, many Jewish communities have their own, in-group bilingualism involving Hebrew, the tongue of sacred texts, and a colloquial language, itself a fusion of several linguistic sources linked to the immediate ethnic surroundings of a given Jewish community. Added to this inbuilt multilingualism is the need to acquire one, often several, local non-Jewish languages for trade and daily social intercourse with surrounding populations.

In the Mediterranean area, the Jews are Sephardic, that is, descendants of the Jewish population of Spain which was expelled five centuries ago as part of Christian reconquest of Iberia from Muslim rule. These Jews moved along the entire Mediterranean littoral, from Morocco to Egypt, Turkey, and the Balkans. Musical multilingualism was a way of life for the Sephardim, articulated differently in each local area. The Israeli writer Amnon Shamosh has vividly described the situation for his native town of Halab (Aleppo), Syria, and the musical consequences:

> Halab . . . was the meeting point of three cultures. . . . It was Arabic at home, French in society and on the street, and Hebrew in the synagogue. . . . We spoke a jargon which was composed of Arabic, in its unique Allepine accent, with touches of French, Ladino [the pan-Sephardic, Spanish-based language] and Hebrew. To this day, a Jew from Aleppo is easily recognized by his speech, be his birthplace Mexico, Panama, Japan, Buenos Aires, or Brooklyn [Shamosh 1979:5].

> I sensed all this many years before I comprehended it. Already at the age of five, when I commenced my first "career" as a singer to entertain celebrating adults, I chose my songs accordingly: there would be one by Abdul Wahab, another of Maurice Chevalier, and *Adon Olam* [a Hebrew hymn] to round off the repertoire. And if an encore was demanded, I would let them beg a little, shut my eyes artistically, begin with *Mipi-El* [Hebrew], go on with *Ala Dal'una* and end with the *Marseillaise*. . . . I'd descend from my chair to receive my favourite reward: praise, kisses and sweets [Shamosh 1979:6].

Why the acclaim? Presumably because the precocious child has grasped the essence of his family circle's culture, which lies in an unruffled eclecticism. It is part of their heritage as well as of their toolkit for strategic survival in an alien, often threatening non-Jewish culture. For the individual, the process of selecting a personal edition of the available cultural encyclopedia becomes an understood fact of life.

A recent study (Shallon 1982) of the Turkish-Sephardic community of Seattle underlines and amplifies the point just raised. Linguistic and musical eclecticism was part and parcel of the life of these people in Turkey, yet varied enormously from individual to individual, depending on personal context. One informant was extremely proud of his ability to chant long passages of the Qur'an, learned while temporarily attending the local Muslim school. Obviously, there is nothing typically Jewish about such behavior, but it underlines a strong desire to use one's potential for multilingualism, even in the case of a culturally inappropriate repertory.

In fact, what is distinctive about this group of Sephardim is not so much their retention of fifteenth-century Spanish balladry, the trait for which they are coveted by scholars, but their heavy investment in eclecticism. For some singers, it meant recording careers in the early decades of the twentieth century, when Jewish musicians performed in a variety of languages for commercial release. However, in the American context this versatility is no longer of strategic value. Rather, it has tended to isolate the older generation of Sephardim. Multilingualism as a musical way of life makes sense only in the presence of the formative linguistic and musical communities, which simply do not exist on the coast of the Pacific Ocean the way they did along the Mediterranean. Thus, the question of transmission to the next generation becomes highly problematic. In the Seattle case, it is via Hebrew alone, which still continues as the sacred tongue, that such handing down is possible, as Ladino, Turkish, Arabic, and Greek are not viable choices for the American-born generations. The multilingual context that spawned a set of musical biographies has vanished; communal continuity must be rephrased in a set of choices involving only Hebrew and English. A new eclecticism emerges on American soil.

From this fairly broad picture of how individuals fit into a complex web of multilingual music-making, I would like to move, in conclusion, to the highly personal factors involved in song selection. For a number of Eastern European Jewish singers we have ample documentation of the slow accretion of repertory.[2] The case of a woman like Lifsha Schaechter Widman is typical in its singularity. Born near the turn of the century in a Bukovina village, she was located on the far edge of the Austro-Hungarian cultural-administrative sphere. At the other end of the bridge across the nearby river was the Russian Empire, where her relatives grew up in a markedly different cultural, linguistic, and musical context. The early phase of Widman's life, through age thirteen when she left for America on her own, was a time of avid song acquisition from a wide variety of sources and languages. She learned German early from aunts and in her one year of formal education. The stock of German songs thus acquired became crucial in her emigration experience. As her route to America lay across German-speaking territory and via a German shipping line, her ability to perform songs stood her in good stead on numerous occasions. She became something of a leader among her refugee group at temporary detention centers and on board ship where, for example, singing for the German crew was rewarded with coveted oranges for Widman and her friends. Such experiences leave their mark on folksingers, charging particular items with special electricity.

Widman's American phase lasted through 1914, when, unluckily, she returned to Europe to find a husband just in time to be delayed for thirty-odd years due to the outbreak of World War I. From this brief New York period she remembers an Irving Berlin song as peddled by a street singer. It was the song Berlin wrote on losing his first wife, "When I Lost You." Perhaps it is not too speculative to imagine Widman tying Berlin's sense of loss to her own situation. Upon surviving two world wars and the Holocaust, she returned to America. Each phase, each locale, and a great many key people in her life continued to add items in a number of languages to her expanding repertory. For Widman, as for so many multilingual singers, material is not necessarily stored by language, but by association. It is not enough to say that since she lived in a multiethnic world, she ended up with a patchwork repertory. Eclecticism does not mean indiscriminate absorption of diverse sources, but rather choosiness in building a personal musical world. Multilingual singers, like polyglot speakers, may not be aware of slipping from one language to another in singing unless the exact memory or bond to the song text is brought up by the interviewer. Such attitudes go against an assumption of clear lines of demarcation between "our" music and "their" music. That this is the case among Jewish singers is striking, since this is a group well known for maintaining, and/or having forced upon them, strong ethnic boundaries.

The assimilation of the same "outside" item into the repertories of two different Eastern European Jewish folksingers drives home the point of personal choice and context. Lifsha Schaechter Widman sang the Schubert song "Ständchen" ("Serenade"), because it was in the air in her Austro-Hungarian village. In performing the song, as I have discussed elsewhere (Slobin 1980), she effectively turned Schubert into an Eastern European Jewish songwriter through musical adaptation, cutting short the composer's through-composed structure to form the standard Yiddish-language folksong quatrain. This truncation also retains the minor mode as the prevalent key, typical of her group's repertory. In addition, her singing style introduces glides and ornaments in places typical of the Jewish folksong.

---

[2] The research cited is from the data of the YIVO Yiddish Folksong Project, a NEH-funded project directed by Barbara Kirshenblatt-Gimblett and cited with her permission.

Henryk Rubinlicht, a Polish urban Jew, was interviewed for the documentary film *Image before My Eyes* (1980), a chronicle of pre-Holocaust Polish Jewish life. He discusses his sadness at being drafted into the Polish Army in 1919. He speaks of parting from his girlfriend, and of the song he sang to her that evening. This is the "Ständchen," with a Polish text he himself composed for the occasion. The fact that he was able to sing it in a tender, dreamy manner sixty years later echoes the poignancy of that moment. That he used Polish indicates his urban Jewish origins: one sister became a sculptor, another a prominent actress, all cultural activities far removed from Widman's rural village. What is striking about the contrast of the two Schubert variants is that it is the singer who was more removed from the source of high culture and concert life who was faithful to the Schubert original in text, but less faithful in music. The man from the city took the melody for granted, including the modulation from minor to major, and used the text as the arena for creativity. Once again, one has to view language and music as equal, interactive systems to grasp the nature of folksong process, and to take the existence of multilingualism as a basic component of the equation.

In this brief study I do not pretend to state impressive conclusions on multilingualism in folk music cultures. What I have tried to show is how subtly multilingual singers handle their linguistic resources; they seem to use them as a factor for creative choice. A similar situation seems apparent from the little work that has been done for folk music cultures as a whole. The analysis could easily spread into the domain of popular music as well. In his study of Ukrainian-Canadian "country" music, Robert Klymasz (1972:376) carefully delineates stimulus diffusion from English song texts to Ukrainian among bilingual songwriters. Just as Kolessa showed common metric schemes in Western Slavic languages to aid in adaptation of song texts, so Klymasz points out that similarities in prosody between Ukrainian and English leads to similar transplanting. Broadening our survey to include such popular song processes reinforces my belief that multilingualism is both widespread and significant, yet neglected, in our continuing study of the world's music.

References Cited

Baumann, Gerd
   1981   "Language Music and the Discourse of Myth." Paper delivered at the International Symposium on Music and the Language Mode, Kolobrzeg, Poland, May 1981.

Dakubu, M. E. Kropp
   1979   "Other People's Words: An Aspect of Style in Ga Songs." *Language and Society: Anthropological Issues*, ed. W. McCormack and S. Wurm, pp. 89-110. The Hague: Mouton.

Elatov, V. I.
   1977   *Pesni Vostochno-Slavianskoi Obshchnosti*. Minsk: Nauka i Tekhnika.

Klymasz, Robert B.
   1972   "Sounds You Never Heard Before: Ukrainian Country Music in Western Canada." *Ethnomusicology* 16:372-80.

Kolessa, F.
   1932   "Karpatskii tsikl narodnikh pisen." *Sbornik praci I. Sjezdu slovanskych filolgu v Praze 1929*, part 2, pp. 93-114.

Shamosh, Amnon
1979   *My Sister the Bride.* Tel Aviv: Massada.

Slobin, Mark
1976   *Music in the Culture of Northern Afghanistan.* Tucson: University of Arizona Press.

1980   "The Uses of Printed Versions in Studying the Song Repertoire of East European Jews: First Findings." *The Field of Yiddish: Studies in Language, Folklore, and Literature, Fourth Collection*, ed. B. Kirshenblatt-Gimblett, D. Miron, R. Wisse, pp. 329-70. Philadelphia: ISHI.

Shallon, Michele
1982   "Sephardic Music in Seattle." B.A. thesis, Wesleyan University, Music Department.

Musical Diffusion and Linguistic Diffusion

Leanne Hinton
University of California, Berkeley

> What we've been calling musicology and ethnomusicology might better be
> called "mixmusicology": the term would remind us that the process of music
> making is the process of change and the assimilation of new ideas. . . .
> For the most part, this process goes on unabashed. Living musics are not
> concerned with aesthetic purity. They simply rejoice in any lovely new
> sound that catches the ear of the composer [McAllester 1979:182].

Every culture in the world presumably has language, and every culture also has
music. These two departments of human culture have some important
similarities and points of contact; perhaps the most obvious of these lies in the
fact that language and music are the two most important ways in which man
uses sound. . . . We can distinguish two main types of link between language
and music: their mutual influence in singing, and their structural similarity. The
remainder of this paper will discuss these two topics, which, although logically
distinct, both constitute areas for cooperation between linguistics and musicology
[Bright 1963:26].

There can be no doubt that music and language are overlapping phenomena, as is
especially obvious in song — the genre that combines the two. This essay[1] investigates areal
studies in music and language — showing how these studies have proceeded in the two fields,
and what sorts of new insights can be reached by an approach combining them.

Linguistic and Musical Areas: Ecology or Diffusion?

In a recent monograph, Herndon (1980) addresses the issue of musical areas and their
relation to linguistic areas. Since her discussion is based on some widely held but misleading

---

[1] I am grateful to many people for their help on this essay, provided mainly in the form of conversations. Among
those who have had input into some of the ideas expressed here are David Fredrickson, Mark Hansell, Margaret
Langdon, Pamela Munro, Mike Nichols, David Shaul, Joel Sherzer, Donald Bahr, Richard Haefer, and all the
participants of the recent Workshop on Ritual Music, organized by Ellen Basso and hosted by the University of
Arizona, March 4-6, 1982. Most of them, I should add, will find things they disagree with in this essay; they are
not to be blamed for my errors.

assumptions about areal studies in general and linguistics in particular, I beg her forgiveness for bringing up some of her points here only to disagree with them. To begin with, she states that "the assumption underlying the creation of areas is basically ecological . . . in that it is assumed that the physical characteristics of a region will exert similar influences on the people who inhabit the area . . . " (ibid.: 93).

No one can doubt that the physical environment plays an important role in certain fundamental aspects of culture. However, few modern scholars — especially those studying language or music — would place ecology at the head of the list of factors responsible for the areas their studies delineate. Instead, *diffusion* — a primarily social phenomenon[2] — is seen as the major source of similarity between neighboring groups of different origins. Language, in particular, has been shown to be quite free from environmental influences in all but the most shallow respects (for example, languages spoken in areas where the salmon run will have a word for salmon). Few phonological or grammatical traits of language have been shown to have an origin in the biophysical environment. An exception is onomatopoeia, wherein sounds are used to imitate the sounds of processes in the environment. Frequently such utterances utilize sounds that are not otherwise present in the language — such as a child's imitation of a machine gun or a siren. As will be seen later in this essay, onomatopoeia and related phenomena do play a role in linguistic diffusion.

Music, more than language, may have some indirect ties to the physical environment. Some scholars have attempted to show the relations between some aspects of musical style and social structure (Lomax 1968); and many anthropologists have closely examined the relationship between social structure and ecology (see Vayda 1969). To the extent that these studies are found to be valid, there might be said to be a very indirect relationship between the physical environment and music, via social structure. Nevertheless, whether a group in North America has "paired-phrase patterning" or "the rise" has no direct relationship to the physical characteristics of the region in which it lives. In music, as in language, the major source of similarity between neighboring groups must be found in diffusion.

Linguistic Families and Linguistic Areas

A second quotation from Herndon is a critique of Nettl's areal studies of music (e.g., Nettl 1954):

> Nettl identifies six regional [musical] styles. These style areas coincide, to some extent, with cultural areas previously identified by others; however, they are at variance with language families. Since most Native American music is vocal, this raises a number of questions about the validity of culture traits, particularly musical ones [ibid.: 107].

Herndon's doubts about the validity of musical areas are based on two questionable assumptions: (1) she equates musical and cultural areas with linguistic *families* rather than linguistic *areas*; (2) she assumes that because Native American music is primarily vocal, it must therefore behave like language does in terms of its distributional patterns.

---

[2] Diffusion itself is, of course, a process which needs explanation. No one knows why it is that out of a hundred possible traits, it is a particular five or six that diffuse. Some of the explanation for diffusion may itself be environmental, but the larger portion is explained by social factors rather than environmental ones.

Comparison must be made between musical areas and linguistic *areas*, rather than linguistic families. Linguistic families are groups of languages that can be traced to a common ancestor, such as Portuguese, French, Italian, and Spanish which all derive from Vulgar Latin and are called the Romance family; or, in North America, Navajo, Apache, Hupa, Beaver, and other languages which are all of the Athabascan family. A linguistic *area*, on the other hand, is a geographic area containing a number of languages from different language families, but in which many of the languages share certain linguistic traits. For example, throughout the Northwest Coast and Northern California, most languages have glottalized stops. The languages come from many different families, and members of those same families that are outside the area in question usually do not have glottalized stops. It is believed that the cause for the prevalence of glottalized stops in that area is diffusion.

General Principles of Diffusion

That traits diffuse from one language to another cannot be disputed. Similarly, traits may also diffuse from one musical tradition to another, as must be obvious when one considers such phenomena as the use of European instruments in South American Indian music, the large audiences in any American city attending Italian opera (sung by Americans), and so on. That musical traits diffuse from one language group to another in North America is very obvious when one observes, for example, the deep similarity of musical traditions among Uto-Aztecan languages and Yuman languages in Southern California. Not only are all the traits of the singing style described by Nettl present in both language families, but the styles are the same, right down to having many of the same genres and the same song cycles. Uto-Aztecan and Yuman singers can even be found singing the same songs together at social gatherings.

There is at least a rough correlation between culture areas, linguistic areas, and musical areas. (See Sherzer 1968 for the most general work available on linguistic areas in North America and how they correlate with culture areas.) However, the boundaries between areas are never exact (groups will often show characteristics of more than one culture area), nor can the correlation between linguistic, musical, or cultural areas ever be exact, because different sorts of traits have different sorts of diffusional patterns. Whether or not a given trait diffuses from one group to another depends on the patterns of social interaction between the two groups. For example, material objects (and the words naming them) may be passed from group to group for long distances along trade routes, while other items (such as a particular grammatical structure) may diffuse from one group to another only by means of intensive social contact involving widespread bilingualism.

This brings us to Herndon's second assumption mentioned above: that music and language must behave the same in terms of their distributional patterns. Just as a word for a particular material object may show a different pattern of diffusion than will a grammatical structure or even another word, so may some musical traits show different patterns of diffusion than linguistic traits, or even than other musical traits. The problem of diffusion, which I have argued is the basis of areal studies, is very complex, tied up with all the intricacies of social interaction. I will argue later in this essay that vocal music does indeed diffuse in a way rather different from spoken language, partly because of the differing social roles of music and speech, and partly due to the differing natures of vocal music and speech. I will also argue that vocal music may serve as a hitherto unrecognized source of linguistic diffusion.

Areal Studies in Linguistics and Musicology

It is interesting to note that while linguistic areas and musical areas are analogous, there is nothing in ethnomusicology that corresponds to the linguistic family. Musicologists studying the indigenous traditions of the Americas have concentrated heavily on the delineation of musical areas, and have not attempted to develop the notion of a "musical family" analogous to the "linguistic family." The fact that "musical families" have not been set up is itself an important piece of evidence that language and music have differing diffusional patterns. It might be suggested that musical characteristics spread so rapidly that more long-standing similarities that would show a common heritage between communities tend to be obscured over a relatively short period of time. Languages, in turn, are conservative, sufficiently impervious to drastic change to maintain evidence of common heritage over several thousand years. It is extremely common for communities speaking related languages to have completely different musical traditions. As already demonstrated, one can expect musical styles to have a distribution corresponding roughly to linguistic areas, *not* linguistic families.

Nevertheless, it is possible that an attempt to study familial or genetic relationships between musical traditions could bear fruit. To the extent that it is true that related languages came from a common ancestral language spoken in a single community, it can be inferred that at one time they had a common musical tradition. By searching out musical traits that two linguistically-related communities have in common, it might be possible to infer what some of the traits of the ancestral musical tradition could have been.

Nevertheless, it does seem that the reconstruction that would be allowed by this sort of study will provide us with much less information than does linguistic reconstruction. Musical traits appear to spread faster and further than linguistic traits, obscuring factors of common heritage, sooner than would be the case with languages. This is evidenced by communities that speak languages that are clearly genetically unrelated but still display virtually identical musical cultures.

Linguistic Aspects of Musical Areas

It is not, of course, always the case that musical diffusion results in identical musical cultures. A community may borrow a single song or song style or instrument while still retaining its own independent musical character. In this section, I would like to identify certain traits of music that may spread from group to group without showing complete identity in musical style.

In general, musicologists doing areal studies have concentrated either on instrumentation (Roberts 1936, Brown 1967) or on musical style (Nettl 1954); for example, range and melodic form. Rarely have the song texts themselves been used in studies of musical areas. I will suggest here some aspects of song texts that could profitably be studied from an areal point of view. Sadly, song texts have rarely been studied at all from an analytic point of view of the sort I am suggesting here. Normally (with some notable exceptions such as McAllester 1954, Frisbie 1980, and Bahr and Haefer 1978), ethnomusicologists have concentrated more heavily on musical aspects of songs, and linguists generally consider song texts to be outside their field of study. I am basing most of my suggestions primarily on certain interesting aspects of Havasupai songs that may in some instances show up in areal patterns. When I know of a trait's presence elsewhere in the Southwest or in neighboring regions I will point it out. But these are not to be considered areal traits, but only *possible* areal traits — for the research has not yet been done.

1. *Vocables.* The presence of vocables ("nonsense syllables") are relatively prominant throughout North America, and can well be seen as an areal feature of the continent as a whole. Nevertheless, comparative studies of degree of prominence and type of vocables within North America could be very enlightening. As for phonological type, there are probably universal constraints on vocable form (Hinton 1980a), but nevertheless, within those constraints, the segments chosen for prominence are very likely to show areal patterns of distribution. For example, in the Great Basin, Papago, and in Arizona Yuman, the velar nasal [ŋ] is very common in vocables, but it is absent in most of California and in many other parts of the country.

Another aspect of vocable construction that may have areal significance is the use of affixes as vocables. That is to say, certain grammatical affixes of fairly general meaning (such as demonstratives and aspect markers) may be used so generally in songs that they are obviously semantically empty and there primarily for their sound value. This is described for Havasupai in some detail (Hinton 1980a, 1984), and there is some indication that the phenomenon exists elsewhere, at least in the Southwest (Sherzer 1981). But it has not been studied enough to tell its distribution.

2. *Phonological Considerations.* Many phonological aspects of song texts should be studied for areal distribution. Havasupai, Hopi (Foster 1982), and Papago (Bahr and Haefer 1978) all show a phenomenon of vowel-lowering, so that /i/ approaches [e] and /u/ approaches [o] in quality. As with all the traits I am discussing here, the extent of distribution of this phenomenon is unknown due to insufficient study.

Another phonological trait common to Havasupai, Hopi, and Papago as well as other Southwestern musical styles is a tendency toward a CV syllable-type in songs. In some languages this reflects the same syllable-type found in speaking, but in other languages such as Havasupai, where consonant clusters abound in speech, this syllable-type can only be created through vowel-insertion.

In Hopi and Havasupai, at least, the one exception to the rule of CV syllable structure in songs can be found in line-end position, where an -*m* may be inserted. This pattern of line-end insertion of -*m* may also have areal significance.

Yet another phonological trait of interest is consonant mutation. Havasupai, Hopi, and Papago all show traits such as the replacement of spoken /v/ by sung /w/, and so forth. (See Hinton 1980a for a more detailed analysis in Havasupai; Bahr and Haefer 1978 show the phenomenon in their transcriptions of Papago songs; Foster 1982 describes it in Hopi.) A general study of whether consonant mutation exists and what the specific choices of mutation are would be very worthwhile.

Related to consonant and vowel mutation is the tendency in languages with vowel nasalization to replace nasal vowels with an oral vowel-nasal consonant combination. This is done in Navajo and Shoshone (Booth 1975; in Shoshone vowel nasalization is prevalent but not analyzed as phonemic), as well as in French; it may in fact be universal rather than areal in nature.

Another characteristic that needs to be examined is the differing patterns of stress in song traditions, reflecting and constraining metric patterns. Here Havasupai and Papago differ: Havasupai stressed syllables fall in the penultimate position of a line, whereas Papago stress usually falls earlier. This difference may purely be subject to constraints of the stress patterns in spoken language, but only more detailed study can determine whether or not it has areal significance beyond those constraints.

Another difference between Havasupai and Papago is the treatment of vowel-length in songs. In Papago, long vowels are given greater time-value than short vowels in songs

(Bahr 1982); in Havasupai, vowel-length is neutralized in song. These differing patterns may also show areal distribution.

3. *Grammatical Features.* Certain traits listed above are partially grammatical, such as the treatment of affixes as vocables. Other features that might be looked at include the grammatical structure of texts and the emphasis of particular grammatical features in song.

In Havasupai, a musical line (in songs containing real words) consists grammatically of a single noun or verb plus accompanying affixes and particles. This special construction of a line is related to stress/meter, for it allows only one primary stress per line. We would do well to know to what extent this formula for the stress and grammatical structure of lines shows areal distribution.

Also in Havasupai, auxiliary verbs and demonstrative particles are used very heavily in song, representing well over half of the lexical items present in a song with real words. Of course, this emphasis presupposes the existence of such verbs and particles in the spoken language. But given such existence, we can ask: will all languages bearing such items utilize them heavily in songs? Or if not, will this emphasis on certain grammatical elements show an areal distribution?

I must point out that this heavy use of auxiliaries and particles is confined to certain genres of Havasupai songs—cante-fable, narrative songs, and Old Women's Songs (see below). A very prevalent genre, the Circle Dance Songs, shows a very different pattern—that of a marked reduction in affixes, auxiliaries, and particles. Indeed, it is very difficult to find any lexical item other than full nouns and verbs in these songs. The Circle Dance Songs are inspired from the Great Basin, most of them being from the 1890 Ghost Dance era, which had its origin among the Uto-Aztecan peoples of the Great Basin region. Interestingly, Papago songs have also often been described as having a "reduced" grammar, leaving out auxiliaries, particles, and affixes. (See Shaul 1981 for a discussion of the relevant literature.) We can speculate (on the basis of this very insufficient amount of data) that reduced grammar might be a family feature of Uto-Aztecan songs, a feature that has diffused to Havasupai in the Circle Dance Songs.

4. *Semantics and Content Features.* Havasupai songs containing real words (except Circle Dance Songs) are virtually all in first-person form. Songs represent the emotions and expressions of people and spirits and mythical characters, and as such must always be in first person. What is the areal distribution of this rule?

A phenomenon that may be related is one found in Seri, reported by Hine (1982). Seri songs have an interesting quotative particle translating as "he said." Most phrases end with this particle, demonstrating that the rest of the song is a quotation from someone else. I have not heard of this use of a quotative in other song traditions (although in Havasupai songs within stories, each song is followed directly by a spoken quotative that translates "so he said"). However, one might expect to find other traditions near Seri to show this device. Sherzer (1982) reports a similar phenomenon among the Kuna of Panama. Only careful research could show whether this is an areal phenomenon stretching from Northern Mexico to Panama (and beyond?) or whether we are seeing two unrelated smaller areas exhibiting similar phenomena.

Havasupai also exhibits a genre of song often labelled as "cante-fable" which entails a story-telling style where quotations of all characters are in song-form. Cante-fable was described by Sapir (1910) for Southern Paiute (in close contact with Havasupai), who suggested that the device diffused from Yuman tribes into Paiute. The full distribution of this trait could tell us a great deal about prehistoric contact between tribes.

Another genre of song that shows areal distribution is the "song cycles," exhibited in all Yuman communities except for Havasupai, Yavapai, and Walapai (Havasupai and Walapai now have these song cycles, but they borrowed them only in the twentieth century), and also exhibited in the Uto-Aztecan tribes of Southern California, in close contact with Yuman. Yet another tradition is the composition (usually by women) of insulting songs — called "Enemy Songs" by the Cupeño (Hill 1982), "Mocking Songs" by the Shoshones (Shimkin 1964), "Hateful Songs" by the Cahuilla and "Old Women's Songs" by the Havasupais. The genre has not been reported for other tribes, but the distribution suggests a spread at least throughout Southern California and the Great Basin, and Havasupai. The Hopis exhibit a more "gentlemanly" version called Grievance Chants (Black 1967). The "War Songs" of the Northwest should also be mentioned here: these are Insult Songs sung by groups of men to each other during a ceremony to settle a dispute (Bright 1978).

One other trait to study is a device defined as "couplets," which Bruce Mannheim (1982) discusses. Mannheim distinguishes two different sorts of couplets: one that presents itself in the form of grammatically parallel lines (typified by Quechua couplets), and one that is characterized by referentially parallel lines (typical of Mesoamerica). Couplets of either sort do not seem to appear in North America: they appear to be an areal feature of Central and South America.

These are just a few suggestions out of many possibilities worthy of investigation from an areal viewpoint.

Problems in Areal Studies

Studying the areal distribution of linguistic or musical features presents certain difficulties. The greatest difficulty, of course, is the lack of available data. But beyond that, all sorts of difficulties of interpretation occur. One major problem is the determination of what constitutes a trait. On a concrete level, grammatical couplets and referential couplets are two separate traits, as are Insult Songs and Grievance Chants. Yet on a more abstract level, they might be seen to represent a single trait of wider areal distribution. The fact that the regions exhibiting the referential and grammatical forms of parallelism are all in Central America and Northern South America suggests that these different forms do show a diffusional pattern, perhaps an ancient one. Similarly, Hopi is in contact with the communities that have Insult Songs. Yet the abstract level carries less certainty with it; it is not certain that two traits alike on an abstract level are alike due to diffusion.

This problem is also present in musical features, not just textual ones. For example, the "rise," characteristic of the California-Yuman musical area (Nettl 1954), is characterized by a phrase of tonal material sung higher than the other phrases. A prototypical form containing the rise is

A B A B A B A B A B *R* B A B A B . . .

In Yuman territory, during the rise the rattle accompaniment changes from a rhythmic pulse to a constant shaking; during the first rise the singers, who have been seated, get up and begin dancing, and continue to dance throughout the rest of the song.

Next door to some Yuman tribes having the rise in their musical tradition live the Papago, who lack the rise. The formal structure of Papago songs is described by Haefer (1981:134):

> Papago songs exhibit a two-fold pattern of repetition in the manner of
> complete and incomplete modes: AA'BC AA'BC A'BC A'BC A'BC or ABCDE

ABCDE BCDE BCDE. Piman singers refer to a song as having a *ṣon* "beginning," *ku:g* "end," and *noḍag* "turning." The turning refers to the shift from a complete to an incomplete mode and is usually signaled by a change in the way the accompanying instrument is played.

What the Papago and Yuman styles have in common is a repetitive form much like a "verse" which is interrupted and changed somewhere in the song. Both groups change the way the instrument is played at this point. While Papago is rightfully excluded from the area containing the rise, its formal song structure bears certain tantalizing similarities to the Yuman tradition that might suggest diffusion of some ancient pattern that subsequently developed in two different directions.

Certainly the safest approach is a conservative one that deals only on a relatively concrete level. Yet one might miss out on very worthwhile insights by ignoring more abstract levels of similarity.

The Role of Music in Linguistic Diffusion

The previous sections of this essay were primarily addressed to issues of interest to ethnomusicologists. In the final sections I will address issues of concern to linguists, to show what role music may play in linguistic diffusion.

I am particularly concerned here with the mechanism of diffusion of phonemes. As illustrated previously with glottalized stops, a phoneme may diffuse across language boundaries. There are many ways in which this may occur. One way is for the phoneme to enter a language through loanwords. Another way is for the element to preexist phonetically in certain environments but to be reinterpreted as a phoneme through a combination of language-internal processes and stimulation from its presence as a phoneme in an influencing language.

The development of a voiced-voiceless distinction in English fricatives provides an example for both processes. Originally [v] was an allophone of /f/ found only in environments surrounded by voiced segments. Similarly, [z] was an allophone of /s/, [ð] of /θ/, and so forth. Alternations based on this allophony are still found in pairs such as wi*f*e - wi*v*es, or alternate pronunciations such as "exit": [ɛksɪt] ∼ [ɛgzɪt].

Two things happened then, approximately simultaneously. One event was the borrowing of many French loanwords such as "vast" and "zealous" which did not conform to the rules of positioning for voiced fricatives. Secondly, some of the environments in which voiced fricatives occurred began to deteriorate, leaving word-final voiced fricatives behind. Words with "silent e" provide examples: the "e" was once pronounced, but was dropped in words such as "slave," "pave," "bathe," and "craze." Thus both word-borrowing and phonological change acted together to cause the reinterpretation of voiced and voiceless fricatives as different phonemes.

It appears that both the processes of reinterpretation (stimulated by contact) and of the introduction of a new segment through word-borrowing usually involve bilingualism. For the latter process, in particular, if bilingualism is not involved, the borrowed word is merely changed to suit the phonological system of the borrowing language. For example, English has borrowed many words from Arabic, but these sport no phonemes foreign to English — the pharyngeals and other segments distinguishing Arabic from English have been replaced by English phonemes. It appears, then, that a foreign segment is retained in a loanword only when the speakers of the borrowing language are also able to speak the donor language.

There is no doubt that bilingualism and multilingualism were very common in traditional North America. But is that the *only* way a new phonetic element can enter a language in a contact situation? I would like to suggest that an alternative mechanism for the entry of a new phoneme is through songs and similar genres of oral literature (such as rhythmic formulaic speech).

Diffusion of Songs in Nonbilingual Settings

There is rich evidence in most cultures of borrowing of songs from one language to another without the presence of a noticeable amount of bilingualism in the receiving community. In English, we need only look at the children's repertory to find a number of songs in other languages. Most popular are the round "Frère Jacques" and the French-Canadian song "Alouette." In adult popular music, we find that songs in other languages sometimes hit the Top 10, such as "Volare" and "Guantanamera." Retention of a product of very ancient contact may be found in the nursery counting-out rhyme "Eeny Meeny Miney Mo," reputed to be borrowed from the Celtic languages by early English speakers in Great Britain.

As an example of obvious song-borrowing in North America, I might briefly summarize the foreign genres of song present in the musical traditions of the Havasupais. They sing songs from the following tribes: Hopis, Paiutes, Chemehuevis, Navajos, Walapais, Yavapais, and Mojaves. The latter three languages belong to the same family as Havasupai (Yuman); the rest belong to the Uto-Aztecan and Athabascan families. Some linguistic influence is demonstrable on Havasupai from Hopi, Walapai, and Mojave — for example, a few words are loanwords from Hopi and Mojave — but there is no demonstrable linguistic diffusion from the other tribes, nor are modern Havasupais bilingual in any of these languages. Besides singing songs directly borrowed from these tribes, the Havasupais also sing songs created by Havasupai composers but sung in one of the borrowed styles. The most obvious example is the Havasupai Circle Dance Songs, which were developed during the 1890 Ghost Dance Cult, already discussed above. Havasupais were converted by the Paiutes, and they borrowed some Paiute songs and composed many of their own songs in the same style.

In summary, Havasupais sing many songs in styles borrowed from other cultures, including some cultures whose languages have had little or no observable effect on the Havasupai language.

The mechanism of musical diffusion was illustrated to me once when I accompanied some Diegueños from San Diego on a visit to the Kiliwas in Baja California. The Diegueños and Kiliwas had no language in common. Communication was through translation involving four languages: a monolingual Kiliwa would make a statement which was translated by a bilingual Kiliwa into Spanish; this would be translated by someone knowing both English and Spanish into English, and then someone bilingual in English and Diegueño would translate the message into Diegueño. However, the need for such cumbersome translation was rare, for most interaction was entirely through various forms of celebration: eating, drinking, music, and dance. Many of the songs sung that night were already known to both tribes. Other songs were led by someone who knew them, and picked up during the singing by the others. By the end of the visit, several songs had been learned by each group, in a situation where linguistic diffusion did not occur at all.

Songs diffuse from one language to another with relative ease, and, while in many cases they are changed drastically from the original, there is usually still enough retention of the original character for their origin to be discernible. A case in point in Havasupai is the Navajo Horse Songs, borrowed a hundred years or so ago. The account of their arrival in the Havasupai community is an interesting one: it is said that a Havasupai baby was kidnapped by Navajos in a raid and raised as a Navajo. As an adult he learned of his origins and traveled back to rejoin the Havasupais. He carried the Horse Songs back with him, and they were subsequently learned by generation after generation of Havasupais. While the general melodic style and form has been transformed to conform to Havasupai traditions, and the words altered significantly, there is still enough of the original Navajo present in some of them so that key words were recognized by Navajos when I played the songs for them. The songs were identified as being from Blessingway, and many of them fit the wording of the Blessingway Horse Songs (kindly provided by David McAllester; see Hinton 1984 for a full description).

Retention of Alien Phonetic Elements in Borrowed Songs

Because of the fact that *sounds* become important for their own sake in a song context, there is a strong tendency for songs and related genres of oral literature to retain phonetic elements of the original rendition even when sung by speakers of different dialects or languages. For example, people singing Country and Western Songs sing with a southern accent regardless of the dialect they speak. Folksingers singing blues retain aspects of black English in their rendition. Caribbean English songs have also been popular among American folksingers, and are sung retaining elements of the Caribbean dialects.

In some cases even composition of new songs will have characteristics of the dialect or language which first produced the genre, even when the composer speaks a different language or dialect. A case in point is the songs of the Beatles, where little trace remained (especially in the earlier songs) of the Liverpool English spoken by the group, and American pronunciation was prevalent.

In songs borrowed from other languages, retention of foreign phonetic elements is also common. In both "Frère Jacques" and "Alouette" there are words with initial /ž/; in spoken English, /ž/ may never occur initially. The song "Guantanamera" has often been sung in translation, but the chorus retains the word "Guantanamera" pronounced the Spanish way, with an initial [ɣ], a sound not present at all in English.

As for American Indian languages, I can cite several examples of foreign phonetic elements found in the songs and formulaic utterances of languages. Nichols (1982) has kindly provided me with examples of formulaic utterances found in Northern Paiute stories in Oregon, containing segments alien to Paiute.

pubúpʔmubúpʔm	"bobbing or nodding of head"
sažáʔwažáʔw	"moving back and forth"
šizíŋazíŋ	"shuffling of the feet"

In Oregon Northern Paiute [z] never occurs before /i/ and [ž] never occurs before /a/; nor do we find glottalized consonants, nor voiceless nasals at the end of the words. All these are found in neighboring languages, however; and though they do not appear in loanwords, in Paiute they do appear in these formulaic onomatopoetic utterances — where, as in song, sound for its own sake is foregrounded.

Another fascinating example of a borrowed segment showing up only in songs and onomatopoetic utterances is the segment [ŋ] (a velar nasal consonant) in Yuman languages. /ŋ/ is a well-installed trait in Uto-Aztecan languages, and reconstructable at least for Northern Uto-Aztecan. It is not reconstructable for Proto-Yuman; therefore its presence in any Yuman language can be seen as a probable instance of diffusion from Uto-Aztecan into Yuman languages.

It is in fact present in six Yuman languages: Havasupai, Walapai, Yavapai, Mojave, Yuma, and Maricopa. However, its presence is so limited and specialized that it is rarely included as part of the phoneme inventory. Its major presence is in songs and song-related areas. It is found in words for musical instruments, and in onomatopoetic formulas (e.g., Havasupai /giŋagiŋ / "the ringing sound made by a small bell"). In songs, it is exceedingly common in vocables.

It is only in Havasupai and Walapai that any other instance of /ŋ/ occurs: the second-person verb construction contains two contiguous morphemes *g* + *m*, which coalesce to [ŋ] in casual speech. The younger generations have reinterpreted the construction as having underlying /ŋ/ (Hinton 1980b). The role of /ŋ / in the morphophonology of Havasupai and Walapai has resulted in its recognition as a phoneme by most scholars. It could be argued that the presence of /ŋ/ in songs and onomatopoetic words has allowed its reinterpretation in Havasupai grammar, partly catalyzed by continued contact with Uto-Aztecan languages.

The areal spread of /ŋ/ in songs and music-related words extends also to Papago, a Uto-Aztecan language that lacks /ŋ/ elsewhere in the language. In Papago, /g/ becomes [ŋ] in songs as part of a general pattern of replacing oral consonants by their nasal counterparts (Saxton and Saxton 1973). In the North, it seems quite reasonable to assume that its presence in Yuman languages derives from the Great Basin languages, especially since most of the songs containing /ŋ/ are claimed by the Yumans themselves to come from that region. Its presence in the South, however, is less clearly explained, since none of the languages—either Yuman or Uto-Aztecan—have /ŋ/ in their phonemic inventories; nor do contact patterns suggest that it came from the north. Papago, along with other agricultural groups in Arizona, show influence from the south in their musical instruments (Brown 1967). It is possible that the Papago /ŋ/ (or the general rule of which /ŋ/ is one result) has its origin in the south as well. Further research is definitely indicated here.

We can summarize this discussion by the presentation of a model of the musical avenue of linguistic diffusion:

1) Some foreign phonetic elements are retained in diffused songs and onomatopoetic utterances, due to the foregrounding of sound for its own sake.
2) This allows the subsequent possibility of the development of a foreign segment in other aspects of the language, especially when contact with the donor language continues. Such development may occur by borrowing other words, and the foreign sounds may be retained due to "acclimatization" through their occurrence in songs and onomatopoetic utterances; or they may occur through language-internal phonological processes.

There is, of course, no necessity for the second step to occur at all, and there is no claim being made here that language diffusion *must* occur first through music. What I am claiming is that this mechanism of sound diffusion can be seen as one way a new sound may diffuse without bilingualism necessarily playing a role.

Scholars hailing from our own departmentalized culture, where music is listened to by many but made by very few, might believe that the musical mechanism of linguistic diffusion must be rare and quite unimportant. But before making such a judgment, it is necessary to understand the role that music has traditionally played in intertribal relations. In most of North America, the occasions of contact between native speakers of different languages almost always involve festivities with music and dance. Almost all festive celebrations are attended by more than one language group, and these celebrations play a very important role in contact between groups: they are the occasions of trade, selection of marriage partners, and so on.

Certainly, all those parts of North America renowned for intense language convergence have many such intertribal gatherings every year. For most of the people in these areas, song was and still is a primary form of vocal contact across languages.

It is not usually possible to separate out the effects of the musical mechanism from the bilingual mechanism of diffusion, since the two co-occur in most cases. But when one understands the importance of music in contact situations, one realizes that, indeed, music may well have played an important role in linguistic diffusion.

References Cited

Bahr, Donald
  1982   Untitled presentation at the Workshop on Ritual Music, March 4-6, Tucson, Arizona.

Bahr, Donald M., and J. Richard Haefer
  1978   "Song in Piman Curing." *Ethnomusicology* 22/1:89-122.

Black, Robert
  1967   "Hopi Grievance Chants: A Mechanism of Social Control." *Studies in Southwestern Ethnolinguistics*, ed. D. H. Hymes and W. Bittle, pp. 33-53. The Hague: Mouton and Company.

Booth, Curtis
  1975   Personal communication, March.

Bright, William
  1963   "Language and Music: Areas for Cooperation." *Ethnomusicology* 7/1:26-32.

  1978   "Karok." *Handbook of North American Indians,* volume 8: *California,* ed. Robert F. Heizer, pp. 180-89. Washington: Smithsonian Institution.

Brown, Donald N.
  1967   "Distribution of Sound Instruments in the Prehistoric Southwestern United States." *Ethnomusicology* 11/1:71-90.

Foster, Anne
  1982   "Observations Concerning Sung Hopi in Hopi Katsina Songs." Unpublished paper written for Linguistics 255, University of California, Berkeley. Available from Foster or Hinton.

Frisbie, Charlotte J.
  1980   "Vocables in Navajo Ceremonial Music." *Ethnomusicology* 24/3:347-92.

Haefer, J. Richard
  1981   "Musical Thought in Papago Culture." Ph.D. dissertation, University of Illinois at Urbana-Champaign, Department of Music.

Herndon, Marcia
  1980   *Native American Music.* Norwood, Pa.: Norwood Editions.

Hill, Jane
1982   Personal communication, June.

Hine, Charles
1982   "Five Seri Spirit Songs." Ms. prepared for the Workshop on Ritual Music, March 4-6, Tucson, Arizona. Available from Hine.

Hinton, Leanne
1980a   "Vocables in Havasupai Song." *Southwestern Indian Ritual Drama*, ed. Charlotte J. Frisbie, pp. 275-306. School of American Research Book. Albuquerque: University of New Mexico Press.

1980b   "When Sounds Go Wild: Phonological Change and Syntactic Re-analysis in Havasupai." *Language* 56/2:320-44.

1984   *Havasupai Songs: A Linguistic Perspective*. Ars Linguistica, 6. Tübingen, West Germany: Gunter Narr.

Lomax, Alan
1968   *Folk Song Style and Culture*. Washington, D.C.: American Association for the Advancement of Science, 88.

Mannheim, Bruce
1982   Untitled presentation at the Workshop on Ritual Music, March 4-6, Tucson, Arizona.

McAllester, David P.
1954   *Enemy Way Music*. Papers of the Peabody Museum of American Archaeology and Ethnology, Harvard University, vol. 41, no. 3.

1979   "The Astonished Ethno-Muse." *Ethnomusicology* 23/2:179-90.

Nettl, Bruno
1954   *North American Indian Musical Styles*. Memoirs of the American Folklore Society, 45.

Nichols, Mike
1982   Personal communication, May.

Roberts, H. H.
1936   *Musical Areas in Aboriginal North America*. Yale University Publications in Anthropology, 12.

Sapir, Edward
1910   "Song Recitative in Paiute Mythology." *Journal of American Folklore* 23:455-72.

Saxton, Dean, and Lucille Saxton
1973   *O'othham Hoho'ok A'agitha: Legends and Lore of the Papago and Pima Indians*. Tucson: University of Arizona Press.

Shaul, David L.
1981   "Piman Song Syntax: Its Historical Significance." *Proceedings of the Seventh Annual Meeting of the Berkeley Linguistics Society*, pp. 275-83.

Sherzer, Joel
1968   *An Areal-Typological Study of American Indian Languages North of Mexico*. Amsterdam: North Holland Publishing Co.

1981   Personal communication, March.

1982   Personal communication, March.

Shimkin, Dmitri B.
1964   "On Wind River Shoshone Literary Forms: An Introduction." *Language in Culture and Society*, ed. Dell Hymes, pp. 344-55. New York: Harper and Row.

Vayda, Andrew
1969   *Environment and Cultural Behavior*. Ecological Studies in Cultural Anthropology. Garden City, N.Y.: Natural History Press.

Cultural Analysis, Linguistic Analogies, and the Study of Dance in Anthropological Perspective

Adrienne L. Kaeppler
Smithsonian Institution

Prologue — Analogy and Analysis

When doing research in Tonga my informants often "explained" answers to my questions by giving analogies. Such an analogy usually had little to do with the subject at hand, but somehow made me understand what had previously been confusing. My informants made it clear, however, that analogies only worked if one's "audience" had the cultural knowledge to experience or understand the parallel being made. This kind of explanation gave both the questioner and the answerer an aesthetic pleasure — a kind of *heliaki* in which one could say one thing but mean another.

Western modes of argument, on the other hand, do not usually proceed by analogy. Rather, by straightforward questioning, answering, and observing and by hypothesizing, inducting, and deducting, the process is analytical — mentally (or physically) breaking things down, taking them apart, and putting them back together again. Perhaps the difference can be characterized as "parallel versus discrete." The latter is not as much based on specific cultural knowledge as the former, but requires a kind of discipline particularly well suited, it seems, to Western thought.

My point is that analogy and analysis are not the same thing, and though Tongans and Westerners (as well as other societies) both analogize and analyze they have different preferences and different contexts in which they do them. In short, analogy and analysis should never be confused; and with reference to this essay,[1] linguistic analogies and linguistic analyses are not the same thing.

Cultural Analysis — Human Action and Interaction

Anthropologists are interested in human action and interaction as well as the products of human action and interaction. Dance — or to put it into a larger frame of reference, structured movement systems — is both a product of human action and interaction as well

---

[1] An early version of this essay was presented at the annual meeting of the Society for Ethnomusicology in Honolulu, Hawaii, October 1981. I wish to thank my colleagues Ives Goddard, George Grace, William Sturtevant, Paul Taylor, and Judy Van Zile for helpful comments and suggestions.

as a process through which action and interaction take place. Music, of course, is also a product of action and interaction and a process through which action and interaction take place. But I will restrict my remarks here to movement.

I believe that a cultural analysis of structured human movement can contribute greatly to our understanding of the human behavior that has generated diverse sociocultural systems. A major task of an anthropologist of movement (or any anthropologist) is to elucidate what the movement dimensions of various activities or activity systems are, as well as what they are communicating and to whom. These movement dimensions of various activities should be recognized as an integral part of that activity, described, analyzed, and used in formulations about the form, function, and meaning of that activity, as well as in constructs about the deep structure and cultural philosophy of that society.

A cultural analysis of structured movement should begin with the analysis of activities — of human action and interaction in various contexts and the movement products created through these activities. The end product of such an analysis should elucidate the structure and content of the movement itself, the creative and social processes which produced the movements according to the aesthetic precepts of a specific group (or subgroup) of people at a specific point in time, the components which differentiate cultural conceptions about how movements are grouped or separated (e.g., into "dance" and "non-dance" or into genres), and how the movements relate to cultural deep structure and philosophy.

Cultural Analogies in the Study of Language

During the 1960s, anthropologists became more and more aware of the methodological and theoretical advances of those linguists who systematically applied Kenneth Pike's conceptualization of "emic" analysis. According to Pike (1954:8), it was "an attempt to *discover* and to describe the pattern of that particular language or culture in reference to the way in which the various elements of that culture are related to each other in the functioning of the particular pattern." He went on to say that ". . . emic criteria savor more of relativity, with the sameness of activity determined in reference to a particular system of activity" (ibid.: 11).

Such concepts were not really new to anthropology but have their roots in the research of anthropologists who wished to understand the functioning of a society in terms of the participants of that society. Malinowski (1922:25), for example, told us long ago that our goal should be "to grasp the native's point of view, his relation to life, to realize *his* vision of *his* world." And Boas (1943:314) succinctly stated that "if we choose to apply our [Western] classification to alien cultures we may combine forms that do not belong together. . . . If it is our serious purpose to understand the thoughts of a people the whole analysis of experience must be based on their concepts, not ours." The "post-Bloomfieldean linguists" who emphasized this concept evolved a methodology through which it could be applied and used it to produce grammars that grouped morphemes into classes in a way that was inherent or natural to the languages themselves. One of the crucial concepts was the etic/emic distinction through which it was possible to apply Boas's wish to understand the "thoughts of a people" to the sound (or phonological) element of language. It is important to remember in this context that such analysis is based on minimal contrastive units of sound and how they are combined, according to a particular group of people, into meaningful sequences.

Linguistic Analogies in the Study of Culture

Language, although it can be analyzed separately, is an inseparable aspect of culture and the methodology developed by linguists, based preeminently on contrastive analysis, re-entered broader anthropological thought with what came to be called the "new ethnography." Conklin, Frake, Gladwin, Goodenough, Sturtevant, and others realized the potential of applying contrastive analysis and other techniques such as componential analysis to cultural domains other than sound. Kinship systems, color categories, religion, botany, and dance were subjected to "emic" analysis in order to make theoretical statements about social structure, religious systems, botanical classifications, and movement systems that embedded the native's points of view. The new ethnography had its roots in ethnoscientific analysis that employed linguistic analogies.

In spite of the heavy criticism by Harris, Burling, Keesing, and others, the ethnoscientists have made significant contributions to the study of culture using and refining methods borrowed back into anthropology from linguistics. Furthermore, the criticism of ethnoscience made by transformationalists may be considered irrelevant because the ethnoscientists and the transformationalists are not attempting to understand the same thing. In short, ethnoscientists do not use linguistic analysis or even linguistic models, but they do use linguistic analogies which were taken into linguistic analyses as cultural analogies sometime earlier. The borrowed linguistic analogies lie primarily in the application of contrastive analysis, as developed by linguists, to cultural forms other than language. It should also be noted that, although semiologists employ linguistic methods and theories in their analysis of society, they are thoroughly grounded in the cultural basis of these linguistic analogies.

Deriving Dance Structure — Linguistic Analogies

Anthropology students of the mid-1960s were exposed to the methodological and theoretical techniques used by linguists and ethnoscientists. My own study of the structure of Tongan dance used etic/emic distinctions based on analogies with structural linguistics (Kaeppler 1967). It goes back much further, however, to the Saussurean distinction between acts and system, and my cultural analysis required that the structure or system thus derived be recognized by members of the society.

Starting with the assumption that only a small segment of all possible movements is significant in any single dance or movement tradition, and that these significant units could be discovered, I used ethnoscientific concepts, as mediated through linguistic methodology, the notion of isolating minimal units (i.e., movement emes which I termed "kinemes") using the process of contrastive analysis (i.e., are kinetically different movements considered by individuals of a specific group of people the same or different). Through this process it was possible to make an inventory of the significant movements of Tongan dance. Just as language can be committed to paper in a phonetic notation and the allophonic variations noted for each phoneme, human movement can be committed to paper in a kinetic notation (e.g., Labanotation) and the allokine variations noted for each kineme. As I have noted above, these techniques of analysis are not strictly linguistic, but are methods that can be productive in the analysis of various cultural phenomena including linguistics, society, art, and dance.

Kinemes are minimal units of movement recognized as contrastive by people of a given dance tradition. Although having no meaning in themselves, kinemes are the basic units from which dance of a given tradition is built. Another level of structural organization was termed the morphokinemic level. A morphokine is the smallest unit that has meaning (not necessarily narrative or pictorial meaning) in the structure of the movement system. Only certain combinations of kinemes are meaningful. Unlike oral language in which linear sequences of contrastive sounds (phonemes) form meaningful elements (morphemes), a number of kinemes often occur simultaneously to form a meaningful movement. Thus, even at this low level of analysis a linguistic model is not very useful. Further analogies with language, such as lexemes or sememes, were not found to be useful in the analysis of dance structure. Instead, morphokines (which have meaning as movement but do not have lexical meaning) were found to be organized into a relatively small number of motifs, which, when ordered simultaneously and chronologically (i.e., choreographed), form dances.

Meanwhile, a similar cultural analysis was being carried out in Eastern Europe. Here, too, researchers found that techniques derived from structural linguistics were useful at the lower levels. The minimal units in this Eastern European study were called "elements or dansemes" which were combined into cells and organized into motives, phrases, stanzas, sections, and parts (Study Group for Folk Dance Terminology 1975). This structural analysis was derived by Eastern Europeans analyzing their own dances from their own emic point of view.

Neither of these studies was a linguistic analysis. They were cultural analyses in the ethnoscientific mode that used two analogues from linguistics: the derivation of minimal units by contrastive analysis, and the analysis of observations and statements about ways in which minimal units were combined into meaningful groupings.

Understanding Linguistic Analogies

It is apparent, however, that such studies are not necessarily viewed as methodological analogies. Both Singer and Freedman feel that the studies use *linguistic concepts*. Singer (1974:381) notes that "linguistic concepts, from both phonology and syntax, have occasionally been applied to the analysis of dance forms. Such studies indicate some pitfalls of inappropriate analogies, as well as the potential for productive efforts." Singer then goes on to make her own analogies in which she develops a "theory of metrics . . . in which the analogies to linguistic theory are as formalized and as explicit as possible" (ibid.). The affinities of Singer's study are consistent with Chomsky and the transformationalists as well as the linguistic analysis of poetic meters. She uses concepts derived from linguistic theory and assumes that others have done so as well. But this is not the case. Emic analysis may have been done by linguists, but its concepts, rather than deriving ultimately from linguistic theory, are embedded in cultural theory as elaborated by Pike and Dell Hymes (1962:22), who notes that it involves "a moral commitment to the inductive discovery of units, criteria and patternings that are valid in terms of the system itself."

In a review of Nadia Chilkovsky Nahumck's book *Introduction to Dance Literacy,* Diane Freedman (1980:86) makes the following statement:

> From a theoretical perspective, the term "literacy" posits an analogy between the systems of dance and language that is more significant than comparing only the notational systems devised for each. This analogy leads directly to the implication that a linguistic model is appropriate for the study of dance and, by extension, all movement. While this notion is not a new one in studies of either dance (Kaeppler 1972) or body movement (Birdwhistell 1970) it is still arguable.

Freedman does not indicate on what grounds it is arguable, but she goes on to say that the "analogy between language and dance must be qualified by an understanding of each as a separate mode of communication in which the symbolic meaning of one mode is not directly translatable to another" (ibid.). Apparently she feels that Birdwhistell, Nahumck, and I do not understand that language and movement are separate modes of communication, but I cannot imagine why she thinks we do not, especially as my work (as summarized above) does not deal with communication or meaning, but *structure*. Nor does it follow that simply because we use methodological analogies for *analysis* that we posit "an analogy between the systems of dance and language." Surely one would not posit an analogy between dance and color categories simply because they both have been subject to emic analysis. In a further exchange about Nahumck's book with Ann Hutchinson Guest, Freedman says that "Guest's response is based on the undefended assumption that language and movement are precisely analogous" (Guest and Freedman 1980:96). Guest, however, makes no such assumption; the question that she raises is about literacy, which after all, really deals with being learned or educated in. How would Freedman's remarks apply, for example, to visual literacy? Labanotation, and especially Nahumck's rendering of it, deals as much with visual literacy (learning to see) as it does with learning to write. But the point is that neither Nahumck nor Guest are dealing with communication in the way conceptualized by Freedman.

Freedman (1980:86) also notes that "the symbols used in Labanotation represent discrete units of a movement sequence, but these units are complex composites of many dimensions, not at all analogous to linguistic phonemes." As far as I am aware no one has suggested that Labanotation symbols are analogous to linguistic phonemes (which incidently are also complex composites of many dimensions). Labanotation symbols are a tool for committing human movement to paper—at most a kinetic "alphabet" analogous to a phonetic "alphabet." Kinemes like phonemes and other emes, are culture-bound minimal units derived by contrastive analysis; and techniques for writing them down in etic symbol systems are irrelevant to their existence (important as they may be as tools).

It is obvious that there is a problem here of misunderstanding. The problem seems to arise from an unsystematic use and indiscriminate interchange of concepts that do not have equal explanatory functions: analysis, analogy, and model. Analogy is a powerful explanatory technique, but it will certainly result in confusion and inappropriate explanation if it is substituted for analysis. Analogy only clears away confusion if the "audience" has the necessary cultural knowledge to experience the parallel. Linguistic analogies are only useful if the audience or reader understands the linguistic analysis from which the analogy is drawn. The specific quality of analogy is not a resemblance between things themselves, but a resemblance of attributes, circumstances, or effects. An argument by analogy is not based simply on similarity of two things but on similarity of their relations. The importance of the work of Eastern Europeans, my own work, and the work of Nahumck and Guest does not lie in communication theory or in postulating similarities between dance and language, but rather in exploring methods for analyzing dance structure and ways in which information about dance movement and structure can be communicated among scholars. Often this is done with the use of analogy. The relation between dance and language is in fact not only analogic but metaphoric, a process by which the qualities of one form are imaginatively ascribed to another, the forms often being essentially unlike. Analogies between language and dance have their basis in metaphor—indeed the concept of "nonverbal communication" was probably originally metaphoric. Finally, the use of the term "linguistic model" appears to compound the confusion. The "model" employed (if one must use that term) is an emic model, not a linguistic model. An emic model—that is, one derived by contrastive analysis—is a conceptual scheme useful for analyzing language as well as other cultural forms such as dance or kinship or plant taxonomy. I believe that it has been shown empirically (Kaeppler 1967), that an emic model (stemming from cultural/linguistic models) can account for the facts in the powerful manner stipulated as a criteria of explanatory adequacy by Feld (1974:201). Delineating the structure or form of a movement system would seem to be logically prior to relating structure or form to its cultural context and deep structure.

It is probably because many dance analysts or music analysts do not have a thorough background in linguistic or cultural analysis that they find emic analysis so mystifying. It is really not mysterious. At the risk of the pitfalls involved in attempting to make the complex simple, there are primarily two processes involved which are based on both observation and questioning. One process is to derive the emic units by observing behavior and questioning which etic behaviors can be grouped or separated into emes (i.e., if they are considered the same or different). There may, of course, be disagreement within the society, and the analyst with the help of informants will have to figure out how to deal with it. A second process (which may proceed simultaneously) is to derive the system by observing and questioning how the emic units are structured and what is the relationship between them. The system may include subsystems which depend on levels of formality and/or context. Both of these processes are part of the ethnoscientific mode. The importance of such analysis was stated by Edward Sapir in 1927. He notes that a person who simply observes

> . . . will be guilty of all manner of distortion. His emphasis will be constantly askew. He will find interesting what the natives take for granted as a casual kind of behavior worthy of no particular comment, and he will utterly fail to observe the crucial turning points in the course of action that give formal significance to the whole in the minds of those who do possess the key to its understanding [Sapir, in Mandelbaum 1949:546].

Further Analogies

There remains to examine the proposition of whether linguistic analogies are appropriate for the study of dance or movement. As noted above, analogy is a potentially powerful explanatory tool if the audience understands the discipline from which the analogy is drawn. Ideally, one could simply analyze movement in terms of movement, give the cultural inventory of minimal movement emes, and state how they are combined and the principles of the system according to the people who use that movement tradition in their everyday or ritual activities. At the moment, however, an analogy with language seems to make these concepts more easily understandable to a wider range of individuals.

On another analogical level, like language, movement communicates. But what does it communicate and to whom? Does the process of moving communicate in the same or different ways as the product itself? This is not simply communication in the literary or narrative sense, but communication about social space, aesthetics, and philosophy of cultural forms. If we think we can understand the product "dance" of other cultures without taking into account the processual and subtle communicative elements that are culture bound, we are only fooling ourselves. Analogically, we can appreciate or admire the difficulty or gracefulness of another society's dance just as we can appreciate or admire the sound of another society's language. But understanding is something else. An anthropological perspective of dance, like language, requires not simply the ability or aptitude to see or make the movements or to hear or say the words but to understand what one is moving, seeing, hearing, or saying.

Grammar (or more specifically, syntax) is a term usually employed for the principles used to put words (or more specifically, morphemes) together in an order considered correct for a specific language. Grammar, however, may vary within a language depending on context and level of formality. Thus, delivering an oration and talking to one's family may use different principles, all of which must be explained. Movement, too, has a grammar, a set of principles used to put movements together in an order considered correct for a specific social group. Thus, wrestling and petting a cat use different movements which are culturally learned and, more important in this context, each dance genre within a society may use different principles. In language comparison two languages may use the same inventory of phonemes, but the grammar may be entirely different; the languages will be mutually unintelligible until the grammar and vocabulary of each is learned. So it is with dance. The kinemes of Tongan and Samoan dance, for example, are very similar but the grammar is different and they are mutually unintelligible until the grammar and motif vocabulary of each is learned. In addition to the difference in grammar, however, there may also be a difference in energy. The use of energy has no good analogue in language, although one might consider "stress" or "tone." Perhaps a more suitable analogy would be with timbre in music.

Poetry is to ordinary conversation as dance is to ordinary movement and perhaps formal speech is analogous to ritual movement. In many societies language, movement, and structured sound or "music" are conceptually related and there are many useful analogues that would enable an analyst attempting to understand one of these cultural forms to understand the others. For example, societies that use honorific language may also use dance or music to convey the same message. This does not imply that two or three of these cultural forms take place simultaneously. Often they do not. A linguist might, however, obtain useful insights into language by also examining dance and music. The similarity of these cultural forms may be in the fact that these domains participate in the more basic cultural process of human interaction.

The systematic features of language, music, and dance as surface structures are likely to embody the same features of the deep structure or underlying principles of a society. Analysis of dance or movement in an ethnoscientific mode, drawing upon analogies, where useful, from language and music can result in an ethno-theory of dance. The use of Western dance theory for analysis of non-Western dance is as inappropriate today as is the use of Western language theory for the analysis of non-Western languages. Every society has a right to analysis of its culture and parts thereof in terms appropriate to its own structure. An ethno-theory must search for a set of movement propositions which include such things as the isolation of pieces of movement and postures and how they can and cannot be combined, a vocabulary of motifs and a grammar for their use, the notions about energy and how it should be visually displayed, if and how on the basis of movement dance can be separated from ritual and, more basic still, if a culture even has such concepts.

But even this is not the final goal of ethnoscientific research or the use of analogy. As Steven Feld (1981) has pointed out, and I will adapt here for movement,

> the ultimate goal of ethno-theoretical research is certainly to articulate the WHAT of a [movement] theory with the WHY. Only in this way can we comprehend, for any specific society or for cultural areas, the nature of how [movement] structures are social structures, how [movement] organizations are social organizations, how [movement] is not just *made* but is in fact *formulated*.

Movement analysis in the ethnoscientific mode has not yet reached this level of sophistication, although I made attempts in 1975 and 1980 (Kaeppler 1978; 1985). This essay is an attempt to clarify the anthropological and linguistic background of ethnoscientific analysis and its application to the study of dance as well as to indicate some of the current directions of my own research on ethno-theory and choreographic grammar. These concepts have so far had little popularity in the study of movement but are analogous to the studies of Melanesian music by Steven Feld and Hugo Zemp (1979). In a larger sense, however, this emphasis is part of the anthropological perspective of the "astonished ethno-muse" (McAllester 1979).

References Cited

Birdwhistell, Ray
1970   *Kinesics and Context*. Philadelphia: University of Pennsylvania Press.

Boas, Franz
1943   "Recent Anthropology." *Science* 98:311-14, 334-37.

Feld, Steven
1974   "Linguistic Models in Ethnomusicology." *Ethnomusicology* 18/2:197-217.

1981   "Music, Cognition and Metaphor: Aspects of Kaluli Musical Theory." Paper presented at the IFMC colloquium at Kolobrzeg, Poland, May 25-30, 1981.

Freedman, Diane C.
1980   Review of *Introduction to Dance Literacy: Perception and Notation of Dance* by Nadia Chilkovsky Nahumck. *Visual Communication* 6/1:84-87.

Guest, Ann Hutchinson, and Diane C. Freedman
1980   Letter to the Editors. *Visual Communication* 6/3:96.

Hymes, Dell
1962   "The Ethnography of Speaking." *Anthropology and Human Behavior*, ed. Thomas Gladwin and William C. Sturtevant, pp. 13-53. Washington, D.C.: Anthropological Society of Washington.

Kaeppler, Adrienne L.
1967   "The Structure of Tongan Dance." Ph.D. dissertation, University of Hawaii, Department of Anthropology.

1972   "Method and Theory in Analyzing Dance Structure with an Analysis of Tongan Dance." *Ethnomusicology* 16/2:173-217.

1978   "Melody, Drone and Decoration: Underlying Structures and Surface Manifestations in Tongan Art and Society." *Art in Society: Studies in Styles, Culture and Aesthetics*, ed. Michael Greenhalgh and Vincent Megaw, pp. 261-74. London: Duckworth.

1985   "Structured Movement Systems in Tonga." *Society and the Dance: The Social Anthropology of Performance and Process*, ed. Paul Spencer, pp. 92-118. New York: Cambridge University Press.

Malinowski, Bronislaw
1922   *Argonauts of the Western Pacific*. New York: E. P. Dutton and Co.; reprint, 1961.

Mandelbaum, David G., ed.
1949   *Selected Writings of Edward Sapir in Language, Culture, and Personality.* Berkeley: University of California Press.

McAllester, David P.
1979   "The Astonished Ethno-muse." *Ethnomusicology* 23/2:179-89.

Pike, Kenneth
1954   *Language in Relation to a Unified Theory of the Structures of Human Behavior.* Glendale, Calif.: Summer Institute of Linguistics.

Singer, Alice
1974   "The Metrical Structure of Macedonian Dance." *Ethnomusicology* 18/3:379-404.

Study Group for Folk Dance Terminology
1975   "Foundations for the Analysis of the Structure and Form of Folk Dance: A Syllabus." *Yearbook of the International Folk Music Council for 1974*, 6:115-35.

Zemp, Hugo
1979   "Aspects of 'Are'are Musical Theory." *Ethnomusicology* 23/1:6-48.

Some Historical Thoughts
on the
Character of Ethnomusicology

Bruno Nettl
University of Illinois

Recent articles by Stephen Blum (1975) and K. A. Gourlay (1978) have examined the work of ethnomusicologists in part in accordance with who they are, in cultural and individual terms. These authors make the point that ethnomusicologists bring to their work certain values, aims, and purposes which come from their own cultural backgrounds, and therefore we should thus, as Blum (1975:209) says, examine the "past and present relationships between the European and American social structures which have generated such aims, and the non-Western societies placed under investigation." I should like to follow the suggestion rather informally, looking at some of the kinds of things that ethnomusicologists have done. Blum's suggestion seems to refer primarily to social factors, but these are surely intended to include the more specifically musical ones. It is difficult to generalize about the approaches and methods of ethnomusicology, but I believe that in the not-too-distant past there was a mainstream of thought and activity, and that to greater and lesser degrees we are all heirs to it. More specifically, I am talking about the so-called Berlin school which began with Stumpf and Hornbostel, and consisted of their students such as Herzog, Kolinski, Bose, and Wachsmann, along with other scholars connected in one way or another with this group such as Robert Lach, Jaap Kunst, Marius Schneider, Curt Sachs, and Charles Seeger, and perhaps also a number of less closely associated folk music scholars such as Béla Bartók and Cecil Sharp. If we ponder some of the values which these scholars, as a group, brought to their work, we can perhaps get some indication of why it is that ethnomusicology moved in certain directions, and not in others.

One place to look is in the typical family and social background, and even more, the educational background, of those who gave ethnomusicology its start. The period in question is roughly 1880-1910, and the most important area, Germany and Austria. There is not much biographical information published about these scholars. Standard encyclopedias of music such as *The New Grove* and *MGG*, obituary notices in scholarly periodicals, occasional autobiographical notes (e.g., Adler 1935) or brief essays in scholarly biography (e.g., Gerson-Kiwi 1974) must suffice; but they are augmented with numerous bits of oral tradition (available to me through older colleagues and relatives), the literature dealing with the state of education in central Europe during the period in question (e.g., Müller 1977, Höfele 1967, and Ringer 1969), and of course the instructional materials on music from that time.

While the early ethnomusicologists were not usually born into families of professional musicians, their parents seemed in most cases to be musical amateurs and music lovers. In some cases, the scholars began early to point to careers in music or musical scholarship; but in most, the study of music seems to have been something carried out on the side. One found them studying piano, music theory, and, particularly, composition. They came from families in which Western classical music was practiced, loved, esteemed.

Although it is easier to document their musical education, there is also evidence that they typically came from backgrounds in which the natural and social sciences, then making rapid advances, were stressed. The family background was rarely artistic, but more typically involved social studies or science of some sort. Hornbostel's father was an attorney; Lachmann's, a teacher in a Gymnasium or college-preparatory school; Lach's, an administrator in the postal service; Stumpf's, a physician. These scholars had a background in middle-class urban life. If one can attempt to generalize about a diverse group of individuals, the scholars who first gave direction to ethnomusicology had a characteristic kind of background, in a culture with a particular set of values: a sense of discipline, the idea of learning as something in which one could and must learn to do intellectually difficult things (see e.g., Höfele 1967:254-56), which in music might include the discipline of theory and the ability to write fugues; a sense of the importance of science, and its influence on social thought including social Darwinism (Höfele 1967:348-50); a sense of history, derived from the influential works of scholars such as Leopold von Ranke, implying less a critical view than a relativistically flavored desire to learn "how it actually was" (Ringer 1969:98) and to describe past epochs in their own terms; the notion that Western culture was somehow in essence different from all others, derived in part from growing colonialism of the time, with the relationship encapsulated in dichotomies between superior and inferior, changing and static, polluted and idyllic, but also a growing sense of national identity and purity. There may have been also the romantization of the countryside, perhaps visited regularly in summers, and a keen sense that it is different from the city. Considering the time with which we are concerned, it seems reasonable to suppose that they grew up admiring Beethoven and Brahms, and learning that there was a history of medieval, Renaissance, and Baroque musical treasures, many being unearthed in their own time. But, given the amateur musical status of their families, musical taste may not have gone in the direction of the avant-garde of their time. This all seems obvious enough, but we need to remind ourselves that early ethnomusicologists did not come, for example, from rural or working-class families, or from radical movements, or for that matter from devout Christianity, or an artistic avant-garde. They grew up in a particular social and cultural milieu, most commonly German and Central European, and the values of this milieu seem to me to be reflected in their work and continued in that of some of their successors.

Duckles (1972:39) suggests a group of motivating factors in the development of musicology which include interest in the music of the ancients, the discovery of a national song, national approaches to scholarship, and the idea of preserving a heritage, which represents cultural values. My purpose here is to try to ferret out some of the values of our musical culture, particularly as expressed shortly before and after 1900, and to see how they affected the development of ethnomusicology.

What are some of the musical counterparts of these cultural values? Among them are authenticity, the idea of purity of styles, and what I sometimes call an athletic view of music. Much of the literature up to the 1930s and beyond views the world's musics as a group of separate units, stylistically distinct and internally homogeneous. In the work of Hornbostel, one reads about the music of the Thompson River Indians, of Tunisians, of the Kubu of Sumatra, of the Japanese, each as a unit, all treated more or less in the same way, each discovered with the use of a small sampling. A paradigm of musical description promulgated by Stumpf and Hornbostel (see Stumpf 1886 and the articles in Hornbostel *Opera omnia*, vol. 1, for examples), this unitary way of dealing with many musics may be interpreted as the result of ethnographic naïvete and the lack of more material. But it also, I think, results from the belief that cultures are discrete and can be sharply characterized, and that all the products of one culture are bound to reflect the same principles. Such a belief would be typical of a Germany in which diverse parts were struggling (or had recently struggled) to become unified, and which was trying to establish a national character, something that was happening in a number of smaller European nations as well. The idea that each tribe has its distinctive musical style seems to me to correspond to the idea, however unrealistic, of a distinctively German, Czech, Hungarian, or Norwegian music. And from this may also stem the avoidance of the study of mixed and hybrid forms, and the belief that such mixtures may cause the appearance of unsuccessful and undesirable forms of music, a notion tied to many sides of the nineteenth-century configuration of European thought.

To do that which is difficult is a major value in Western academic music, and in many other cultures as well. In the typical training in Germany and central Europe of the late nineteenth and early twentieth centuries, it seems to have been the intellectually difficult which was particularly stressed. This was, after all, the period of Wagner's *Meistersinger*, of Brahms and Bruckner, and of the renewed discovery of Bach and the late Beethoven. The difficulty in this kind of music seems to me to have comprised mainly linear procedures involving the development of melody and contrapuntal simultaneity. And so, when we look at the way in which some of the earlier leaders of our field approached non-Western music, we see special attention paid to matters of form and polyphony, with some disappointment in the absence of the latter sometimes coming to the surface. But more important, special attention given to the music of India and the Middle East (with less to China and Japan, for example) seems to me to reflect an interest in the study of music with thematic development very different from that of Brahms, but like his, complex music in which one can trace the fate of a single musical idea over a long period of time.

I call some of this the athletic approach, and it includes emphasis of the composer's ability to create effects through the use of simultaneous pitches and to lead independent voices simultaneously in such a way that particular kinds of interrelationships — harmony, counterpoint, polyphony — are established. Typical of the scornful statements I used to hear about a new piece is that "the composer surely hadn't had to study counterpoint" in order to write it. For the academic musician around 1900 and later, normal music was music in which several pitches could be heard simultaneously. In Western culture, there existed some monophonic music, but it was clearly outside the mainstream, and the hegemony of polyphony is shown in the desire even by some distinguished scholars such as Cecil Sharp, to write harmonizations of folk songs, the concern of music historians regarding the origins of polyphony in medieval Europe (e.g., Ambros 1862, vol. 2), and the tendency among ethnomusicologists to divide music into two categories, monophonic and polyphonic (Roberts 1936, for example). Thus, that the world of polyphony may consist of many completely incompatible phenomena was not an issue in early ethnomusicology perhaps until the work of Marius Schneider (1934), nor was the existence of folk taxonomies which made no such distinction or made it elsewhere in the continuum. Theory texts early and recent attest to the enormous importance of harmony in Western academic music.

The early ethnomusicologists dealt with music in which polyphony, if it existed at all, was very different from ours. And if normal music, to us, is polyphonic, in the broad sense, the concept of polyphony was used to show on the one hand that the non-Western music was worthy of attention because it did have, one said rather defensively, polyphony, with people performing together in incomprehensible fashion, nevertheless knowing what they were doing; but on the other hand, most of this exotic music was worthy of study precisely because it was so different, had no polyphony (see Sachs 1943:48-51 for an — unintentional — contrast of Western and "primitive" polyphony). And so we can occasionally read that polyphony, as a category, existed in musics such as American Indian (Roberts 1936:38-39). The idea of a systematic polyphonic practice — and of systematic music making in general — was high on the list of values among our forebears. I'll not go further, except to suggest that had ethnomusicology begun in an atmosphere like that of the new music of the 1960s, the idea of control, of knowing what one is doing, proceeding systematically, might have played a smaller role among the things for which ethnomusicologists were looking. There is no doubt in my mind that early ethnomusicologists wanted to show that non-Western musics were systematically organized in good part because they had learned their own music with this value in mind. By contrast, the interest of composers since 1950 in non-Western music has on the whole been completely different; some of them stress what they perceive as un-systematic, indeterminate, mystical, and many try consciously not to intellectualize, again bringing their values to their approaches.

In other respects, too, the ways in which the early ethnomusicologists analyzed music had much to do with the way in which Western musicians were trained, and with the characteristics of nineteenth-century Western musical thought. Let me say a word about melody and rhythm. I know that it is impossible effectively to separate the two, and yet there is no doubt in my mind that the nineteenth century in Western academic music represents enormous achievement in the melodic aspects. Motivic development, thematic transformation, complex harmonic structure — all have rhythmic implications, but the development of strong conscious rhythmic perception seems to have been neglected. Certainly the formal training of musicians involved these far more than rhythm (see e.g., the theory texts of Hugo Riemann). Even in the 1940s, theory classes gave short shrift to rhythm, telling little beyond the existence of a few standard meters, being attentive to scale, mode, and melody, and lavish in the treatment of harmony (as shown by the widely used texts of Allen I. McHose). It is little wonder, therefore, that Alexander J. Ellis's study of the musical scales of various nations, published in 1885, came to be viewed as the clarion call for ethnomusicology, while a similarly seminal work, Bücher's *Arbeit und Rhythmus* of 1896, attracted far less attention among musical scholars. Again, a look at Hornbostel's procedure confirms the impression. The study of the music of the Thompson River Indians by Hornbostel and Abraham (1906), for example, devotes about four times as much attention to melody as to rhythm. And this balance of values continued to be maintained, as, for example, in the works of George Herzog, his students who followed his procedures closely, and, for that matter, in many others among the first half century of ethnomusicological publication.

The Western musician's sensitivity to scales and intonation made it possible for the early ethnomusicologists to establish comparative frameworks for the intercultural study of these phenomena. And so, the study of those aspects of music which involve movement in pitch came to dominate. I'll mention only a couple of bits of evidence: the studies of M. Kolinski (e.g., 1961, 1965) whose purpose is to make possible the classification of any music within a system of all imaginable scalar and melodic configurations, and the studies carried out with the melographs in Norway, in Israel, and at UCLA which emphasize melody over rhythm, although the latter is not totally neglected.

The point to be made is that the lack of Western rhythmic sophistication has caused rhythm to be treated differently by ethnomusicologists. Perhaps that has not been all bad. Again going back to Hornbostel, let me mention his and Otto Abraham's study of the music of India (1904). The individual transcribed pieces are described in terms of their melodic aspects; there is a discussion of scales in typical Hornbostel style, along with some paragraphs about the concept of raga. Rhythm is also discussed, but this is done almost entirely within the framework of Indian music theory; that is, of tala. For other cultures where native theory is less readily available, Hornbostel and his successors discussed rhythm rather impressionistically but not systematically, giving examples of the kinds of things one might find. Kolinski, who did so much to make possible melodic and scalar analysis, did much less with rhythm and on the whole was content with broad categories such as commetric and contrametric structure (Kolinski 1973). By contrast, in the period since the 1950s, in which so much progress has been made, those (usually younger) ethnomusicologists who had not been handed a simple and comparatively-oriented way of describing rhythm by their scholarly tradition came to use much more culture-specific approaches and thus perhaps avoided many of the problems stemming from ethnocentrically derived procedures from which many studies of melody suffer. Authors of the typical ethnomusicological literature on rhythm, it seems to me, see this aspect of a culture's music much more in terms of its own cultural background.

One reason for the lack of rhythmic sophistication in Western culture may be sought in an ambiguous aspect of our rhythmic notation. Melody is notated, for the practical musician up to 1960, in a way so as to be heard; rhythmic notation — note lengths, bar lines, and so forth — tells you how to perform the music, but also, we might put it, how you should feel. The existence of meter, sometimes opposed to the actual rhythm of melodic material, is taken for granted as an undercurrent. In using Western notation for transcribing non-Western music, we often impose this dual structure where it does, but also where it does not, apply. One reason for all this may be the degree to which notation, and notability of a music, is itself a major value in Western musical thought. I'm inclined to think that had ethnomusicology developed in sub-Saharan Africa or for that matter in India, it might not have become a field whose central task seemed at one time to be transcription. But for the Western musician, real and true music is music notated. Learning to transcribe was for long the central activity of the ethnomusicologist's arsenal, and a major purpose of the profession was to get the world's music down on paper.

The peculiar history of transcription is an interesting and vast topic. Let me say here only that of course it was Western notation that was used, and of course this notation to a large extent reflects Western academic musical values. It is a system that is good for pitch, moderately good for prescribing rhythm, poor for much else. And so, of course, we came in our study of the world's musical systems for a time to concentrate on those aspects of music on which Western notation and its readers could concentrate.

We are sometimes told that historical musicology takes a diachronic view, while ethnomusicology takes a synchronic one (see Simon 1978:27-29 for discussion). But in fact, ethnomusicology, particularly in its early decades but later as well, has had a strong interest in matters which are, broadly speaking, historical. Let me quickly mention three: the interest in origins, an approach to musics derived from early cultural evolutionism, and the association with movements in anthropology whose purpose was the understanding of human and cultural history. There are no doubt many reasons for this historical proclivity, but I suggest that one of them may be the view that late nineteenth-and twentieth-century musicians had of their own music as historical artifact. Actually, European musicians did not become enormously interested in their own history until late in the nineteenth century. Certainly there were earlier moves in this direction, but in the nineteenth century composers began to be self-conscious about the matter of progress, to see themselves as points in a line of succession, while performers sought for earlier materials in archives and libraries, and scholars began to study and write history in earnest (Duckles 1972). After all, musicology as a formally constituted profession goes back only a little over one hundred years, perhaps to 1869, the date of the establishment of a chair in Prague. But with the rise of musicology, with the rapid and often incomprehensible changes in musical style from Wagner to Schoenberg and Stravinsky and on, with the invention of recording, the Western musical establishment suddenly found itself unprecedentedly in a music culture which lived to a large extent on products of its own distant past. The early developments in ethnomusicology participated in this view of what a proper musical culture should be, and this attitude can still be found.

A few examples of the above will suffice. Some of the early surveys of tribal music, those of Wallaschek (1893) and Stumpf (1911), were given titles implying that they dealt with the beginnings of music. A considerable amount of other literature also concerned itself with origins, not only of music in general, but of individual phenomena such as instruments (Sachs 1929), polyphony (Adler 1909, Schneider 1934), and rhythm (Bücher 1896).

The concept of evolution played a greater role. There is no doubt that most of the literature which sees the various non-Western musics as way-stations along an evolutionary line does not simply draw on the theory of biological evolution, which was often misunderstood. And yet, the idea that present forms represent stages of the past surely comes ultimately from Darwinism. Not as common is the more correctly Darwinian notion that musics and indeed individual compositions may change and adapt and thereby survive, but one can find this too, sometimes in curious places. Let me mention, as an anecdote, a small classic, Wilhelm Tappert's book *Wandernde Melodien* (1890), which already in the nineteenth century noted the distribution of a musical theme in many widespread and diverse musical and social contexts. First published in 1868, it is really a contribution to the understanding of diffusion and variation. But Tappert makes it clear that he is using Darwin's ideas to show how a melody survives by adaptation to various musical and social environments. Almost a hundred years later, one may be amused to find that Tappert wrote, in the preface to his second edition, 1890: "This introduction [a defense of socio-cultural Darwinism] was written in 1868. At that time, opinion about Darwin's theory of evolution was still divided. Today, no one argues about it any more" (trans. by BN). Incidentally, Tappert was neither biologist nor social scientist, but a choral director!

But of course later, through the work of people like Lach, Sachs, and Schneider, the interpretation of music history via unilinear evolution became part of the mainstream of early comparative musicology, and this continued into the 1940s, in a period in which cultural evolution had come to be of low esteem among anthropologists as an explanation of how things came to be (see Harris 1968 for a broad exposition of these issues). I believe that many ethnomusicologists stuck to this explanation because they came from a world of music with an intense interest in origins and history. In the late 1940s, ethnomusicologists were confronted by anthropologists (e.g., Radcliffe-Brown or Ralph Linton) who said, in effect, that's all very nice about history, but we want to know about structure and function. But many of them failed to comprehend how anyone could relegate history to second place. Only when ethnomusicology began, in the 1950s, to add what I'll call a *musical* to its more specifically *musicological* approach did the historical emphasis decline.

A third result of the historical bent of early ethnomusicology was its close association with the German school of diffusionist anthropologists, the so-called Kulturkreis school. The rather important role of musical studies in the development of this school has been traced in a recent book by Albrecht Schneider (1976). The findings of Hornbostel and Sachs, their use of the Kulturkreis concept to delineate the history of instruments in Africa (Hornbostel 1933) and even in the world (Sachs 1929) were considered to be major contributions to Kulturkreis anthropology. German diffusionism was abandoned in the 1940s, though it continued to be admired by scholars such as Clyde Kluckhohn (Harris 1968:389-90) and within limits it was even praised by Merriam (1964:289). But curiously, some ethnomusicologists stuck to it even as anthropologists were in the process of leaving it; as examples one might cite Sachs's late works (1940, 1962), Schneider's history of polyphony (1934), even a study of Jaap Kunst's about Balkan-Indonesian relations (1954). Again, it seems to me that the reason must lie in part in the ethnomusicologists' strong interest in history, a legacy of their typical background in the world of Western classical music.

Finally, Western music in the nineteenth and early twentieth centuries was taught as a compact system; by the middle of the twentieth century, it was labeled as the "common practice" period. It could expand, but only within limits, and the experiments of a Debussy, a Schoenberg, an Ives, or a Stravinsky were first at best barely tolerated by theorists and teachers (see again the theoretical works of Riemann and Heinrich Schenker). It followed, I believe, that non-Western music was perceived within a framework of an "ours-not ours" dichotomy which can be related to the concept of nationalism. Non-Western music could not make itself felt within the value structure of Western music and thus came to be valued precisely because it was different. And thus, the more different, the better. By contrast, I suspect that today's musicians would seek for accommodation, but not eighty years ago. But if early ethnomusicology was informed substantially by Western academic musical values, there were some respects in which these values caused non-Western music to be treated quite differently from Western music. The view of the integrity of the Western classical system supported the idea of comparative study, a kind of exoticism, and the belief that small samples were adequate. Comparative study resulted from the world view of a colonialist culture and the approaches of early anthropology, based on social Darwinism, missionary activity, and the amassing of museum specimens also played their part. But let's look at Western music.

Of what earthly use could it be to make a detailed inventory of the scales and rhythms of a small Indian tribe? What could this have said to the then modern musician? He or she would not have wished to emulate the Indians, and only in cases of severe nationalism would their songs have been considered an influence. I think it was because they were so different that they were considered potentially interesting. Here was a music that did not in any way share the values of Western art music, had no harmony, and was thought to be used only in conjunction with rituals and other activities. One analyzed it with methods derived from Western music study, but one was first and foremost impressed by the differences. It could not be appreciated for its own sake, but rather because, in a comparative perspective, it shed light on the nature of non-Western music as a unit, as something inherently different from Western music and thus in important ways like other non-Western music. Comparative study may have been motivated by cultural evolutionism, but it also had important perceptual connotations.

And so, as well, the one outstanding feature of the Western musician's approach to the art was omitted, the concentration on the great man, or woman, as the central thing about a musical system. Students of Western music looked to Bach and Mozart, and felt that in some way all other Western musicians emulated these great masters and were judged by how they succeeded. The contrastive avoidance of concentration on the role of the individual in non-Western, especially tribal, music has to do with the belief that non-Western music is in essence so different from the compact Western system that one cannot expect it to share any characteristics. This is all rather curious in view of the fact that so many early studies were carried out with the help of perhaps one or two informants-great persons, surely, at least in the history of research. Western music was studied because it was great, and one looked at its greatest representatives; non-Western music was different, not worthwhile as art, and thus studied because it represented a culture. And from this also stems the excessive emphasis on functionality in non-Western and folk music as stated in early ethnomusicology.

But the love of Western art music also drove the early ethnomusicologists into an attitude of exoticism. Many of us have marveled at the neglect, until recently, of the world's urban popular musics by ethnomusicologists. The line of reasoning fifty years ago may have been like this: It is worth studying non-Western music because it is so utterly different, and not because it is an inferior kind of music within an essentially Western, if broadened, system. For this reason, at least in part, those kinds of non-Western music that exhibited real or imagined relationships to Western music were neglected. I include here the by now well-known acculturated phenomena, or musics which by chance approximate Western-like sounds. The early scholars, and many later ones, tried to draw sharp lines between the ours-not ours categories. And so, for many decades, a vast proportion of the extant music in the twentieth-century third world was ignored. As we know, only recently have various popular and urban musical phenomena received attention.

To conclude: I've surely overstated my point. There are many other reasons that could be advanced to explain the way in which ethnomusicology developed. But I am convinced that, whether it was a good thing or not, ethnomusicology grew up under the aegis of Western classical music, and out of the culture of many of its practitioners and devotees in the period from 1880 to the 1930s. It is here that we must seek the reasons for the particular ways in which our field first developed, and the roots for some of the methods and approaches still followed today.

References Cited

Adler, Guido
  1908   "Über Heterophonie." *Jahrbuch der Musikbibliothek Peters* 15:17-27.

  1935   *Wollen und Wirken: Aus dem Leben eines Musikhistorikers.* Wien: Universal-Edition.

Ambros, August Wilhelm
  1862   *Geschichte der Musik.* Breslau: F. E. C. Leuckart.

Blum, Stephen
  1975   "Towards a Social History of Musicological Technique." *Ethnomusicology* 19:207-31.

Bücher, Karl
  1896   *Arbeit und Rhythmus.* Leipzig: Teubner.

Duckles, Vincent
  1972   "Musicology at the Mirror: A Prospectus for the History of Musical Scholarship." *Perspectives in Musicology*, ed. Barry Brook and others, pp. 32-49. New York: Norton.

Ellis, Alexander J.
  1885   "On the Musical Scales of Various Nations." *Journal of the Society of the Arts* 33:485-527.

Gerson-Kiwi, Edith
  1974   "Robert Lachmann: His Achievement and His Legacy." *Yuval* 3:100-08.

Gourlay, K. A.
  1978   "Towards a Reassessment of the Ethnomusicologist's Role." *Ethnomusicology* 22:1-36.

Harris, Marvin
1968   *The Rise of Anthropological Theory.* New York: Crowell.

Höfele, Karl Heinrich
1967   *Geist und Gesellschaft der Bismarckzeit, 1870-1890.* Göttingen: Musterschmidt.

Hornbostel, Erich M. von
1933   "The Ethnology of African Sound Instruments." *Africa* 6:129-57, 277-311.

Hornbostel, Erich M. von, and Otto Abraham
1904   "Phonographierte indische Melodien." *Sammelbände der internationalen Musikgesellschaft* 5:348-401.

1906   "Phonographierte Indianermelodien aus Britisch-Columbia." *Boas Anniversary Volume,* pp. 447-74. New York: G. E. Stechert.

Kolinski, Meiczyslaw
1961   "Classification of Tonal Structures." *Studies in Ethnomusicology* (New York) 1:38-76.

1965   "The General Direction of Melodic Movement." *Ethnomusicology* 9:240-64.

1973   "A Cross-Cultural Approach to Metro-Rhythmic Patterns." *Ethnomusicology* 17:494-506.

Kunst, Jaap
1954   *Cultural Relations between the Balkans and Indonesia.* Amsterdam: Koninklijk Institute voor de Tropen, Mededeling No. CVII.

Müller, Detlev
1977   *Sozialstruktur und Schulsystem: Aspekte zum Strukturwandel des Schulwesens im 19. Jahrhundert.* Göttingen: Vanlenboeck und Ruprecht.

Riemann, Hugo
1890   *Katechismus der Harmonie- und Modulationslehre.* Leipzig: Hesse.

Ringer, Fritz K.
1969   *The Decline of the German Mandarins: The German Academic Community, 1890-1933.* Cambridge: Harvard University Press.

Roberts, Helen H.
1936   *Musical Areas in Aboriginal North America.* New Haven: Yale University Press.

Sachs, Curt
1929   *Geist und Werden der Musikinstrumente.* Berlin: J. Bard.

1940   *The History of Musical Instruments.* New York: Norton.

1943   *The Rise of Music in the Ancient World, East and West.* New York: Norton.

1962   *The Wellsprings of Music.* The Hague: M. Nijhoff.

Schneider, Albrecht
1976   *Musikwissenschaft und Kulturkreislehre.* Bonn: Verlag für systematische Musikwissenschaft.

Schneider, Marius
1934   *Geschichte der Mehrstimmigkeit.* Berlin: J. Bard.

Simon, Artur
1978   "Probleme, Methoden und Ziele der Ethnomusikologie." *Jahrbuch für musikalische Volks-und Völkerkunde* 9:8-52.

Stumpf, Carl
1886   "Lieder der Bellakula-Indianer." *Vierteljahrschrift für Musikwissenschaft* 2:405-26.

1911   *Die Anfänge der Musik.* Leipzig: J. A. Barth.

Tappert, Wilhelm
1890   *Wandernde Melodien.* 2. Ausgabe. Leipzig: List & Francke.

Wallaschek, Richard
1893   *Primitive Music.* London: Longmans, Green. (Published in 1903 as *Anfänge der Tonkunst.*)

PART II THE QUESTION OF CHANGE

The Changing Role
of the
Bauls in Modern Bengal

Charles Capwell
University of Illinois

The Bauls are members of a religious sect in Bengal where they are well known for their songs. Being casteless, in the strict sense, the Bauls are similar to some religious orders in India which require their initiates to abandon conventionally organized society, including the caste structure, in order to devote themselves to other worldly pursuits. Being house-holders, however, the Bauls usually raise families,[1] and these, because of the transmission of Baul traditions, including the profession of singing to some of its members, have something of a caste-like position in society.

> The importance of Baul songs lies in the fact that they represent one of the most popular and distinct forms of Bengali folk songs, and this popularity is not confined to any region. There is scarcely any district in Bengal (including Bangladesh) where such songs are unknown. Moreover, it is not at all difficult to recognize a Baul song because . . . it has some distinct features or qualities which mark it out from other forms of Bengali folk song [Bose 1967:46].

This description of Baul song (Baul-*gān*) was given by the folklorist Sanat Kumar Bose; his opinion about the popularity and ubiquity of Baul-*gān* in Bengal makes it evident that it is a significant element in Bengali culture and one which is easily recognizable to Bengalis.

Despite their being, at times, arcanely sectarian, Baul-*gān* have a profound appeal for a large number of Bengalis as the following appreciative comments by several of them will illustrate. "That longing for the remote, that passion, that restless psychological overflowing is their gift to Bengali literature" (Jāhāṅgīr 1964:32). Such is the assessment of Bōrhānuddin Khān Jāhāṅgīr, a folklorist of Bangladesh, while Hemango Biswas, his colleague in Calcutta, has written that "the basic philosophy of the Bauls—their robust humanism—remains an ever-lasting inspiration for us" (1967:169). Of the tunes, Santidev Ghosh, the great interpreter of the songs of Rabindranath Tagore (*Robīndrosoṅgīt*) says that in them there is "an emotion of pain and resignation like that of the flute" (Ghōṣ 1962:100). The flute to which he refers, of course, is an instrument of the countryside, not of the concert hall; it is the instrument

---

[1] The religious practice of the Bauls involves the ritual performance of *coitus reservatus*. As a result of this discipline they are able to practice birth control and either produce no children, a desired goal for some, or to limit children to a number decided upon personally or through the instructions of a guru. "Accidents," as unplanned children are sometimes called by Bauls themselves, however, are not unknown.

with which Krishna makes the respectable women of Vrindavan forget their responsibilities and self-respect, just as the Bauls can give care-worn and world-weary urbanites of Bengal at least a momentary opportunity to be carefree and other-worldly.

The quality of *mon udās karā*, making one's mind indifferent to mundane matters, is well-illustrated in the text of the following Baul-*gān* which describes Radha's decision to abandon the home of her in-laws and her wifely duty for the sake of her ungovernable attraction to Krishna:

> Go, go dear, go back; I'll not go again
> to that wicked house.
> How shall I endure again and again
> such calumny of Krishna?
>
> My sister-in-law's sharp words have cleaved my breast
> and pierced my heart.
> My good name has floated away
> on that dark sea of infamy.[2]
>
> Tell my sister-in-law, tell her this--
> "He to whom Radha belongs, to him has she gone."
> This mad (*khēpā*) Baul says, "Oh, what has happened
> in coming to this material world?"

As sung by Purna Chandra Das (on *The Bengal Minstrel*, Nonesuch H-72068), the most famous contemporary Baul, the tune, with its weeping appoggiaturas and melancholy scale, perfectly conveys the pathetic affect of the situation in which Radha finds herself (Ex. 1).

Example 1. A Baul-*gān*.

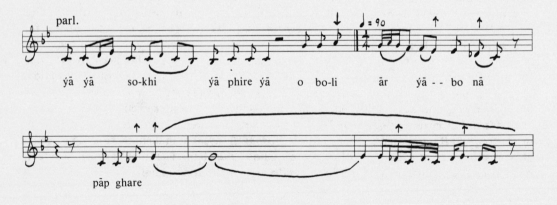

---

[2] A pun here involves the word *śyām*, an epithet for Krishna meaning "dark."

Figure 1. Bengali Child Dressed as Baul.

The fact that their music has brought the Bauls wide recognition and an affectionate, if condescending, regard may be deduced from the photo reproduced *opposite* which was once displayed in the show window of a Calcutta photographer's studio (Fig. 1). Here the treasure of a middle-class Bengali family is charmingly immortalized as a singing and dancing Baul in the manner in which an American child might pose as a cowboy or some such figure of American folklore.

Their eccentric behavior — as well as their music — elicits a favorable interest in the Bauls from other Bengalis, and they are called *ulṭo pathiks*, "contrary pilgrims," because they flout social and religious conventions. They may also be called *khēpā*, "mad," with the same indulgence as the little boy in the photo would be were he to behave in a naughty, but captivating, manner. *Khēpā*, in fact, is a highly-prized epithet among the Bauls who grant it to but a few of their number. In the song quoted above, for example, the poet refers to himself by this title in the final verse, the so-called *bhoṇitā*, or signature verse.

Another word very similar in meaning to *khēpā* is *pāgol*, and it is one which continually recurs in the speech and the songs of the Bauls because they consider it admirable to be *pāgol* by the standards of conventional behavior. This, for example, is how one song text begins:

> An inspired *pāgol* came and caused a sensation
> in Nadia city[3] — go have a look yourselves.
> I'll go with that *pāgol*, become *pāgol* myself,
> I'll look upon a new source of inspiration.
>
> Brahma is *pāgol*, Vishnu is *pāgol*, and a third *pāgol*
> doesn't allow himself to be caught.
> Shiva on Mt. Kailasa is *pāgol*, too; having eaten he is *pāgol*,
> for he lives on marijuana and jimsonweed.

Another *pāgol* song begins with the complaint *nakol pāgol sakol deśe/āsol pāgol kayjonā* — "there are false madmen everywhere; how many are the genuine madmen?" As an example of the false madmen, the song reports that:

> Some are *pāgol* for love, others are *pāgol* after material
> possessions; men *pāgol* for wealth, fame, and followers are
> everywhere.
>
> They are of every cut and color, who can keep track of them?
> Their intellects are clouded by self-deception, they do
> not understand Truth and the Eternal.

---

[3] This refers to Caitanya, a Bengali Hindu revivalist of the sixteenth century.

As for the genuine madman—

> It's a difficult matter to get a *pāgol* like Shiva,
>> he who has given up ambrosia and takes poison for food.
>> He has an ox for a mount, a hide for a seat,
>> and snakes for jewelry.
>
> Shiva left his brick house and everything in it
>> and made the burning-ground his living room.
>> For what reason does Shiva go begging,
>> He in whose house resides the Goddess of Plenty?

The tune to which this text is sung has none of the *mon udās karā* quality of the previously quoted one but expresses rather the infectiously witty and lively side of Baul character which the Bauls themselves refer to as *rosik*—in fact, in the refrain, the word *pāgol* is qualified with this adjective (*rosik pāgol*, translated here as "inspired madman") (Ex. 2). This type of tune is one which the singer is likely to provide with a physical counterpart in the form of a droll, hip-swinging dance.

Example 2. A "Pagol" Song.

Through their unconventional performances, the Bauls have become something like culture heroes for many Bengalis who view them as encapsulating an admirable aspect of a traditionally Bengali way of life. They have not always been viewed so favorably, however, for not only was their cult considered obscure not so long ago (Das Gupta 1969), but disreputable as well. In the book *Hindu Castes and Sects* published in 1896, for example, Jogendranath Bhattacarya gave this description of them: "The Bauls are low class men and make it a point to appear as dirty as possible. They have a regular costume which consists of a cone-shaped skull cap and a long jacket of dirty rags patched together extending from the shoulders to the lower part of the legs" (1968:381). Though they no longer wear this "cone-shaped skull cap," some Bauls do still wear the quilted jacket which is called *guḍhori*.

Bhattacarya did not stop with mentioning the low class and dirtiness of the Bauls; his indictment went further:

The Bauls are spoken of as Vaisnavas, but properly speaking they are a godless sect. They do not worship any idols, and on that account, their religion may be regarded as a very advanced one. But according to their tenets, sexual indulgence is the most approved of form of religious exercise, and it is said that they have been known to drink a solution made from human excretions. The moral condition of these and some other sects . . . is deplorable indeed, and the more so as there is no sign of any effort in any quarter to rescue them [ibid.].

Bhattacarya's description of them was not wholly disapproving, however, and he did at least grant that they were amusing and an attraction to the low classes:

Not only their dress but their musical instruments, their dancing, and their songs are all characterized by a kind of queerness which makes them very amusing. . . . The quaint allegories and the rustic philosophy of their songs are upon the whole so enjoyable that, in most of the important towns of Bengal, amateur parties of Bauls have been organized who cause great merriment on festive occasions by their mimicry [ibid.].

From Bhattacarya's comments it is evident that while the Bauls traditionally appealed to the rural lower classes, the urban gentlemen of the late nineteenth century had begun to find them appealing as objects of parody. In the same year that Bhattacarya published his work, the doyen of Calcutta's musical life, Raja Sir Sourindro Mohun Tagore, published his *Universal History of Music* in which he also mentions that "Amateur parties are sometimes found in imitation of the Bauls, a sect of religious mendicants who dance and sing" (1896:84). These amateur Bauls must have been something like the Bengali equivalent of the black-faced minstrels of the West.

A more profound interest in the Bauls than this parodistic one had already been manifested in 1883 by Rabindranath Tagore, who was just twenty-two at the time. Ultimately Rabindranath did more than anyone else to rehabilitate the image of the Bauls and to make it worthy of respect rather than ridicule. At this age he began his championing of the Bauls in a review of an anthology which included some of their song texts. In the review he authoritatively took to task those Bengali writers who sought to translate into their own language the themes and idioms of English literature as well as those who tried to counteract foreign influence by "purifying" Bengali grammar and vocabulary with heavy doses of Sanskrit. As an inspiration to those who wanted to find a congenial and forceful vehicle for genuine expression in their own language, he pointed out how the Bauls' songs deal with the weighty themes authors were seeking in foreign literature and how direct and fitting is their use of Bengali:

> How natural the Bengali, and how straightforward
> the affect . . . without giving it a thought, we let
> them enter the innermost part of our souls —
>
> I have seen on the Lake of Love the Man of my Heart,
>   purest gold.
> Thinking to catch him, I went to catch him and missed.

> Universal love and other such great ideas sound
> well to us from the mouths of foreigners, but how is
> it that the beggars who go about singing of these things
> in front of our very doors do not reach our ears?
> [Tagore 1966a:269].

It is well known that Tagore's ears were sharply attuned to what these beggars had to say and how they said it. The thematic content and diction of his own poetry, however refined it may have become, is permeated with the flavor of Baul texts as was clearly demonstrated by Edward Dimock (1959) in his article "Rabindranath Tagore, the Greatest of the Bauls." Perhaps even more important is the extent to which Tagore's ears were sensitive to the tunes the Bauls used to carry their texts. Though he found inspiration in the texts, it was the music which seemed the more meaningful to him. Of the words, he would say, in the preface to a later collection of folk texts (1942:x), that "all those Baul songs gotten from here and there are not worth much whether from the sadhona [spiritual] or literary point of view," but in recalling when he first heard a particular Baul song he goes on to say, "The words are extremely plain, but in conjunction with the tune, their meaning flashes up in an unprecedented brilliance . . . like the sobbing air of a child who cannot find its mother in the dark."

For Tagore, and partly through him, for the urbanized classes of Bengal, the Baul came to represent the naïve expression of truth unencumbered with social or sectarian bias. The most direct means of expressing this truth, according to Tagore, was in melody. Evidence for the importance of the tunes in Tagore's way of thinking can be found in his plays. In *Phālgunī*, for example, an allegory on the loss of innocence, the acceptance of death, and the reaffirmation of life, an irrepressible Band of Youths is confronted by a constable who gets snatches of song in reply to his queries; in mild exasperation, he says:

> C: I gather that to answer a question you sing a song?
> Y: Yes! If we don't, the answer doesn't come out right.
>   If we speak in plain words, it is terribly unclear,
>   can't be understood.
> C: Do you believe your songs are so clear then?
> Y: Of course! Don't they have tunes? [Tagore 1966b:54-55].

Later the Youths meet a Blind Baul, a man who is blind not only in the physiological sense but also in the sense that he has lost sight of those things which constitute conventional social and religious propriety. As he himself says of his blindness: "While the sight of those with eyes was setting, there arose the sight of the blind. When the sun had gone, then I saw the light within the bosom of darkness" (Tagore 1966b:71). It is this Blind Baul the Youths ask for guidance to the Old Man who possesses the knowledge of death they must acquire. The Blind Baul consents to lead them, saying "Let me go along while singing, you follow behind. If I do not sing, I can not find the path" (ibid.). As Tagore saw it, the Baul's song leads him onto the path toward a deeper understanding of life.

Elsewhere in *Phālgunī*, the ability of Baul music to achieve the most direct expression of Truth is pointed up in an encounter between the Maharaja, who naturally represents attachment to material welfare and social order with a parallel spiritual obtuseness, and the poet, who is just another aspect of the Baul in this play; indeed, Tagore refers to the Kavi-Baul, the Poet-Baul. First the Maharaja and the Poet converse; the latter says:

P. The mundane world is merely a coming and
going. That man who, while dancing to the sound of
the Baul's drone, simply comes and goes, he is a
devotee, he is a pilgrim, he is the poet-Baul's disciple.
M. If that is so, how shall I find peace?
P. We have no attachment to peace, that's how non-
attached we are.
M. But I want to obtain possessions and riches.
P. We have not even a little greed for possessions and
riches, that's how non-attached we are.
M. What can you mean? You'll cause trouble, I can see
[ibid.: 17-18].

Thereafter the poet sings a song with a paradoxical text, a type of which Bauls are fond. The Maharaja's response to it is: "I do not understand a word of what you say, but your tune pierces my heart" (ibid.: 19). To emphasize the vital message in the Baul's tune, Tagore contrasts the Maharaja's spontaneous reaction with that of the character Srutibhushan, a boring pedant, who, while capable of understanding every syllable of the text, is left completely unmoved by it, or by its musical setting.

In keeping with the tradition described by his older relative Sourindro, Rabindranath himself used to perform as an "amateur Baul" in his own plays. But his impersonation was not mimicry designed to cause "great merriment"; rather, it was meant to arouse admiration since the Baul is often the one character who has genuine wisdom.

Quite some time after he had written *Phālgunī*, Tagore (1942:x) expressed his debt to Baul music in the foreword to a collection of folk song texts, in which he says "In many of my songs I have used the tunes of the Bauls, and in many others consciously or not, they have become mixed with classical modes." The power of the tunes for Tagore was not just their ability to quicken the cold flesh of philosophy but to evoke as well, in his nationalistic songs, a sense of Bengaliness. According to Santidev Ghosh (Ghōṣ 1962:178), the twenty-four nationalistic songs of Tagore's youth, with but two exceptions, follow the style of Hindustani classical music. But in the year 1905 alone, when he wrote twenty-two nationalistic songs, nearly half of them were set to Baul tunes. The catalyst for this sudden upsurge of nationalistic expression and for its particularly Bengali flavor was the Partition of Bengal which occurred in that year. The purpose of the partition was to weaken the effectiveness of demands by the educated and partly Westernized Hindu elite for greater influence on the judicial, educational, and political institutions of the country. But the result was to kindle feelings of violent outrage from the part of Bengali society which had come to view itself as having a legitimate claim to governing power. The Partition was rescinded in 1911 when the capital of British India was moved from Calcutta to New Delhi.

When Tagore published a number of his nationalistic song texts in 1905, he chose the seemingly innocuous title *Bāul*; but while seemingly innocuous, the very title itself was an expression of the regionalistic sentiment which had been so offended by the Partition. Here is the beginning of one of the poems contained in this collection:

My Golden Bengal I love thee,
Forever your sky and breezes play a flute in my heart.
In Spring the scent in your mango groves intoxicates me,
In Fall your full fields I see with a sweet smile.

The rest is in much the same vein — rather sentimental revery on the motherland — until we reach the punch line:

> Whatever wealth a poor man has I will place at your feet,
> I will not buy at another's house a hangman's noose for
> your necklace.

Here Tagore suddenly lashes out at the British monopoly of trade in manufactured goods in India and expresses sympathy with the Swadeshi movement that encouraged a boycott of foreign manufacturers. No Bengali could have missed the point of such a song in those politically sensitive times.

What the British failed to do in 1905 was accomplished in 1947 when Bengal was permanently split between India and Pakistan. In 1971, when East Bengal, then East Pakistan, won its independence and became Bangladesh, it adopted the Tagore Baul song as its national anthem (Ex. 3).

Example 3. Tagore Baul Song.

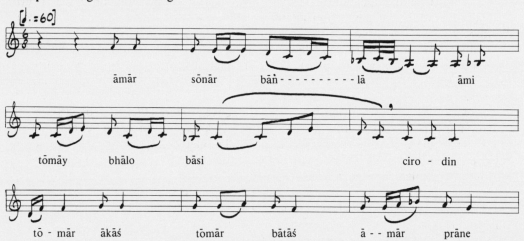

The flowing compound meter of this tune contrasts with the more vigorous type of Example 2. This characteristic and others, such as the descent to the sixth degree below the tonic and the redundant rise and fall to and from the third degree at the cadence in the fifth measure, mark it as an East Bengal tune. Tagore no doubt became familiar with such tunes during his ten years managing the family estates in Rajshahi and Kushtia districts. Of course, it would have been solipsistic of the People's Republic of Bangladesh to use the tune as Tagore had used it — to arouse awareness of Bengaliness among Bengalis. Therefore, as the Bangladesh national anthem, it has been transformed with the colonial legacy of harmony, counterpoint, and the sound of the military band to proclaim the idea of Bengali nationhood abroad in the musical idiom of international politics.

Tagore was not alone in his admiration for the Bauls or in his attempts to make them symbols of Bengali cultural and political identity. His friend and colleague Kshitimohan Sen was even more active as a collector of Baul songs and as an essayist about the sect. He wrote monographs and gave lectures about the Bauls which represented them as being free of caste prejudice and sectarian bigotry, and as being the carriers of a mystical tradition for which he found roots in the Upanishads and ramifications in a number of other North Indian sects. At the time of independence, when Hindu-Muslim antipathy was about to erupt in murderous communal riots, Sen (1949) pleaded for the continuation of the *Hindu-Mussulmāner ẏukto sādhonā*, the Hindu-Muslim cooperation which had contributed so much to the culture of India. In his own province, he saw the Bauls as living apostles of that cooperation, because in their songs Allah and Khuda were to be encountered along with Radha and Krishna and Caitanya. The Bauls, to Sen, were the contemporary inheritors, as well, of a long tradition of heterodox mysticism. To be worthy of such roles, of course, they had to be cleansed of the dirt which Jogendranath Bhattacarya had found on them. Therefore, such Bauls as Bhattacarya had described became, for Sen, *abāul*, "unbauls" (1954:50); the image of the Bauls Sen cherished was that of the *śuddho bāul*, the "pure Baul."

As described by Bhattacarya, the Bauls' "quaint allegories and rustic philosophy" were "highly appreciated by the low classes." But, through the efforts of men of high position like Tagore and Sen, the quaint allegories of the Bauls were found to be cogent and artful means of expression of a sort most natural to the Bengali language, and the rustic philosophy was found to transcend boundaries of a class, sectarian, or communal nature and to be profoundly humanitarian. Compellingly presented with the artistic and belletristic competence of Tagore and Sen, it is understandable that this romanticized image came to have a wide appeal.

The development of the rehabilitated image of the Bauls, along with the development of the media of mass communication, has served to create an ever-widening interest in the Bauls' songs which are to be heard now on radio and television, on discs, in the movies, in hotel cabarets, and on the dramatic stage in a variety of arrangements and sung by a variety of performers as well as by Bauls.

The adaptation of the Baul-*gān* idiom for use in films perhaps best illustrates both the popular recognition of the style and of those associations which have made Baul-*gān* a successful symbol for traditional Bengal. One such song, "O go tomar sesh bicharer," which occurs in the film *Dak Harkara* (*Hits from Bengali Films*, Odeon 3ABX 4001), while having a tune and text that may actually be traditional, is performed in a way that removes it completely from the traditional Baul manner of performance. The voice of the singer has the mellifluous, crooning quality and the rich vibrato that are typical of the vocal style favored by male singers of Bengali popular art song, and the tempo is too slow for a Baul performance. The accompaniment is realized on *mañjira* (a pair of small bell cymbals) and *gopīyantro* (a plucked chordophonic drone) which are commonly used by Bauls, but again, the languid tempo gives the accompaniment a peculiar flavor. The tempo, combined with the vocal timbre, serves to exaggerate—in the manner characteristic of popular art—the "mood of aching resignation like that of the flute," to use Santidev Ghosh's description of Baul songs once again. A similar mood was less self-consciously expressed by the Baul singer of Example 1.

A different and livelier mood, similar to that of Example 2, with its dancelike quality and witty text, is found in another Baul song, "Jemon beni," used in the film *Notun Phasol* (*Hits from Bengali Films*, Odeon 3AEX 4001).[4] Its paradoxical text illustrates the Bauls' belief in full participation in life without being drowned in it:

> The way my braid is, so shall it remain;
> I'll not wet my hair.
> I'll get into the water, I'll splash it around,

---

[4] Purna Das sings this text to a different tune on Nonesuch H-72068.

I'll swim back and forth, and I'll even submerge
myself—but I won't touch the water.
The way my braid is, so shall it remain;
I'll not wet my hair.

In the notes accompanying the record, credit for the tune is given to Nirmalendu Choudhury, perhaps the best-known singer of Bengali folk songs both in India and abroad. The tune, however, may be found notated in collections of traditional songs edited by S. C. Cakroborttī (1962:1, 65) (Ex. 4).

The text, as sung in the film, includes an ascription to a woman in the so-called signature line and is probably meant to coincide with the fact that the narrator in the text is female. The real author of the text, however, was a Baul known as Rasoraj, the *jéthā* or father's elder brother to Purna Chandra Das, the most widely-known Baul today.

Example 4. "Jemon beni."

To Purna, this kind of appropriation by non-Bauls of what he views as the particular heritage of the Bauls is an outrage. Speaking from his own experience in making play-back recordings for a film, he says in a short autobiographical sketch, "Bad luck as it was for us, the picture on release showed no mention of us in its credit titles. It was a lesson to us, however similar shocks were not rare in the life that followed after it" (Das Baul n.d.: [29]). Having learned what value Bengali society had come to place on the Bauls by seeing in his childhood the appreciation that Tagore had had for his father and, later, his own growing popularity, Purna Das feels an injustice has been done Bauls who have received so little in the way of a practical reward for their widely recognized contribution to Bengali culture. His emphatically stated goal for all Bauls is "no more begging!" As an individual he has achieved this goal and more; he lives in his own newly constructed home in a desirable locality of Calcutta and possesses other paraphernalia of a middle-class existence and is able to send his children to good schools. When he sings he does not, like his brethren, receive gratuities more or less at the whim of his audience or patron, but fulfills his part of a contract for which he receives an arranged fee. His wariness of anyone who seeks his services and his use of intermediaries to negotiate terms and to see that they are fulfilled sometimes surprises those who find such manners inconsistent with the other-worldly, carefree character they associate with Bauls. Unlike the Baul in Tagore's *Phālgunī*, Purna Das would probably be more sympathetic to the Maharaja's human desires; for him there is little romance in the life of poverty-stricken minstrelsy and nothing admirable in allowing others to enjoy the heritage of the Bauls for their own ends.

While appreciation for Baul-*gān* is widespread, Purna Das has recognized that there is not much of a commercial public demand for recitals made up of Baul-*gān* exclusively. Only a few urban lovers of folklore take the considerable trouble to visit the annual rural fairs, at which Purna Das no longer performs, in order to sit for hours on end through the night listening to the exuberant performances of Bauls on their home ground. Purna Das, therefore, usually includes on his programs a variety of traditional songs which are sung by his wife and other accompanists. While a number of Bauls come to Calcutta for an occasional opportunity to sing on All India Radio, at a music festival, or for a private gathering, Purna Das has achieved a unique position as a Baul in becoming a commercial artist and a cultural emissary of the Government of India.

However much the role of the Bauls may have changed during the last several generations from that of being low-class clowns to being nostalgic emblems of Bengaliness in the eyes of the public, the Bauls themselves seem not to have altered much. They have passively continued their dual lives in public as traditional entertainers and in private as religious seekers, while only Purna Das has been able actively to exploit the new opportunities inherent in the rehabilitation of the Baul image by the literary, scholarly, and entertainment worlds. Whether others will be able to join him and to establish more firmly the role of commercial entertainer among the Bauls remains to be seen.

References Cited

Bhattacarya, Jogendranath
1968   *Hindu Castes and Sects*. Reprint of 1896 edition. Calcutta: Editions Indian (dist. Firma K. L. Mukhopadhyay).

Biswas, Hemango
1967   "A Glorious Heritage." *Folkmusic and Folklore: An Anthology*, ed. Hemango Biswas, et al., vol. 1, pp. 165-76. Calcutta: Folkmusic and Folklore Research Institute.

Bose, Sanat Kumar
1967   "Baul Songs of Bengal." *Folkmusic and Folklore: An Anthology*, ed. Hemango Biswas, et al., vol. 1, pp. 45-56. Calcutta: Folkmusic and Folklore Research Institute.

Cakrobortti, Surendro Candro
[1962-63]   *Bānlār lōk sangīt*. 2 vols. Calcutta: Bengal Music College.

Das Baul, Purna
n.d.   "Baul: An Enchanting Inheritance." *Introducing Purna Chandra Das, A Baul of Bengal*, ed. Amiya Chatterjee, pp. [27-30]. Calcutta: n.p.

Das Gupta, Shashibhusan
1969   *Obscure Religious Cults*. 3rd ed. Calcutta: Firma K. L. Mukhopadhyay.

Dimock, Edward C.
1959   "Rabindranath Tagore—the Greatest of the Bauls of Bengal." *Journal of Asian Studies* 19:33-50.

Ghōṣ, Śāntideb
1962   *Rōbīndrosongīt*. Calcutta: Viswabharati.

Jāhāṅgīr, Bōrhānuddin Khān
1964   *Bāul gān ō duddu śāh*. Lōk-sāhityo sanrakson granthomālā, 5. Dacca: Bengal Academy, Bardhoman House.

Sen, Kshitimohan
1949   *Bhārote Hindu—Musolmāner Ýukto Sādhonā*. Calcutta: Viswabharati Granthalay.

1954   *Bānlār Bāul*. Calcutta: Calcutta University.

Tagore, Rabindranath [Thākur, Robīndronāth]
1905   *Bāul*. n.p.

1942   *"Āsīrbād." Hārāmoṇi*, ed. Muhammad Monsur Uddīn, pp. viii-xii. Calcutta: Calcutta University.

1966a   *Songītcintā*. Calcutta: Viswabharati.

1966b   *Phālgunī*. Calcutta: Viswabharati.

Tagore, Sourindro Mohun
1896   *Universal History of Music Compiled from Diverse Sources*. Calcutta: N. G. Goswamy.

Musical Innovation and Acculturation
in
African Music

Ashenafi Kebede
Florida State University

This short essay[1] is written as a token to honor David P. McAllester—a scholar/anthropologist, a pioneer in the creation and continuance of the Society of Ethnomusicology, and above all a great teacher, friend, and colleague. This contribution deals with musical change as it relates to African music. Hence, it follows some of the ideas of McAllester (1979) who viewed "change" as "one great constant in human culture."

While research in the area of music change has been considered an important branch of ethnomusicology for a long time, for the past decade it has been pursued by relatively few researchers. Generally speaking, ethnomusicology has really not kept up with the overwhelming changes in music that are taking place in this fast-moving world of mass communication. In fact, many European and American ethnomusicologists and educators of today still approach the study of non-Western music as their predecessors did some thirty years ago. They continue to search for the "pure" and "authentic" musical idioms with the same old erroneous assumption that all non-European traditions form an inferior stage of development to that of Europe. John Blacking (1980a:1) has understood the problem when he correctly states that ethnomusicology has "followed the pattern of imperial growth, so that in 1980 we still have a quasi-colonial situation, in which a majority of Europeans and North Americans import raw music from Third World countries and export journals and largely ethnocentric theories of music and music-making." Because of the Eurocentric foundation and development of the discipline, there has not been sufficient interest in contemporary urban and third-stream styles of African music that emerged as the result of international communication and musical diffusion.

The communications explosion is a far-reaching development in modern African life. It has intensified the extent of aural and visual contact both nationally at the inter-ethnic and externally at the international levels. Human beings of all cultures listen to each other and exchange ideas and creativity through a global dissemination of sound and pictures over the air. Even the peoples of the western world, often taken for granted, probably undergo and experience culture change at a rapid pace, accelerated by the impact of the media.

Narayana Mennon, a respected Indian musicologist who served as president of the International Music Council (UNESCO), said that some 800 million radio sets with a potential

---

[1] Most of the materials for this essay have been taken from chapters 13, 14, and 15 of my book *Roots of Black Music*. I am grateful to Mary E. Kennan, editor, Spectrum Books, Prentice-Hall, for her permission to use them.

three billion or more of listeners — about 80% of the population of the world — are tuned to music programs for something like four to five hours a day. This clearly makes radio the most popular and powerful instrument of music education or miseducation. According to Mennon (1975): "It can make or unmake musical taste, develop or kill musical activity, make or kill individual reputations on a scale unthinkable in the days before broadcasting." The establishment of the communications media around the world has played a leading role in accelerating the process of music change. Most people own, or have access to, radios. Transistor radio owners are confined to the national stations. Since many African city-dwellers own short-wave radios, broadcasts from other countries are popular. For example, radio listeners are familiar with the European BBC, the Voice of America, and other broadcasting stations of neighboring African countries such as Egypt, Sudan, Somalia, and Kenya.

Most African countries run at least two radio stations, each operating on a single band or frequency. Broadcasts are directed to the diverse ethnic groups and classes at different times. One of the two Ethiopian radio stations, for example, broadcasts daily news and music in Arabic from 7 to 8 a.m.; this is intended for the Muslim population. The Amharic program is from 8 to 9 a.m. and, as it is the national language, most societies in Ethiopia tune in. There are programs in English and French for those educated abroad and foreign residents. And since the 1974 takeover of the government by the socialist military regime *Dergue*, programs considered "revolutionary" are broadcast in the languages and dialects of the diverse peoples; it is estimated that there are over seventy languages and 300 dialects spoken in Ethiopia.[2]

Some countries like Egypt, however, own stations operating on numerous bands. Here, radio broadcasting is highly specialized and provides the public with a wide range of programs. In Cairo, for example, one frequency is given exclusively to a single popular vocalist like Om Kalthoom, while another broadcasts only readings from the Koran. This kind of generic broadcasting works best when the society is racially and culturally homogeneous. Muslim societies in many African nations often tune in to Egyptian stations. Western music, particularly black American music, has been widely diffused and made popular by commercial agencies of record and tape corporations. Because of the growth in the number of European-styled adult entertainment centers such as nightclubs, bars, coffee shops, dance saloons, and red-light districts, the demand for, and sale of, prerecorded tapes of popular music have increased dramatically.

Judging by the sale of records, tapes, and playing equipment, the audience for music in general has grown globally. Commercialism has taken advantage of this continuing increase in consumption by mass-producing music appealing to millions around the world. The large part of the global population in Africa and Asia continues to be an excellent market for western goods, including music. It is interesting to learn that the total sales of sound recordings have tripled during the past decade. Sales of popular and urban music have been the most successful. Although some African nations, such as Egypt, Senegal, and Nigeria, have established their own companies, the top six record-producing countries are, according to quantity imported, the United States, Japan, the U.S.S.R., the United Kingdom, the German Federal Republic, and France (Mennon 1975).

When traditional forms of music no longer satisfy the changing needs of society, they are either abandoned or partially modified through the processes of innovation and

---

[2] The repertory of *teramaj musiKa* (progressive revolutionary music), which is fast growing in socialist Ethiopia, can be studied as part of contemporary music. So far, no studies can be documented.

acculturation. The new styles of music, often referred to as urban music or neo-folk, blend African with European, American, and Asian elements. Here we are dealing with what McAllester calls "mixmusicology," a term he used to remind readers "that the process of music-making is the process of change and the assimilation of new ideas" (1979:182).

Problems arise, however, when we attempt to classify urban music in Africa into types and kinds. American-styled dance bands perform acculturated dance music on exclusively European instruments. These bands constitute the most common type of urban music. The African performers are formally trained in European music theory, staff notation, and rudimentary harmony. They employ alien, primarily black American, techniques as vehicles when performing musical items from African traditional sources. In other words, the leaders of the bands write compositions and arrangements based on African folk music. These jazzed-up arrangements use simple harmonic accompaniments, which are often restricted to the tonic, subdominant, and dominant chords. Other external influences on urban music come from Latin America, the Middle East, and Asia as well as from the urban music of other neighboring African countries.

As discussed in a previous article (Kebede 1976), there are also bands that play improvised and memorized music only on authentic or modified African instruments, and which do not use notation. Examples from Ethiopia were given where innovative structural modifications are observed on almost all of the traditional instruments of the *yebahil* ("folklore") orchestra. The *masinKo*[3] (fiddles), contrary to tradition, are not homemade by the individual performer. Instead they are produced in a factory. The three standard sizes now available, small, medium, and large, represent an element of acculturation along the lines of the string section of a European orchestra. The same approach is applied to the other instruments of Ethiopian traditional music. Electronic amplification devices are even attached to the resonators of chordophones; some, like the *krar* (bowl-lyre), are also equipped with nylon and wire instead of the traditional gut strings; they sound like alien instruments, even when performing a native melody. Because of these modifications, the instruments of the *bahil* orchestra produce massive volumes of sound generally preferred by modern city-dwellers.

Change is also apparent in the symbolism of musical instruments. *Bahil* (tradition) often assigned specific roles, extra-musical symbolism, and concepts to musical instruments. The *krar* traditionally possessed the theriomorphic symbolism of a farm ox, the *masinKo*, that of a horse. These and many other similar symbolic attributes of music and musical instruments are ignored and forgotten by today's young performers of urban music. Nketia (1971:330-35) has observed comparable changes in Ghana and the emergence of new musical traditions there as a result of the forces of acculturation.

Highlife is one of the oldest types of urban music of sub-Saharan Africa performed in the dance halls and nightclubs. According to Atta Mensah (1980:187), its origin dates back to the marching bands formed by disbanded Ghanaian and West Indian soldiers before the turn of the century. It certainly became most popular towards the end of the 1960s when most hotels and nightclubs employed resident bands to meet the musical needs of their dancing patrons. American popular, jazz, and calypso have marked influence on highlife. Jazz instruments — saxophones, trumpets, vibes, string basses, guitars — are often combined with a variety of African idiophones and membranophones such as drums, rattles, bells, and so on. The sizes of the bands vary from small combos of four to large orchestras of fourteen

---

[3] The capital letter "K" is here used to indicate the glottalized sound of the spoken Amharic. In this case, it is pronounced like "k" but exploded.

performers. Songs are often sung accompanied by spirited dance rhythms. The themes and texts of these songs are often borrowed from West African traditional songs.

A dance form known as *l'arab* or *tarab* is popular in the Afro-Semitic and Islamized regions, which include the entire north and northeast, as well as the Muslim areas of West and East Africa. It is characterized by the long melismas and highly ornamented melodies of the vocalist accompanied by the oriental instruments such as the *'ud*, *rbab*, and *tabl* mixed with European violins, guitars, and pianos. Unrequited love is the theme of most songs. It is a style of music popular today in many major African cities such as Cairo, Khartoum, Dar es Salaam, Tunis, Morocco, and Mogadisho. (Very similar styles, both in music-text content and performance practice, are commonly heard in the cities of the Near and Middle Eastern countries, including the Arab sections of Jerusalem, Beirut, and Teheran.)

Other names of popular dance music of the 1960s and 1970s include Congolese Rhumba, which originated in the Republics of Zaire and Congo. As its name implies, it is strongly influenced by Afro-Cuban and Latin American rhythms. *Kwela*, another powerful dance form among youth, originated in South Africa (Johannesburg) and is now widely spread throughout Central and South Africa. *Kwela* incorporated jazz idioms with African popular musical practices (Blacking 1980b:195-215).

Aside from the modern urban dance music styles, of which there are a few studies, the emergence of extended forms of third-stream music is apparent in the works of today's African composers. These have so far remained beyond the scope of ethnomusicology and musicology. African composers of the third-stream type living in this milieu feel abandoned and ignored both by the artistic and scholarly communities of Europe and America as well as by the people of their native lands. To make matters worse, concert halls, electronic studios, symphony orchestras, trained performers and, most of all, appreciative audiences of serious experimental and new works are almost totally lacking in Africa. Hence, most of Africa's composers of third-stream music have taken residencies in Europe and the United States. (This also applies to most well-known Africans in the visual and performing arts.)

Here follows a brief introduction to a few composers of this genre which I label third-stream music. The oldest African composer, the Nigerian Fela Sowande (born 1905), has written exclusively for European instruments according to western choral and symphonic traditions. Southern (1976:92) tells us that he "was a boy soprano in the Episcopal Church in Lagos, Nigeria, and studied music as a child with T. K. E. Phillips, the church's organist and church master." He obtained his Bachelor of Music degree from the University of London. Sowande's remarkable career has earned him, besides international recognition, numerous honors and awards. In 1956, Queen Elizabeth II bestowed upon him the M.B.E. (Member of the British Empire) for "distinguished services in the cause of music"; in 1972 he earned an honorary doctorate of music from the University of Ife, Nigeria.

Fela Sowande lived in London and worked as a jazz musician in the 1930s; he introduced a series of programs in African music for the BBC in the 1940s. His career as a composer-conductor reached its high point when the BBC Symphony Orchestra premiered his work *Africana* in 1944. Sponsored by the State Department, he came to the United States in 1957 to give organ concerts. He later became a permanent U.S. resident, and has taught at many universities as professor of African and Afro-American music. He has also conducted many major orchestras, including the New York Philharmonic. Sowande's best known compositions include *Africana, A Folk Symphony*, and *African Suite*.[4]

---

[4] Fela Sowande's *African Suite* is included on Columbia's *Black Composers Series*, performed by the London Symphony Orchestra conducted by Paul Freeman (Columbia M 33433).

Akin Euba is another Nigerian composer who holds the diploma of Fellow of the Trinity College (London) in piano performance and composition. He studied with Nketia and obtained his Ph.D. from the University of Ghana at Legon. Since 1963, Euba has devoted himself to the study of African traditional music, particularly the music of the Yoruba, and has produced compositions making use of elements derived from his ethnic heritage. These compositions include *Chaka* (1970), a setting of a dramatic poem by Leopold Sedar Senghor; *Dirges* (1972), for speakers, singers, instrumentalists, and dancers (using poems by African authors); and *Two Tortoise Folk Tales in Yoruba* (1975), a music-drama for Nigerian instruments using texts by Adeboye Babalola. Professor Euba also composed *Festac 77 Anthem* for the Second World Black and African Festival of Arts and Culture held in Lagos, Nigeria. This particular anthem is written for four-part choir and jazz combo including piano, drum set, congo drums, and string bass. The instrumental parts utilize improvisation in an American swing style. The English text of the anthem, excluding the refrain, is excerpted from a well-known poem by Afro-American Margaret Walker titled "For My People."[5] Professor Euba is currently serving as director of the Center for Cultural Studies, University of Lagos, Nigeria.

Other Nigerian composers of third-stream music include Akinola Akinyele, Samuel Akpabot, Ayo Bankole, Wilberforce Echezona, Lazarus Ekwueme, Adam Fiberissima, Felix Nwuba, Alphonso Okosa, T. K. E. Phillips, and Joshua Uzoigwe.

Many African composers write extended music for listening, coupling the materials of their native tradition with innovative processes. Priority is given to the propagation and advancement of one's heritage rather than to musical originality. Ephriam Amu is a good example of an African composer whose contributions exhibit a close relationship with the stylistic characteristics of his native Ghanaian traditional music. His long career goes back to the 1920s when, as a teacher, he recreated contemporary music using traditional themes in order to meet the new lifestyles of his students. "Besides paving the way for a new type of music," Nketia (1971:334) writes, "he has also helped in establishing a tradition of written African music in Ghana."

J. H. Kwabena Nketia is recognized in Ghana primarily as a composer who interprets the materials of his native tradition into contemporary idioms. Titles of his compositions include *Builsa Work Song* for piano, *Bolga Sonata* for violin and piano, and *Canzona* for flute, oboe, and piano. Author of the textbook *The Music of Africa* and numerous scholarly articles, he is internationally known as a prominent scholar of the music of sub-Saharan Africa and one of the world's most outstanding ethnomusicologists. Professor Nketia has served for many years as director of the Institute of African Studies at the University of Ghana in Legon. In addition, he held a professorial position, and even headed at one time the program of ethnomusicology, at the University of California, Los Angeles, where he has been on the faculty of the department of music for over fifteen years. N. Z. Nayo, Atta Annan Mensah (also a well-known ethnomusicologist), and Ato Turkson are among several other contemporary composers in Ghana.

Francis Bebey, former head of UNESCO's music division, is best known as a guitar soloist. This talented Camerounian is also a composer, poet, author, and administrator. He is well known in the West for his book *African Music: A People's Art*, which is widely read in Europe and America. His musical settings of other people's poems have brought him fame

---

[5] The Afro-American Margaret Walker was born in Birmingham, Alabama. Her poem "For My People" has become a source of inspiration for black people in their continued struggle against oppression and racism in the U.S.

as a performer and composer. His solo pieces include *Tingrela*, a work dedicated to a village in Upper Volta; *Song of Ibadan*; and *Concerto for an Old Mask*. His familiarity with, and knowledge of, African urban music—especially *ashiko*, highlife of the Cameroun, pygmy vocal techniques, jazz guitar (of Segovia), and Cuban *guajiro*—are demonstrated in his settings of "The Meaning of Africa" and "Breaths," poems by Sierra Leone's Abioseh Nikol and Senegal's Birgo Diop, respectively. Bebey's impressive techniques include use of the yodel when he sings (in *Breaths*, for instance) and production of percussive sound effects on the resonator and strings of his guitar.[6]

European missionary schools in particular had a marked influence on sub-Saharan African Christian musical practices and singing of hymns in four-part arrangements. It is, however, the establishment and popularity of Western-styled governments with their defense, educational, and propaganda systems throughout Africa that has accelerated the emergence and popularity of military and school bands as well as college and university choruses. Through foreign economic aid obtained by African cultural departments, musical instruments for military and school bands are often bought at exorbitant prices from abroad, and foreign band conductors are hired at the highest salary scales. Some of these foreign personnel become naturalized African citizens. In most cases, university choruses were started by European bandleaders and continued by their African students.

In Ethiopia, for example, the Armenian musician Kevork Nalbandian started the European-styled band tradition in the early 1940s. He also composed the most popular national anthem sung during Haile Selassie's reign (1930-74). His cousin Nerses Nalbandian, a naturalized citizen of Ethiopia, advanced a four-part choral tradition in Addis Ababa which blended elements from Armenian and Ethiopian urban music. Because of his use of four-part harmony laced with a heavily urbanized boogie-woogie rhythmic background, as opposed to the monophonic-textured non-rhythmic styles of most of Ethiopia's traditional music, Nerses Nalbandian's compositions can be categorized and studied as examples of musical adoption. It is interesting to note here that Nerses systematically incorporates in his compositions ornamental and decorative sound effects borrowed directly from Amhara and Armenian folk music. Most of his song texts, however, are written and sung in Amharic on serious traditional themes that deal humorously with social reform and unrequited love. For example, the text of his *anchi bale-Tela*[7] is on barley and the traditional women who make the barley-mead, called *Tela*,[8] as a livelihood. *Tela*, a native beer, is portrayed in the song as an addictively poisonous beverage that has gradually driven men from mild intoxication to drunkenness and finally to insanity. He describes the barley-mead makers as greedy and ignorant women who rob their clients both of their money and life. Nalbandian's choral works are undoubtedly intended to be both musically and morally educational to high school and college youths who often sing and listen to them.

Ethnomusicologists have often crossed over into the field of third-stream composition or performance/improvisation while undertaking comparative analysis of musical systems of two seemingly diverse cultures far apart in geographical location. While studying koto

---

[6] Bebey's music can be heard on the Philips album *Concert pour un Vieux Masque: Pièces pour Guitare* (Philips P70-4681L).

[7] The capital letter "T" indicates a glottalized Amhara sound which does not have an equivalent in the English language. The tongue is formed as in "t" but exploded.

[8] See note above.

performance techniques, I was pleased to discover cultural proximity between Japanese *sokyoku* and Amhara *azmari* music in the systems of tuning, performance, use of ornamental subtleties, and general aesthetic principles.[9] I was thus motivated to write music based on Ethiopian themes, using the Japanese koto, its tuning, and Ikuta koto notation. In *Koturasia: Penta-Melodic Exposition* for koto, violin, and B-flat clarinet, the koto is tuned to Japanese *hira joshi* tonality which is very reminiscent of the Ethiopian *yetizita zema silt*.[10] Through the use of Japanese notation, the koto also lends itself excellently to the exploration of pentachordal, chromatic, and subtle microtonal sound inflections and ornaments common to both Japanese and Ethiopian Amhara music. *Soliloquy* and *Mot* (both for voices, Japanese koto, and flute) are two of my other compositions written with the same motivation.

A few soloist-composers, like the Sundanese *'ud* player Hamza El-Din, build their entire compositions solely on elaborate Islamic-Sudanic melodic themes. In breathtaking performances, Hamza interprets a Nubian chant in *The Water Wheel*, with hypnotic effect; through the tonal repetitions of the *'ud* he communicates the timeless cycles of pastoral life embodying all the wonder in the infinity of ripples around the majesty of the Nile. His performances in the United States have received highly positive reviews from papers such as *The New York Times*, *The Woodstock News*, and *The New Age*.

Another remarkable contemporary composer from the Oriental African zone is the Egyptian-born Halim El-Dabh, who has published over fifty musical scores. His *Concerto for Durbakka* was premiered in 1959 by the American Symphony Orchestra conducted by Leopold Stokowski. He invented a new system of notation for writing the part of the *durbakka*, a vase-shaped Egyptian drum of clay and fish-skin (which is traditionally symbolic of earth and water). Halim's musical vocabulary is rooted in his Afro-Arabic heritage. His compositions are devoid of Western harmonic progressions. Instead, one experiences heterophonic and polyphonic elements very characteristic of the music of the Nile Valley cultures, elements which have been re-introduced to Western music by Stravinsky. Again following his Egyptian heritage and background, many of El-Dabh's compositions integrate and correlate dance, folklore, poetry, and singing with new meanings in space and sound. His *Clytemnestra*, which premiered in New York with choreography by Martha Graham, is a dance opera which has been hailed as a milestone in American theater. This success led to his symphonic music for the ballet *Lucifer*, performed by Rudolph Nureyev and Margot Fonteyn, choreographed by Martha Graham, and premiered in 1975. Halim El-Dabh is currently serving as professor of music at Kent State University.

Danielou (1969:14) once wrote: "The very term ethnomusicology, employed for the study of African music, already implies a standpoint that is scientifically and culturally unacceptable." He (ibid.: 7) reasons that Africa "is not a remote island where prehistoric cultures have miraculously survived which musical archaeologists can study and classify as one studies and classifies different kinds of chipped flint tools." I have been taught that ethnomusicology is a systematic study of the music of man/woman in the context of his/her

---

[9] For example, listen to *Pentatonism & Microtonality*, which may be obtained from International Music, P.O. Box 20291, Tallahassee, FL 32304.

[10] *Koturasia* has been widely performed by Fusako Yoshida and others in the United States, including locations such as Japan Auditorium, New York City; Colden Auditorium, Queens College, Flushing, New York; Brandeis University Recital Hall, Waltham, Massachusetts; and Florida State University School of Music, Tallahassee, Florida. For the complete score, write International Music, address above.

culture, East or West. If this holds still true, why has there been so much neglect of contemporary music styles in Africa such as the urban and third-stream types? Many Western scholars still approach Africa as though it is an isolated case, erroneously forgetting that Africa has always been part of, and has contributed to, all the intercultural events that have also affected the rest of the world.

Europeans and Americans are always commended when they demonstrate bimusicality, knowledge of African music as a secondary area, through theory, performance, or even composition. The exact opposite often happens when Africans and Asians involve themselves in the mastery of culture areas outside of their own. Africans and Asians are repeatedly told to honor and promote the values of their musical heritage instead of blending it with alien characteristics. In fact, many traditionalist Africans and most ethnomusicologists blindly, without active listening or thinking, consider the contemporary styles of African music discussed in this essay to be inferior forms of music. They forget, when dealing with African and Asian cultures, that technology has turned the world into a global village. They completely ignore the fact that change is an inevitable part of our contemporary lifestyle, East or West. The most rapid musical changes of all are taking place in European and American cultures because they are being daily impregnated by elements coming largely from Africa and Asia. In this age of mass media and worldwide air transportation and communication, most serious musicians anywhere and of whatever racial origin are often involved in the study of world music. Some schools in the United States have even made the study of non-European music a requirement for graduating with a music degree.[11] Yet the names of numerous African composers or their works are not known or mentioned.[12]

There are also those scholars who profess that the diversity and charm of world cultures is being daily threatened as technology standardizes everything in our lives from music, dress, and transportation to food. They discourage the creation, performance, or study of acculturated music in Africa or anywhere else. The well-known Vietnamese musicologist Tran Van Khe (1975) has indicated that we will all be sucked into the mainstream of standardization where life loses all charm, unless some thought is given to the preservation of the great musical traditions that belong to all humans. Alan Lomax has also discussed his fears of a gradual but great cultural grey-out if the processes of acculturation continue at the present rate on a worldwide basis. Using a biological mode, he and Arensberg (1977:679) say: "Reduction of cultural variety limits human variation and adaptability, and thus the continued loss of culture autonomies means a shrinking of genetic resources which will sooner or later threaten our biological future as a species."

McAllester, on the other hand, maintains a different view. He (1979:181) puts it eloquently as follows:

> After all our impulses to cherish and protect, we should realize that human culture is not a flower with fragile petals ready to drop at the first frosty touch of a new idea. Culture is more like an irresistible plague, pandemic to humankind. New ideas are the food it feeds on, and these can no more be stopped than the perpetuation of life itself. The musical manifestations of culture are, by their sonorous nature, highly evident. They give public notice of the spread of culture.

---

[11] At Florida State University, for example, a course in world music is required for all undergraduate music majors working towards a degree.

[12] Due to space limitations, musical examples are not included.

References Cited

Blacking, John
1980a "Purpose, Theory, and Practice for the Next Twenty-Five Years in Ethnomusicology." Draft paper distributed at the 1980 Society for Ethnomusicology meeting, Bloomington, in November.

1980b "Trends in the Black Music of South Africa, 1959-1969." *Musics of Many Cultures*, ed. Elizabeth May, pp. 195-215. Berkeley: University of California Press.

Danielou, Alain
1969 "Cultural Genocide." *The World of Music* 21/1:6-16.

Kebede, Ashenafi
1976 "Modern Trends in Traditional Secular Music of Ethiopia." *The Black Perspective in Music* 4/3:289-301.

Khe, Tran Van
1975 "Present and Future Preservation and Presentation of Music and Dance." Paper distributed and read at the World Music Conference, Montreal, Canada, in October.

Lomax, Alan, and Conrad Arensberg
1977 "A Worldwide Evolutionary Classification of Cultures by Subsistence Systems." *Current Anthropology* 18/4:659-701, 705-08.

McAllester, David P.
1979 "The Astonished Ethno-Muse." *Ethnomusicology* 23/2:179-89.

Mensah, Atta Annan
1980 "Music South of the Sahara." *Musics of Many Cultures*, ed. Elizabeth May, pp. 172-94. Berkeley: University of California Press.

Mennon, Narayana
1975 "The Influence of the Mass Media on Tomorrow's Public." Draft paper distributed at the World Music Conference, Montreal, Canada, in October.

Nketia, J. H. K.
1971 "Modern Trends in Ghana Music." *Readings in Ethnomusicology*, ed. David P. McAllester, pp. 330-35. New York: Johnson Reprint Company.

Southern, Eileen
1976 "Conversation with Fela Sowande, High Priest of Music." *The Black Perpective in Music* 4/1:90-104.

Social Change and the Functions
of
Music in Java

Martin Hatch
Cornell University

Several recent analyses of central Javanese society have stressed the need to understand aspects of Javanese song and instrumental music of the past in order to comprehend fully not only the cultural history but also the economic and political history of central Java (Day 1981; Errington 1979, about Malay *hikayat*, but with clear analogies to Javanese song; Scherer 1975). This need is tied most obviously to an inquiry into the mechanics and effects of Javanese poetry in particular and the history of Javanese literature in general. Evidence of writing in Java — inscriptions in stone — begins with the Taruma inscription, in the fifth century A.D. (deCasparis 1975:19). By the ninth century, the nature and amount of that evidence is such that some scholars assume that writing was widespread throughout Java at that time (ibid.: 28ff. and 72). Other evidence suggests that literacy was not limited to a scribal, priestly, or economic elite alone, but was learned as one of the crafts, as part of the education of many other Javanese as well (ibid.: 72-73). Evidence of widespread literacy before the seventeenth century throughout mainland Southeast Asia and in the Philippines is cited in Furnival (1943) and Francisco (1977). Prior to the middle of the nineteenth century, when commercial printing began in Southeast Asia, all Southeast Asian texts except those written for Western readers were handwritten on paper or palm leaf (Pigeaud 1967:1, 33-36). Almost all of those manuscripts were poems, with contents that ranged from chronicles and genealogies to stories of heroes, from prayers to letters. Scholarship based on these works has been bibliographic, philological, and historical. But scholars have often noted that the poetry with which they were working was, in fact, meant to be sung (Teeuw et al. 1969:7; Pigeaud 1967:1, 20; Kunst 1973:122). Indeed, up until the twentieth century, almost all words written in Javanese were meant to be sung. Names for the categories of different genres of sung poetry have changed throughout the one thousand year history of Javanese literature. The most recent name for the most common form of Javanese poetry is *tembang*. (See Hatch 1980 for a discussion of the history of *tembang* as a musical and literary medium.)

Whatever historical developments a culture has experienced, the differentiation between spoken and sung words has usually involved ascribing some mysterious or magical significance to the sung. Discourse is spoken or written; if written, usually as an outgrowth of or intertwined with the spoken. Most analyses of spoken words which try to ascertain meaning analyze grammatical construction and vocabulary. Tones and rhythms of the words are only minor considerations. If they are considered at all, it is as a part of analyses of poetry. Then tone and rhythm are usually presented as supplements to the analysis of text meanings, as in discussions of metrics. But, in the case of sung words, tone and rhythm can be equal to or more important than grammar and vocabulary in the apprehension of meaning—the effect of the song.

Developments in the politics and economics of Western societies, and in one strong current of educational policy in the West, have produced conditions where analysis of the the mysteries of songs has been divided into consideration of its text and consideration of its tones and rhythms, or its melody. Thus song texts, whether orally communicated and then written down, or originally composed in written form, have often been given value and meaning independent of their melodies, and their melodies have often been analyzed in search for meanings independent from their words. One such approach regards melody as a "setting" of text; another, as an "enhancement."

The developments in Western societies that led to such a schism in consideration of a unitary form, song, also gave rise to the predominant way of perceiving politics and political acts: members of Western societies regard a musician as either a political person or a musical person, and music as either political or transcending politics—one musical tradition or traditional music in the world of musical traditions or traditional musics. This way of perceiving music allows that musicians who pursue their love for music are not political, except perhaps when their love for music has political implications. They may not be aware of these implications, and they may not be held responsible for them.

The power of music has changed for most Westerners over the ages. The singing of a song was, in the past, a powerful act—not for the words alone, but for the words as songs. It is evident that a similar sense of power in tone and rhythm is still felt by most musicians. But now, even most musicians see this power as fundamentally different from the kind of power that "runs the world." This is the case because the weight of established powerful opinion runs against the sense of power that musicians may feel.

If Euro-American societies were the first to adopt this set of attitudes, then many other societies around the world are joining in. It is also possible that the complex of conditions of which these attitudes are a part has become a worldwide epidemic—what can be called the demystifying or rationalizing of human experience. The condition has been most successfully accomplished in Euro-American cultures, but the elites of other societies of the modern world are not far behind.

There is mystery/magic in music. The mystery of song makes speech into incantation. In the view of most Westerners, this kind of mystery is not a proper part of the organization of the state. And some Western analysts of Javanese society have gone so far as to maintain that the belief in mystery, the mysterious, in Javanese cultures has stood in the way of economic and political development—rationalization of modes of production, distribution, and consumption (May 1978:311-35).

Where do Javanese music and other crafts belong in this rationalized scheme of the future? In roles not unlike those into which they have been placed in Western societies that are under pressure from similar forces. In Java, instrumental music and related crafts have been made *seni*, "arts," and institutionalized in art institutes under the rubric of departments of education and culture. Large gamelan ensembles play incidental music at the opening of shopping centers and movie theaters or at the gate-ways to public parks. The great gong is struck to mark the opening of the branch of a bank or a regional economic development office. Gamelan, wayang, and dance are mobilized for tourist displays of the Javanese spirit. Gamelan practice is taught to political prisoners in order to "civilize" or "enculturate" them.

Recent analyses of the politics of Java have revealed that, for at least some important political leaders of the Javanese past, the sense of political organization of society that served as an underpinning for their political activities was analogous to their sense of the organization of Javanese gamelan ensembles. R. M. Soetomo, whom Benedict Anderson calls a "central figure in pre-independence Indonesian politics" (Anderson 1979:223), developed an ideal model of Indonesian society after independence which was based on his understanding of the dynamics of performance in a gamelan ensemble. His view of the glorious (*mulia*) Indonesia of the future was one in which the people performed together according to their achievements and competence in a confluence of energies for the common good. There would be leaders, but they would not pull their followers or force them into submission. Rather they would be guides, like older brothers or fathers to the younger brothers or children in a family (Scherer 1975:218ff. and 231ff.).

Several contemporary Javanese teachers of gamelan performance and theory discuss the organization of gamelan in ways similar to Soetomo's. Martopangrawit, the senior teacher of performance and theory at the academy of Javanese performing arts in Surakarta, divides the gamelan into two functional groups: *pamangku*— those who support or carry—and *pamurba*— those who guide the way. These two groups are further divided into the *pamangku* and *pamurba* of *lagu*—melodic aspects—and of *irama*—rhythmic aspects. The *pamurba* of *lagu* is the *rebab* (spike-fiddle) in most pieces, but could also be the *gender* (10-14 suspended key metallophone) or *gambang*/(xylophone) in other soft pieces, and the *bonang* (pot-gong rows) or *saron* (a 5-7 key metallophone) in louder pieces. The *pamurba* of *irama* is invariably the *kendhang* (drum set). *Pamangku* of *lagu* are other metallophones, zither, *suling* (end-blown flute), and voices. *Pamangku* of *irama* are various larger pot-gongs and several different-sized, hanging, knobbed gongs. All functional groups in the ensemble work together to produce the gamelan piece (Martopangrawit 1975:I, 4-5). Using the metaphor constructed by another important theorist of gamelan, Ki Sindusawarno, this working together in gamelan is like that of a Javanese family working and playing together for the good of each member (Sindusawarno 1955:40).

Soetatmo Soeriokoesoemo, one of the first Javanese nationalists, and admittedly a cultural conservative in his generation of leaders, saw the difference between this Javanese view of the proper organization of social groups and theories of the "people's democracy" that were being advanced in Java at the beginning of the twentieth century. He maintained that "if men had equal rights, they would have no duties to fulfill . . ." (quoted in Shiraishi 1981:103) and that a more appropriate analogy could be drawn between the organization of the state and the organization of the Javanese family. He elaborated on this point in the following passage:

> Equality and brotherhood . . . are also preached by the wise; but not the equality of democracy, which speaks of equal rights, but the equality of the family, where the eldest son plays a more important part in carrying domestic burdens and duties, and so enjoys more rights than his younger, still playing-around, brother. There are no equal right in such a family and yet among the children there rules equality and brotherhood in the fullest sense of the word [ibid.].

It is clear for many historians and political scientists, the structures and practices of Javanese song and gamelan can be essential tools for understanding the structure of Javanese society in the past. It is also clear that, in the present, the relationships between those practices and their social contexts have changed in ways which can only be described as revolutionary. Those changes are indicated by two comments made about gamelan performance by contemporary performers of gamelan and by other members of Javanese society. When asked what are the relationships between music and politics in Java today, most musicians will answer that there are none. They will often say that gamelan is a *seni tradisi* (traditional art) and they are *seniman musik* (musicians) with no interest in politics.

In times past, even as late as the nineteenth and early twentieth century, the linkages between musical and political power were quite close. Particular gamelan sets were associated with sacral power. Particular gamelan pieces had specific associations with the condition of a king's rule. Individual leaders were able to draw to their court centers the most lively and energetic musical craftsmen and craftswomen, and thus to display a rich show of the diversity of their realm. But if, in modern times, music and politics do not mix, is it because present-day political leaders allow no room for the contexts and popular attitudes toward gamelan that thrived in the past?

There are Javanese and Western observers of Indonesian affairs who suggest that gamelan is a part of the feudal Javanese past, and that it has no clear role in a modern Java of present and future. Some gamelan musicians say, in response to this charge, that gamelan is neither a part of a feudal past nor an aspect of modern Java. It is "traditional." The designation "feudal" would imply that the ethos in which gamelan functioned was oppressive, nonparticipatory, and corrupt. But in rejecting the epithet "modern" as well, gamelan musicians are affirming that the traditional functions of gamelan and attitudes toward it are alive for some Javanese, and the possibility remains that the past order of Javanese society which gamelan represents can and will thrive again in the future.

Following the successful violent revolution against Dutch economic and political domination, violent because that was the only way the Dutch could be forced to let go—a Javanese elite with a goal of modernizing the economics and politics of Indonesia quickly asserted its strength. In this sense, Western economic powers came out of the revolution with more than they took into it. (See Akhmadi 1981 for a recent analysis of the relationship between the modern Indonesian elite and Dutch colonial attitudes.) This Javanese elite alternately vied for power or cooperated with the strongest force at that time—the personal power of Ir. Soekarno, accepted as the father (*bapak*) of the revolution.

Soekarno's speeches and public policies most often reflected not only a ruler's graceful acknowledgement of and respect for his own strengths, but also a recognition of the strengths, loves, and needs of the people he guided. Soekarno held tenaciously to a moderate line of balance between ministering to the elite's demands and the people's needs. In balancing the various forces, he may well have placed too much emphasis on the demands of the economic elite for a modern, Westernized structure for the economics and politics of the state. It is possible that his focus on these demands was caused by his awareness of the need for world, mainly American, recognition and the military power that would have been mustered to overthrow his rule had he moved to base his power solely on the sources of power in pre-colonial Javanese society. In this sense, he stepped into a partly "rationalized" power structure and agreed to rule within that structure in order to save his country from further bloodshed. If this analysis of the bases of Soekarno's leadership has a major flaw, it is in his assent to the establishment of a Western-style educational system in Indonesia. His rejection of the more Javanese educational system, called Taman Siswa, was a step away from what would have been another important stage, probably the most important stage, in legitimizing his power and establishing Indonesia as a viable alternative force, a Third Force, in world politics. (See McVey 1967 for a discussion of the political and ideological aspects of the Taman Siswa decision, and Akhmadi 1981 for a recent complaint about the ineffectiveness of Western education methods in Indonesia.)

As part of this decision, the Indonesian arts conservatories, among them the conservatory of Javanese performing arts, were established to re-institutionalize, but in a much different form, these richly endowed and much respected traditional structures and articulations of the Javanese people. The difference in institutional form caused a crucial change in the direction of the development of the Indonesian state in general, and of Javanese "arts" in particular. This development in the arts can still be reversed, because enough venerated artists and enough energetic youth remain to establish the arts in a position resembling their former one. It is improbable, however, that the development can be reversed in the "arts" without it being reversed in the state. Indeed, there are clear indications that the reversal of this development of the arts would present a threat to the present rationalizing trends in the power structure of the state, and thus would immediately be suppressed by modern political forces.

This general analysis of these political developments is given particular substance when we consider a recent incident involving the President of Indonesia, Ex-General Soeharto. On October 28, 1974, the president called together a group of Jakarta journalists to issue a statement on his family origins and distribute copies of his family tree. At that meeting, he introduced to the press the members of his family and other persons who could attest to the conditions, the facts, of his birth and childhood. Soeharto was acting to squelch ideas of his noble origins which might have been prompted by the appearance, a month before, of an article in a Jakarta magazine. The article suggested that Soeharto might be the lost son of a former sultan of Yogyakarta, that he might be another in the traditional pattern of rightful leaders of the Javanese people, that he might be a ruler with another of the traditional powers or rights to rule — the legitimacy of a family connection with the rulers of the past.

There are two main reasons why such an attempt to mythicize Soeharto's rule would have been attempted: to legitimize a rule that had few other traditional claims to power, or to invest the ruler with traditional sources of power in order to prepare to undermine those sources. If the former, the mythicizer would hope to lull an increasingly hostile population into benign acceptance of Soeharto's command. If the latter, the mythicizer would hope to undermine Soeharto's rule by calling to popular attention at a later time the many ways in which Soeharto's rule was corrupt and otherwise historically invalid. In this sense, once the leader was set up, he could be knocked down.

Based on an analysis of other aspects of contemporary Indonesian politics and the traditional historical roots of leadership, one can conclude that the purpose of this attempt to mythicize Soeharto's power was to invest him with traditional power in order to sap him of that power and end his rule. It is clear from the present government's management of popular elections and misappropriation of Indonesian economic resources that Soeharto's power does not arise from popular awe. How does it maintain itself? By military force. And even this force is internally threatened if his rule is not rationalized, for the military force which he leads is corrupt at the top as well. Rationalization of the military stresses chain of command over the "popularity" of an individual leader. Old sources of power, which include personal strength, charisma, and social grace, are rarely found among the highest military leaders. These leaders can justify their rule only by rationalizing the present power relationships and claiming that they are due the respect of those they lead because they are the present leaders — and for that reason alone. (See D. Anderson 1976 for a discussion of one attempt at rationalization, the enforced centralization of authority, in the Indonesian military.)

The present Indonesian military leadership, through its rationalized bureaucracy, has developed a propaganda/educational campaign which stresses the importance of diverse cultures of Indonesia. The complex of buildings and engineered water and land called Taman Mini-Indonesia is a microcosmic construction of this attitude. Built in the 1970s, this "mini-Indonesian park" as the name indicates, is a square mile of water and land bulldozed out of rice fields near Jakarta, west Java, to form a small version of the Indonesian islands and the seas around them. Each mini-island provides the sites for full-sized buildings in the architectural styles of the cultures indigenous to that island. Each building houses exhibitions of arts and crafts, and periodic performances of dance and music, from the home area of the building. A large stone, concrete, and glass building near the entrance to the park serves as a reliquary for retired holy relics (*pusaka*), including collections of *kris* and *batik* from the presidential collections and a room full of gamelan ensembles, with wax musicians attending to all of the instruments. The performing arts of central Java are among the other aspects of Javanese culture that are stressed in this campaign for diversity. These performing arts were institutionalized in mostly government conservatories and academies during the early years of Indonesian independence (Hatch 1979). Aside from the fact that these institutionalizations were based on rationalized views of the functions of the arts—views that are ultimately untenable for artistic activities in any society—they were particularly invalid for the traditional arts of Java, as those arts functioned in the Javanese past. To compound this basic theoretical error, the propaganda campaign stresses the material aspects, the instruments, forms, and structures, over the cooperative, familial processes and attitudes in the artistic activities.

The strength of traditional Javanese music was that it became the expression of a community, the whole self of the community. It told how life was organized for the community. It was not a concert art which separated performers from the audience. As Judith Becker has observed, in the Javanese arts "one finds no star system, no glorification of the category of individuals called artists" (Becker 1979:6). Javanese music had close connections with *slamatan*, ritual assurances of safety, health, and security. It was closely linked to everyday public functions. Gamelan performances aerated the blood of the community. The sound of song knit together the social fabric. Gamelan performance animated sacred functions. This is why early types of gamelan ensembles are associated with priests and teachers, and many of the Javanese names for forms of song refer also to the basic sacred and educative activities in the community.

The skill of Javanese gamelan musicians lies in their abilities to draw, in cooperative play, from the rich repertories of patterns (*cengkok*) in their musical memories, and to inflect those patterns with their own immediate sense of the proper musical statement (*wiletan*). The skill of Javanese singers of *tembang* lies in their abilities to elaborate (with *wiletan*) upon a melodic and textual phrase (*cengkok*) in a process of "ongoing derivation and embellishment which is the very life and substance of art in Java" (Day 1981:19). For both singer and gamelan musician, it is the inflected patterns, not the patterns themselves, which are music. Strength lies not in structure, but in the communal transformation of that structure. If this attitude toward the social aspects of the tradition is being abandoned now, it is because able musicians are being seduced by the glitter of elite status, the virtuoso performer; by the desire for control over the musical riches of the tradition, the expert director; by the lure of the "genius" of individuality, the innovative composer. These enticements, parts of the politics of modernization, are not uncommon in the music of societies of our time. In Javanese music, to succumb to them is to leave the strength of the tradition. Or perhaps the power of the tradition, in social contexts and popular attitudes, is abandoning the musical forms. Is that power flowing into newer genres of Indonesian music, such as *pop* and *dangdut*?

The strength of a ruler in Java of the past lay in his ability to concentrate effectively in himself the free-floating powers, like musical patterns, available in the society he led (Anderson 1972:8ff.). Power in Javanese society was loose in the world; people supported the ruler who was able to draw that power to himself. The ideal leader radiated a sense of *tentrem kerta raharja*—peace, quietude, prosperity—outward to his supporters. When such a condition turns to control by threat of force from the top, then it can be said that the power of the tradition has moved on.

References Cited

Anderson, Benedict
1972   "The Idea of Power in Javanese Culture." *Culture and Politics in Indonesia*, ed. Claire Holt, pp. 1-69. Ithaca: Cornell University.

1979   "A Time of Darkness and a Time of Light: Transposition in Early Indonesian Thought." *Perceptions of the Past in Southeast Asia*, ed. A. Reid and D. Marr, pp. 219-48. Singapore: Heinemann.

Anderson, David
1976   "The Military Aspects of the Madiun Affair." *Indonesia* 21:1-64.

Akhmadi, Heri
1981   *Breaking the Chains of Oppression of the Indonesian People.* Ithaca: Cornell Modern Indonesia Project.

Becker, Judith
1979   "People Who Sing: People Who Dance." *What Is Modern Indonesian Culture?*, ed. Gloria Davis, pp. 3-10. Athens: Ohio University Press.

Day, John A.
1981   "Meanings of Change in the Poetry of Nineteenth-Century Java." Ph.D. dissertation, Cornell University, History Department.

deCasparis, J. G.
1975   *Indonesian Palaeography.* Leiden: Brill.

Errington, Shelly
1979   "Some Comments on Style in the Meanings of the Past." *Journal of Asian Studies* 38:231-44.

Francisco, Juan
1977   *Philippine Palaeography.* Manila: Philippine Journal of Linguistics.

Furnival, John S.
1943   *Educational Progress in Southeast Asia.* New York: Far Eastern Society.

Hatch, Martin
1979   "Theory and Notation in an Oral Tradition: Some Notes on ASKI, Surakarta." *What Is Modern Indonesian Culture?*, ed. Gloria Davis, pp. 11-18. Athens: Ohio University Press.

1980   "Lagu, Laras, Layang: Rethinking Melody in Javanese Music." Ph.D. dissertation, Cornell University, Music Department.

Kunst, Jaap
1973   *Music in Java: Its History, Its Theory and Its Technique.* 3rd ed. The Hague: Nijhoff. Originally published 1934.

Martopangrawit, R. L.
1975   *Pengetahuan Karawitan.* Volume 1. Surakarta: ASKI.

May, Brian
1978   *The Indonesian Tragedy.* London: Routledge & Kegan Paul.

McVey, Ruth
  1967   "Taman Siswa and the Indonesian National Awakening." *Indonesia* 4:128-49.

Pigeaud, Theodore
1967-70   *Literature of Java.* 3 vols. The Hague: Nijhoff.

Scherer, Savitri
  1975   "Harmony and Dissonance: Early Nationalist Thought in Java." M.A. thesis, Cornell
          University, History Department.

Shiraishi, Takashi
  1981   "The Disputes between Tjipto Mangoenkoesoemo and Soetatmo Soeriokoesoemo: Satria vs.
          Pandita." *Indonesia* 32:93-108.

Sindusawarno, Ki
  1955   *Ilmu-Karawitan.* Volume 1. Surakarta: Konservatori Karawitan.

Teeuw, A., et al.
  1969   *Siwaratrikalpa.* The Hague: Nijhoff.

Navajo Ceremonialists
in the
Pre-1970 Political World

Charlotte J. Frisbie
Southern Illinois University
at Edwardsville

Introduction

Ethnomusicological considerations of the political sphere of culture to date remain minimal. Various researchers, using a structural-functional approach, have considered music as political expression, identifying certain genres which express social protest, public opinion, praise for present rulers, or otherwise function in enforcing conformity, and challenging or preserving the existing sociopolitical order. Work on the politics of music within specific cultural contexts, and other topics such as the politics of musicians' groups, has barely begun. Even with the increasing interest in music in its cultural context and in music makers themselves, we have yet to reach the point where the numerous roles music makers have in any culture are fully explicated. While we can speak with some understanding about who is or is not a music maker in X culture, discuss the achieved or ascribed processes by which one becomes or realizes that he or she is a music maker, describe what one does musically as a music maker, and discuss what status music-making has in a specific cultural context, we have yet to know enough about the lives of music makers to understanding the possible associations this role has with comparable ones in other spheres of culture. Yet, in the American Indian world alone, we have past and present indication that music makers, especially when operating in the traditional ceremonial world, may express their influence politically as well as ceremonially by having equal voice with other people of power, participating in councils or, as in the pre-Conquest Pueblo case, in a theocracy.

In Navajo studies, the lack of consideration of possible relationships between traditional ceremonialism and its music-making leaders (herein termed ceremonialists) and politics is just as apparent. Anthropological and ethnomusicological considerations of the power of Navajo ceremonialists have most often focused on the realm of the sacred. After a century of anthropological work and at least three decades of ethnomusicological work, much of which has been conducted by McAllester either singly or in collaboration with others, students of Navajo culture have access to a number of explications of the powers inherent in and available through traditional Navajo religion. Likewise, the status and religious roles of practitioners have been examined to yield a much better understanding of both the bodies of knowledge from which their ritual and spiritual powers derive, and the ritual performance contexts in which these powers are repeatedly demonstrated, reactivated, and reaffirmed. Ceremonialists, as leaders of ritual dramas which entail the knowledge and correct performance of numerous sequenced songs, prayers, ritual acts, recitation and explication of myths, and sandpaintings, are well known. Yet, in all of this work, and maybe because of it, little attention has been given to the other kinds of powers and influence which may be associated with the ceremonialist status. In the area of politics, the lack of effort may derive from an early and apparently continuing acceptance of the Franciscan Fathers' (1910:382) statement, "While the influence of the chanter is felt it has very little, if any, bearing on the government of the tribe as such."

Developments that occurred on the reservation from 1970 to 1980 during my fieldwork suggest that it is time to reexamine this statement. Because of these, and because ethnomusicology as a discipline needs to expand its queries about the political sphere of culture beyond those focused on music as political expression, I have decided to offer a preliminary essay on Navajo ceremonialists in the political world. While spatial restrictions have forced me to limit the present discussion to evidence for past political involvement of known ceremonialists, I plan to complete the discussion by analyzing contemporary trends in a future essay. It is my hope that the present essay[1] and its future counterpart will stimulate further discussion of the political roles and political involvement of traditional ceremonialists, and will provide an impetus for statistically verifiable research on the topic in the years ahead.

Research Problems

The story of the development of Navajo sociopolitical organization is really one of development from band to nation. In order to determine what relationship, if any, existed in the past between ceremonialism and politics, one is faced with reconstructing the political and ceremonial universe through time. While initially this might seem feasible, in reality it is next to impossible. In the past there were numerous avenues to prestige and influence in the Navajo world; among them were warfare, hunting, leadership in peace, wealth in livestock, and ceremonial knowledge. Politically, while one can identify some of the more famous eighteenth and nineteenth-century war and peace leaders and local headmen, and subsequent twentieth-century tribal chairmen, vice chairmen, and tribal council delegates, available records do not allow reconstruction of the total universe. Additionally, autobiographical materials on most of these individuals are either nonexistent or so limited that any assessment of their possible concurrent roles as ceremonialists is impossible.

Trying to reconstruct the known universe of ceremonialists is equally fraught with problems. Life details of very few such individuals are represented in the literature. For those for whom they are known, in some cases it is impossible to tell if political activity was also part of their world and, if so, at what point in their lives it became important.

While these problems will, of necessity, remain impenetrable, the available information does suggest a few insights. To explicate these, let us examine what is known about the universes to determine what can be said about their relationship.

Original Leadership System

Origin myths offer a variety of prototypes for political leadership in the present world by recounting the situation as it existed in earlier worlds. For example, Van Valkenburgh

---

[1] I would like to thank David M. Brugge, Bruno Nettl, and Mary Shepardson for their helpful suggestions and critical comments on an earlier version of this essay. I, of course, assume full responsibility for the present version.

(1945:64) discusses four leaders in the Lower World, each of whom was paired and associated with a direction: Big Wolf and wife-east, Coyote and wife-west, Badger and wife-north, and Mountain Lion and wife-south. These leaders functioned as intermediaries between the People and the supernaturals and helped maintain and enforce certain behavioral laws. After the Emergence, Changing Woman appointed four chiefs who again had directional affiliations as well as the job of organizing the present world, holding council, and directing work. East, of course, had priority. According to Shepardson (1963:7-8) the mythological materials, despite their variations, give some indication of a democratic council, the possibility of women chiefs, and a dual division between war and peace leaders.

Leadership roles during the early foraging band period in Navajo history can only be hypothesized. Analogies based on ethnographic descriptions of contemporary foragers suggest that leadership roles were temporary, ever-changing, and event-specific. The possible existence and role of a council of elders in addition to such leaders must remain a matter of conjecture.

Leadership after Arrival in the Southwest: Before Fort Sumner

Oral histories become especially useful for the eighteenth and nineteenth-century parts of this attempted reconstruction. Most scholars agree that the tribe did not exist as a political entity in these times; leadership was expressed at multiple levels and few, if any, coalitions between local and/or regional leaders can be documented. The underlying arrangement appears to have been dual, with war and peace leaders at regional levels supported by local leaders or headmen. Additionally there existed an assembly known as the *naachid*, the very nature, function, and significance of which remain problematical for researchers.

REGIONAL LEVEL

Of all the available sources, Hill's (1940) discussion of war and peace leaders remains the most effective. Hill sees the natural, geographic community as the major economic unit and fundamental political entity among the Navajos. Leadership in this community was vested "in one or more individuals whose duties involved the direction of domestic affairs and warfare" (Hill 1940:24). Since these activities were viewed as distinctive, it was rare for one person to fill both offices. Both the war and peace leadership positions had ritual knowledge requirements, and central in both were oratorical skills — the ability to speak, talk, advise, guide, exhort — reflected in the words *naat'áanii* (speech maker, orator, moves head from side to side, makes speeches, leader, headman) and *nanisht'á* (to orate). Both kinds of leaders spoke for groups larger than kin aggregates and both positions were open to women as well as men.

War Leaders. The choice of war leaders (*natini*) (or *hashkééjí naat'ááh* — Young and Morgan 1980:1060)

> was entirely dependent upon ritual attainment. Anyone who had acquired the knowledge of one or more of the War Ways, upon which the success of any punitive venture was thought to depend, was eligible as a leader. Because of practical field experience these individuals were also in charge of defense operations, if the occasion arose [Hill 1940:24].

These war leaders, who led attacks when groups "went to war" became the object of mixed attitudes as history unfolded; as Hill (ibid.) indicates, feelings toward them ranged from respect to the assigning of blame for incarceration at Fort Sumner. Van Valkenburgh's (1945) criteria for war leaders are comparable to Hill's; the former, however, makes it clear that women could be war chiefs if they had participated in raids or fights with the enemy (Van Valkenburgh 1936:22).

Peace Leaders. In addition to the war leaders, the People recognized peace leaders or *naat'áanii* (*hózhǫ́ǫ́jí naat'ááh* – Young and Morgan 1980:963). Hill (1940:25) summarizes the skills considered to be prerequisites:

> Factors governing the choice included exemplary character, oratorial ability, personal magnetism, and proven ability to serve in both the practical and religious aspects of culture. It was a foregone conclusion that the chosen individual would be a practitioner and it was necessary that he [*sic*] control at least the Blessing Way Ceremony.

Others mention similar factors: wisdom; the ability to speak to the People and for them after a consensus had been reached; rhetorical competence which included the ability to persuade, discuss, debate, be eloquent, and use mythological knowledge to explain and rationalize decisions. On a personal level, one had to be discreet, discriminating, respectable, and wise.

Hill also describes the selection process and subsequent ritual induction. Like that of war leader, the job of peace leader was neither hereditary, remunerative, nor clan-linked. Although the job might pass from father to son or sister's son, new leaders had to have all proper qualifications of experience and knowledge. Tenure in the elective positions was for life, as long as one acted in ways beneficial to the public and in ways that inspired confidence and resulted in successful outcomes. Leaders had no powers of coercion; their following was voluntary and they were not allowed to dominate, order others around, or to direct matters in ways that satisfied personal whims or led to personal gain. Should they fail to exercise their powers in ways beneficial to the group, they could be deposed or forced to resign (Young 1978:15). Leaders could also resign due to old age and could recommend specific successors. If such a person proved unworthy, he or she could be ignored by the community or informed that the term was up. Hill (1940:25-26) says that women might occasionally be chosen as *naat'ánii*; while some aspects of their roles are clear, it is "difficult to determine" whether they "acted in the full capacity of [their] male counterpart[s]."

Induction proceedings were accompanied by at least one Chief Blessingway and possibly other ritual actions. The Chief Blessingway protected the leader "from misfortune and insubordination" (Franciscan Fathers 1910:424); however, this ceremony appears to have been defunct by 1910, at least according to the Franciscan Fathers (ibid.). Additional ritual actions, described by Hill (1940:26-27) and the Franciscan Fathers (1910:41, 424), are augmented by Young (1978:26-27). Upon their completion, the new leader addressed the crowd, asking for cooperation and assistance.

The job of *naat'áanii* is better described than that of war leader, just as are the desirable attributes associated with the position. One's success depended not on coercion, force, or authoritarianism, but on the power of persuasion and the ability and willingness to lead by example. One was influential in all aspects of culture except warfare. One of the jobs was to speak effectively to one's own people and to other communities, often at large gatherings such as those held in conjunction with Enemyway, Nightway, Corral Dances, or secular occasions. These speeches were directed at specific problems and were expected to have moral scope and ethical overtones. "A primary function was that of expounding on moral-ethical subjects, admonishing The People to live in peace and harmony" (Young 1978:25). Leaders were expected to give advice, instruction, and to look after the welfare of the People. The importance of one's oratorical skills was paramount; one was expected to speak fluently in ways comprehensible to crowds, to hold their attention, to organize speeches so that main points were clear, and to ground them in tradition and mythology. Peace leaders were expected to stand for and to emphasize peace, hard work, and righteousness.

The job also had economic aspects; the peace leader was viewed as an economic director. He or she was expected to encourage all toward productive activities. That meant planning and organizing, telling people where to move, when to plant, setting dates for such events, and giving instruction, assistance, and supervision at communal projects such as construction of irrigation ditches or work on fencing.

Peace leaders also had legal roles; *naat'áanii* were expected to mediate and arbitrate legal disputes and resolve arguments. According to Williams (1970:6), this sphere also included the right to decide and pronounce death sentences in witchcraft cases.

Finally, a *naat'áanii* was expected to assume responsibility for indigent people who had no relatives to assist them, to be hospitable to all, and to represent his or her group by speaking for it after consensus had been reached, thereby acting as an intermediary with and representative to other communities, and later, the tribe and the federal government (Hill 1940:27-28).

To the information above a few other things may be added.[2] The Franciscan Fathers (1910:424) and Van Valkenburgh (1936:20) suggest that such leadership roles were marked by distinguishing dress and insignia, and the Franciscan Fathers (1910:453) also mention specific mourning customs. Van Valkenburgh (1945:64-65), when discussing *naat'áanii* who led family groups, says that these leaders could be males or females who were virile and eloquent. They were expected to direct gathering, hunting, good living, and to lead by example. They were guided by the wisdom of elderly men and medicine men and were dependent on the approval of both of these groups. Bingham and Bingham (1976:5) suggest that the influence of both kinds of early leaders was in part due to the strength of their clans (in addition to skills and attributes named by others). They also say that "the best leaders knew many prayers and ceremonies and were not afraid of witchcraft."

The Naachid. The *naachid*, first described by Matthews (1890:94-104), has been discussed by a number of authors including Reichard (1928), Hill (1936), the Franciscan Fathers (1910), Van Valkenburgh (1936, 1945, 1946), Wyman and Kluckhohn (1938), Kluckhohn and Wyman (1940), Brugge (1963), and Young (1961, 1978). Discussions are so wide-ranging that the only conclusion to be drawn is that the function and significance of the *naachid* are unclear. To introduce the *naachid*, consider Young's (1961:371) description; according to legend, the People were "once more closely knit politically under the *naachid*, an organization reportedly composed

---

[2] Shepardson (1963:52-53) has made valuable comments about the value conflicts associated with various authority roles in Navajo culture.

of twelve Peace Chiefs and twelve War Chiefs, *elected* for life. . . . The *naachid* gathered periodically for ceremonials and council"; meetings were dominated by whichever category of *naat'áanii* was appropriate. Van Valkenburgh (1936:21) says that the word *nah-sit* described the ceremonial enclosure associated with the event. He describes the gathering as an archaic tribal assembly held in two or four-year intervals, or more frequently if necessary. The timing was seasonal; the event began after harvest, opening with a four-day dance led by respected couples. These dances were continued throughout the winter with appropriate intervals of rest (some say twelve days) until spring arrived. Ceremonially, the *naachid* was a "prayer for abundant water and soil fertility" (ibid.: 21), and ritually it included trips to the sacred mountains, prayers, trips to Zuni Salt Lake, and use of clay from there on the dancers' lips to bring rain. Later Van Valkenburgh (1945:66) refers to it as "Throwing Out of Earth." Politically, it allowed the gathering of war and peace leaders for debate and discussion of tribal business during the days of rest with which the dances were interspersed. Control of discussions alternated according to the circumstances of war or peace.

Reichard's (1928) description of the *naachid* attributes rainmaking and curing as well as political functions to the assembly. Her informants described it as a sacred and important event which brought the People together in a central place. Twelve peace chiefs and twelve war chiefs (some say six and six), who were in positions of honor for life, comprised the council. Among their ceremonial duties were those of naming infants and doing rituals associated with war and peace (1928:30). The political part of the *naachid* included harangues in favor of either war or peaceful activities such as planting and conservation. Her informants made it clear that, ceremonially, one purpose of the *naachid* was to increase the water supply by having sings for rain; one informant remembered one of the songs involved.

Hill's (1936:18) informants suggested that the *naachid* was a gesture dance or a victory celebration held after the successful avenging of the murder of a Navajo. They all denied the political characteristics suggested by Reichard and suggested that the *naachid* originally derived from the Plains (ibid.: 19), unlike Van Valkenburgh (1945:67) who believed it derived from the Pueblos. Further, Hill's informants said that it was a tribal affair in that all helped build the ceremonial hogan in the fall or winter. A notable warrior was picked as a patient and a Hopi scalp was used regardless of the identity of the enemy. The gesture dance was held regularly until spring when the *naachid* was closed with a five-day War Dance and then replaced by spring planting. Hill doubts that the *naachid* had political significance, being of the opinion that political developments were more recent. The name "gesture dance" derives from the alleged practice of a man making obscene gestures while dancing.

Wyman and Kluckhohn (1938:7) also use the gloss "Gesture Dance" when classifying *naachid* as one of three subgroups of War Ceremonials in their discussion of Navajo song ceremonials. Using data from Hill, Reichard, Haile, and their own fieldwork, they note that by the 1930s the *naachid* had not been performed for at least two generations, and indicate doubt concerning its real nature (ibid.: 35). These comments are augmented later by remarks from another Navajo: "[The *naachid*] was held after a war party got back. Men and women moved their arms and hands in time together inside the hogan" (Kluckhohn and Wyman 1940:190).

Matthews (1890) states that the event was a curative rite or a healing dance. He reports such a dance held at a sacred place in the San Juan Valley for Big Knee and comments that some Apaches observed some of the winter events. Matthews also says that by 1890 the *naachid* had fallen into disuse.

Information on the last *naachid* is also variable. Van Valkenburgh (1946:4-7) reports one held in 1856 for Yanbaa, famed woman warrior (Woman Who Met the Enemy); during this *naachid*, Manuelito preached war and Zarcillos Largos opposed it, prophesying defeat.[3] Brugge (1963) documents a *naachid* held in 1840 on the other side of Chinle, at which the focus was on peace. He also provides a cogent summary of ethnographic information, identifies gaps, reviews the numerous names for the event, and suggests that it had both political and ceremonial overtones and that all or most of the People attended at least part of any *naachid*.

Young (1961:371) suggests that the *naachid* was apparently no longer a potent force by 1846 and indicates that some doubt its existence at any point in time. However, in 1978 he says that the last one was in the 1850s and describes the *naachid* as a general meeting held partly for ceremonial purposes. Informant accounts (1978:20-23) suggest that the *naachid* was a type of political organization during which planning for war or for cooperation in growing and storing food took place. Young (ibid.: 24) believes that we will never know if the entire tribe assembled in *naachid* or if it had political significance.

The models of leadership given in such discussions are also divergent. Van Valkenburgh's information suggests a hierarchy headed by one speaker higher than others under whom were the regional peace and war speakers (elected for the reasons and attributes specified above), the local or lesser speakers, and finally, runners and attendants whom leaders could appoint to help and advise them. The Franciscan Fathers (1910:422) report that in earlier days the tribe was represented by twelve chiefs who in council were subject to four spokesmen, as in the Lower World. This council decided all matters. Kluckhohn and Leighton (1960:73) believe that reports of twelve war and twelve peace leaders are reflections of myths and "ideal patterns with a strong element of retrospective falsification."[4] Young (1978:15) presents *naat'áanii* and a council as the oral history model; the chiefs talked, advised, and guided, and called together a council to discuss problems and danger.

Local Level. At the local level, leaders were also called *naat'áanii*. A review of the available discussions of this position suggests that, in essence, these *naat'áanii* were local versions of peace chiefs. There is no indication that qualifications, selection processes, or functions differed from those already delineated for the peace leaders recognized at the regional level. Historically there is good evidence that it was at the local level that the traditional system of leadership endured the longest, and that during the post-Fort Sumner years government appointed "chiefs" depended heavily upon the cooperation and effective functioning of these leaders.

---

[3] In this same report, Van Valkenburgh (1964:4, 6) mentions an earlier *naachid*, allegedly called by Nahabani (Narbona) in 1849 to encourage war on Mexicans and Americans who were building the log-sod fort at Fort Defiance, a place of sacred springs used by ceremonialists for offerings and medicine. I have not been able to reconcile Van Valkenburgh's account of this *naachid* with either the original orders to establish the fort, issued by Colonel Edwin Vose Sumner in September of 1851, or with any of the available accounts of Narbona's activities or of Navajo skirmishes with Lieutenant Colonel John M. Washington and his troops.

[4] Brugge (1982) points out that the number twelve occasionally appears in historic period documentation and that as one of the numbers important in Navajo religion, it deserves further thought in these contexts. The instance he cites occurred during negotiations of the final treaty at Fort Sumner. Transcripts of the negotiations show that the Commissioners asked the Navajos to elect a council of ten chiefs, which they did. But on the next day, they came up with two more names. The Treaty, as reproduced in Brugge and Correll (1971:88-98) shows that the Navajo signers included twelve chiefs and a seventeen-member council. The twelve chiefs included Barboncito, Armijo, Delgado, Manuelito, Largo, Herrero, Chiqueto, Muerto de Hombre, Hombro, Narbono, Narbono Segundo, and Ganada Mucho.

Historical Information. The Spanish period (1598-1821), the Mexican period (1821-42), and the early American period (1842-64) were stormy times in Navajo history. Dominant governments had no understanding of the traditional leadership system and continually failed to comprehend why treaties negotiated with one or more "leaders" were not binding on all Navajos. The Spanish tried to elevate some of the local leaders to higher positions, creating the "chief of all Navajos," a title which they coupled with the Army title of "general" as the case of Don Carlos illustrates. Such attempts, and comparable American attempts, were distinct failures despite the canes, badges, and other symbols of office bestowed on these designees. The only Navajo who is known to have become totally committed to supporting the Americans, Antonio C. Sandoval (1807-59) of the Mount Taylor area, became known as "Enemy Navajo" to his own people for his actions (Correll 1970a:39). Herrero Delgadito, sanctioned by the Americans as "the leader," had little influence; instead, leadership remained in the hands of local headmen and regional war and peace leaders.

A number of the latter are well known from the pre-Fort Sumner period; recall, for example, Zarcillos Largos (?-1860), Narbona (1766-1849), Antonio el Pinto (?-1793), and Barboncito (?-1871), known as peace chiefs, and Manuelito (1818-93), known as a war leader. Of these early leaders, Hoffman and Johnson (1970) indicate that both Zarcillos Largos and Barboncito were well-known medicine men; the former performed Mountaintopway and Enemyway, and Barboncito practiced Beautyway. Both continued practicing their ceremonies throughout their lives, sometimes singing over other leaders, such as when Manuelito was a patient of Zarcillos Largos. Their biographies also suggest that some of them teamed up politically, such as Zarcillos Largos and Barboncito, and later, Manuelito, Ganado Mucho, and Barboncito, and that they assumed political positions upon one another's retirements, such as Zarcillos Largos' succession to Narbona's job and Manuelito's to Zarcillos Largos' (Brugge 1970). While the ceremonialist status of Narbona, Antonio el Pinto, and Manuelito is not discussed by Hoffman and Johnson, in the two cases wherein dual political/ceremonial roles are affirmed (Barboncito and Zarcillos Largos), it is clear that ceremonial knowledge was acquired early, probably before political activity, and that the reputation and oratorical skills in this area plus military prowess in Zarcillos Largos' case combined to lead to these men's natural assumption of political leadership roles.

Relationships between Politics and Ceremonialism in Pre-Fort Sumner Times. Despite the variety of reconstructed models for pre-1864 Navajo leadership, it seems clear that ritual leadership and knowledge were among the qualifications necessary for those selected to be either war or peace leaders at the regional level or as headmen at the local level. Since these were prerequisites, the implication is that political activism and involvement came later in life, after the acquisition of ceremonial knowledge and the establishment of a personal and professional reputation. Hill and others make it clear that the position of war leader was ritually related to knowledge of the War Ways, while that of peace leader was tied to knowledge of the Blessingway. Additionally, rituals surrounded installation of these leaders. That there should have been an association between politics and ceremonialism seems natural in some ways, given the fact that many of the skills required for successful leadership in both worlds were similar. Both jobs depended on eloquent oratory and rhetoric; knowledge of Navajo mythology and legends; the ability to relate such knowledge to the present world, its inhabitants, and events; the ability to set an example, be righteous, hard working, hospitable, trustworthy, to hold an audience's attention, to lead by example, to inspire confidence, to handle small and large gatherings, and to serve as mediators, be it between patients and supernaturals or local groups and others. Both jobs did, indeed, imply the necessity of being "a person of the world." Van Valkenburgh's (1945) discussion of local *naat'áanii* suggests additional ties since, according to him, a leader's fate depended on the continuous approval of the wise, nonpolitically active elders and medicine men.

The other major set of evidence for ties between ceremonialism and politics among the Navajos, pre-1864, can be found in the problematical *naachid*. Whatever interpretation one gives to its political and ceremonial functions, it is clear, I think, that it represented a fusion of elements of both, a time when groups participated in both ritual activities and secular discussions, alternating between the two and being led throughout by people who were individually qualified in both the religious and nonreligious leadership areas. Van Valkenburgh (1936:21) expresses similar ideas when he says that the *naachid* indicated that "there was a close association between the ceremonial and political life of the early Navajo."

All of this is important in view of the Franciscan Fathers' (1910:422-23, 382) insistence on the negative correlation between ceremonial skills and political leadership. A review of their comments, in light of the above, suggests that perhaps these are valid only as descriptions of attitudes and practices that prevailed *after* the Fort Sumner incarceration and, more importantly, only as descriptions of agents' attitudes toward the unreformed war leaders. (Recall that Hill [1940] also documented equivocal Navajo attitudes towards these leaders.)

The Franciscan Fathers (1910:422-23) tell us, "It would seem, too, that the government of the tribe was not, as a rule, entrusted to the singers or medicine men, unless they showed unusual ability and peaceful dispositions." Then they state that singers who normally accompanied raiding and war parties individually instituted these without the knowledge or approval of local headmen with such frequency that, for the protection of all, "the necessity was felt of filling *the ranks of the chiefs* with men making no profession of singing, unless they showed unusual consistency" (ibid.: 423—emphasis added).

Elsewhere the Franciscan Fathers (1910:382) tell us, "While the influence of the chanter is felt it has very little, if any, bearing on the government of the tribe as such. Apparently, their influence is due to their greater or lesser authority on a given chant. Very few of the existing headmen are chosen from the ranks of the *chanters*." While this statement has been accepted as valid by Shepardson (1963) and Henderson (1982), I suggest that it is valid only as an etic description of the 1868-1938 period. To explore that idea, let us turn to a brief examination of the development of political leadership after the incarceration and a documentation of what is known about identifiable political leaders and ceremonialists during this later period.

Leadership after Fort Sumner

While the Fort Sumner incarceration is viewed by some as destroying the old leadership system (which is certainly true in the case of the *naachid*), what it really did was add an alien system, designed by the Americans, on top of the continuing traditional pattern of Navajo leadership. Upon release in 1868, the People were placed under the control of a U.S. government agent. This agent, and the more numerous ones in later years, added a superstructure by appointing a head chief and chiefs to serve as liaisons with the People. These appointments were approved by the Secretary of the Interior, and the agent's right to make such appointments was, of course, sanctioned by the Army stationed at Fort Wingate. While the alien nature of the head chief/chiefs superstructure might lead one to suspect that these chiefs, whom Shepardson (1963:14) dubs "Agency Indian Chiefs," had no popular support, it is obvious that over time some agents did, in fact, turn to former peace leaders and/or recently reformed war leaders when searching for appointees.

The first such head chief was Barboncito from the Canyon de Chelly area. "One of his duties was to lecture the people who assembled for the ration distributions at Fort Defiance on the value of peace and hard work" (Shepardson, ibid.). Barboncito's role was supported by the efforts of others, designated as "chiefs"; thus, one finds Manuelito as chief of the east (east of Chuska Mountains), Ganado Mucho-chief of the west (Chinle Valley-Kinlichee), and Mariano-chief of the Fort Wingate-Dutton Plateau areas, as well as Haskeneinii of Kayenta-Oljeto Valley, Largo, Delgadito, Francisco Capitan, Becente of the east, and countless others.

The appointed chiefs, who in many cases were also natural leaders, were occasionally called to Fort Defiance by the agent when it was necessary to relay information about government policies, territorial expansion, rations, law enforcement, or compulsory education. In these "assemblies," the chiefs served as representatives of their people; they could bring up matters of concern to the People and evidently could negotiate certain matters of policy implementation. While it is easy to see how these assemblies could have led to the development of tribal government, there is no evidence that they did.

At the local level, leadership remained in the hands of *naat'áaii*, "wealthy stock owners, ceremonial practitioners, and heads of large family groups" (Shepardson, ibid.). The chiefs held their own meetings with these local leaders and counted on them to continue the activities formerly associated with the peace leader role. According to Williams (1970:16), these local leaders were selected by the People who favored those with a modest amount of wealth, those who were mature and male, and who had "the knowledge and ability to perform one or more Sings."

Upon Barboncito's death, Manuelito was appointed head chief and many sources report that the wise, wealthy Ganado Mucho was second in command. Manuelito was reportedly deposed by the agent in 1884, whereupon Henry Chee Dodge was appointed head chief by the Secretary of the Interior. With this appointment, one sees the first indication of preference for a man of both worlds, one who was cooperative, effective, and able to operate with both Americans and Navajos. Preceding this appointment, one can document the addition of a number of other American institutions such as scouts, policemen, courts, and interpreters. The formal superstructure was indeed expanding, but, in some cases anyway, prestigious peace leaders from the Fort Sumner period and reformed war leaders were chosen to fill leadership positions such as those involved in Army scouting and enforcing internal law and order. By 1900, some thirty regional *naat'áanii* were recognized with titles and cards (Shepardson 1963:78; Van Valkenburgh 1945:71); underneath this structure, the local leadership patterns remained intact.

Pressure mounted from a variety of external directions in the early part of the twentieth century and combined to result in what can be called "the Dawn of Tribalism" for the People (Young 1978). At the federal level, the Navajo Agency was divided into multiple agencies. The earliest attempts at a Business Council, artificially created to deal with resource allocation rights (1922) and including Chee Dodge, Charlie Mitchell, and Dugal Chee Bekiss, was followed by a twelve member council in 1923 and the creation of the Chapter system in 1927. The latter, while based on local leadership patterns, formalized these with election of officers, specific meeting times and places, and all the rest. Initially most of the people "chose their old leaders to be chapter officers," but in cases where this was not done headmen continued to serve as examples, arbitrators, and helpers of the people at their own camps and at ceremonies. Those installed continued to be orators and arbitrators of land, stock, and witchcraft disputes (Bingham and Bingham 1976:10, 11).

The twelve delegate council was replaced by one consisting of twelve delegates and twelve alternates in 1928. Meanwhile, evidence that the superstructure was losing touch with local leadership continued to grow as delegates served more as intermediaries between the U.S. and the Navajos than according to older, traditional customs. The final result of this increasing dissatisfaction with the alien forms of government was a reservation-wide canvas in 1936-37 (in which Father Berard Haile played a major role), a Constitutional Assembly in 1937, and the formulation in 1938 of many of the basic rules by which the present Navajo Tribal Council operates, including the idea of a central council consisting of seventy-four delegates elected at the community level to four-year terms.

It is clear that in the latter part of the nineteenth century and the early part of the twentieth, when local headmen leadership had yet to be replaced by elected formal leaders at the chapter and tribal levels, the traditional leadership system thrived. Some of these leaders, such as Peshlakai from Crystal, are known historically for contradicting agents or for taking stands and "causing trouble"; recall Black Horse at Round Rock (1892), Ba'álílii of the Shiprock agency, Tadidiin of Kaibeto, and Bizhoshi of Beautiful Mountain. In certain instances, agents chose to ignore such headmen, while at other times these uncooperative leaders were replaced. As Shepardson indicates (1963:78), sometimes government recognition destroyed a local leader's prestige.

The expansion of the tribal council, continuing erosion of local leaders' powers by agents, the traumas of stock reduction, accelerated involvement in state, national, and international affairs, and other factors combined to bring about new definitions of leadership. In the 1930s and 1940s many Navajo elders stopped being politically active at the local level, sometimes by choice and sometimes because they were blamed for the miseries of stock reduction, accused of witchcraft, and voted out of office. Williams (1970:39-40) provides interesting data on the number of ceremonialists and politicians involved in witchcraft accusations during this period.

By the 1950s one is looking at a new concept of leadership. At the council level, the story is one of an alien institution that takes hold and increases in political stature to the point where now, in the 1980s, it is viewed as the "traditional" instrument of government as well as one which is capable of becoming an instrument of self government. At the community level, the chapter president is the elected leader of the community. While "in some places the Chapter President is still like one of the *naat'áanii* in the old days" (Bingham and Bingham 1976:37), in many cases this is not true. As Young (1978:165) says, the tribal government of today is "a far cry from the Headman system of a generation ago, and even of the Council organization of a bare 25 years in the past."

Assessment of Relationship between Politics and Ceremonialism after Fort Sumner. It appears that until the 1938 establishment of a tribal council system based on community selection of delegates, traditional leadership patterns continued with great strength at the local level, and that these were often also reflected in appointments of head chiefs and chiefs, scouts, policemen, and other functionaries of the alien superstructure.

Locating personal information about these numerous local leaders is an impossible task, especially if one is trying to evaluate a possible connection between politics and ceremonialism. Various life histories identify some of these leaders in a few regions of the reservation and also contain information on a few better known ceremonialists. In most cases, however, it is impossible to tell whether a person who was a singer was also active politically, whether a headman was also a ceremonialist, or, in cases where a double role is clear, what the sequence of the influential skills may have been.

Frank Mitchell's life history (Mitchell 1978) mentions Charlie Mitchell, Silversmith, and Chee Dodge as important leaders, Weela as a Fort Defiance headman/non-singer, and fifteen others as headmen, two of whom were obviously also policemen. Of these leaders, Long Moustache and Two Streams Meet Curly were singers as well as politicians, as were both Frank and his father-in-law, Man Who Shouts. In *Son of Old Man Hat* (Dyk 1938), the subject's father is described as knowing songs, prayers, and cures, and as a headman. Four other singers are mentioned: Giving Out Anger, Stutterer, Old Man White Horse, and Slow; two of these, Giving Out Anger (Hashkeneinii) and Slow, were also definitely headmen. In *Left Handed* (Dyk and Dyk 1980), Supernatural Power (Ba'álílii; see Correll 1970b) was both a singer and a headman. Of the seven other singers mentioned herein, some appear to have functioned as headmen, but their exact political roles are unclear. In the autobiography of Old Mexican (Dyk 1947), wherein some of the characters overlap with *Son of Old Man Hat*, ten headmen are listed but it is unclear if nine of them were singers as well. Supernatural Power, mentioned above, is the only person whose double role can be confirmed. In *Gregorio* (Leighton and Leighton 1949), five singers are identified but information on their political roles, if any, is not included. "A Navaho Politician" (Kluckhohn 1964), makes it clear that Bill Begay was not a singer, but gives the example of Jacob Morgan, Navajo leader in the Farmington area, who was ordained as a Methodist minister. Finally, in "A Navaho Personal Document" (Kluckhohn 1956), Mr. Moustache (who is Grandfather B in Roberts 1951) was definitely a Blessingway singer and headman.

To the above list may be added a few other individuals: Pete Price (Young 1978); Denetsosie (Johnson 1969); Smiler (Williams 1970:14); Father A (Roberts 1951), a singer/policeman who is also Victor in *Gregorio*; and Gordo (singer/judge), Old Man Sam, and Gordo's Father, singers and local leaders in the Rimrock area (Vogt 1951). In the case of these and the individuals named earlier, double roles as politician and ceremonialist can be documented. In the cases of Denetsosie, Smiler, Mitchell, and Man Who Shouts, it is clear that ceremonial knowledge and reputation preceded involvement in politics, whether at the tribal, chapter, or headman level. Dick (Johnson 1977) gives us evidence of a contemporary ceremonialist who also serves as president of a school board. For those leaders who lived during the shift from headman leadership to tribal council delegates and the chapter system, political activism often shifted accordingly, moving from the elected headman role to that of elected delegate or chapter officer, appointed law enforcer, and/or occasionally also to elected or appointed judgeships.

Those who appear on the basis of literature now available to have been singers rather than political activists include, in addition to those discussed above, Tom Ration and Buck Austin[5] (Johnson 1977) and John Honie (Carlson and Witherspoon 1968). Those who appear to have been leaders but not ceremonialists, in addition to the individuals named above, include Thomas Clani, Charles Brown, Howard Bogoutin and Tillman Hadley (Johnson 1977), as well as Taayooni and Ganado Mucho's sons, leaders in 1926 in Ganado (Young 1978).

At the tribal level, the picture is equally unclear in many cases. The list below (see Table 1) documents the terms of various chairmen and vice-chairmen and what is known in information currently available about their traditional ceremonial training.

---

[5] While Austin's self presentation (Johnson 1977) contains no reference to political activism, I know from my own work that in the 1970s he was very active in hearings concerned with potential defamation of sacred places.

TABLE 1

CHAIRMEN AND VICE-CHAIRMEN

Term	Chairman	Ceremonialist	Vice-Chairman	Ceremonialist
1923-28	Chee Dodge	no	– – –	– –
1928-32	Deshna Chischillige	no(?)	Maxwell Yazzie	no
1933-36	Thomas Dodge	no	Marcus Kanuho	?
1937-38	Henry Taliman	no(?)	Roy Kinsel	?
1938-42	Jacob C. Morgan	no	Howard Gorman	no
1942-46	Chee Dodge	no	Sam Ahkeah	no
1946-50	Sam Ahkeah	no	(Chee Dodge) Zhealy Tso	(no)?
1951-54	Sam Ahkeah	no	(John Claw) Adolph Maloney	(?)no
1955-58	Paul Jones	no	Scott Preston	yes
1959-62	Paul Jones	no	Scott Preston	yes
1963-66	Raymond Nakai	no	Nelson Damon	no
1967-70	Raymond Nakai	no	Nelson Damon	no
1971-74	Peter MacDonald	no	Wilson C. Skeet	no
1975-78	Peter MacDonald	no	Wilson C. Skeet	no
1979-82	Peter MacDonald[6]	no	Frank E. Paul	no

The Hoffman and Johnson (1970) biographies include those of Chee Dodge, Sam Ahkeah, Paul Jones, and Raymond Nakai from the above list and indicate no ceremonialist roles for any of these individuals. The only reference to ceremonial affiliations is the statement that Sam Ahkeah's grandmother was a medicine woman. From my own fieldwork I know that Scott Preston was a Blessingway singer, but the total repertory and sequence of politics and ceremonialism in his life are unknown to me. Williams (1970:26) lists both Paul Jones and Scott Preston as medicine men "who could perform sings" and also says that Chee Dodge was able to perform sings. Information from my informants does not substantiate his claims about either Dodge or Jones.

It is obvious that in post-Fort Sumner times ceremonial knowledge remained an important prerequisite for leadership at the local level, if not also at the alien level of appointed head chief and chiefs. Williams (1970:26) suggests that traces of this were still obvious in 1962, when thirty-nine medicine men were among the seventy-four Tribal Council delegates and when Grazing Committee members were oriented toward the traditional lifeway, being "active in traditional curing ceremonies either as Singers or as guest speakers" (ibid.: 38). Shepardson (1963:70) reports that the old traditional leaders still exerted informal authority through local discussions and decisions. By then, however, new leaders were being chosen on the basis of criteria different from those used in the past, a trend which I believe was first indicated in the appointment of Chee Dodge as head chief. The Tribal Chairman,

---

[6] In the November 1982 election, the MacDonald-Paul team was defeated by Peterson Zah and Edward T. Begay, respectively, the candidates for Chairman and Vice-Chairman. Zah and Begay would both be classified as "No" on this chart.

for example, was expected to be at least middle-aged, bilingual, and culturally a member of both the American and Navajo worlds, but yet modest and conciliatory as were the old *naat'áanii* (ibid.: 75). Qualities expected of council delegates were less well-defined; those elected were supposed to be closer to the traditional system and involved at the community level and not to campaign openly. They were not expected to be educated or to speak English. One community's assessment of the situation was that for a delegate they wanted a good man, one who was trustworthy, a good speaker, one who talks things over with the people (ibid.: 100).

Data available from two communities help illustrate persistence and change in leadership patterns. In Navajo Mountain in the 1960s, aged informants did not agree in their identification of former leaders or headmen except in the case of Hoskinini and his son Atene (Shepardson and Hammond 1970:157). Among those named were "Singers, heads of large extended families, policemen, one 'seven-dollar-a-month judge,' and one woman" (ibid.). It is clear, however, that Whiteman Killer (who moved into the area in 1892) was an important leader, as was his son-in-law Endishchee in the twentieth century. While Whiteman Killer's other roles are unknown, it is clear that Endishchee was also a medicine man.

The first council delegates from Navajo Mountain were "traditional, non-English speaking tribesmen" among whom were some descendants or affines of both Whiteman Killer and Endishchee (ibid.: 158, 159). Among the ten identified by Shepardson and Hammond's (ibid.: 37) collaborators as having served between 1923 and 1950 were three singers—John Fat, Charley Drake, and Leslie Tomasyo (Endishchee's stepgrandson), and one hand-trembler, Segony (Shepardson 1975, 1982; Chisholm 1976). Tomasyo, the 1938 delegate, was English-speaking. Although the identity and exact terms of delegates before 1950 were not ascertainable from tribal records (Shepardson 1983), it is known that from 1950 to 1966 the Navajo Mountain council delegates were English-speaking non-singers, and that the 1962 delegate was "the best-educated man in the community" (Shepardson and Hammond 1970:160).

In Navajo Mountain, the older "political system" was an informal one wherein leadership was vested in singers, headmen, and respected leaders of large kin groups. Decisions were made by consensus among adults; leaders provided advice, counsel, and mediation. To this system have been added "more modern authority systems" including the Tribal Council, the chapter, federal government, and the states of Arizona and Utah. A blurring of the traditional and modern was becoming apparent by 1938; by the 1960s, Shepardson and Hammond (1970:161) found "a blurring of the lines between formal and informal leadership by Chapter officers and councilmen, who [were] exercising both *de facto* and *de jure* political leadership." Also by the 1960s the authors found that singers held no positions of leadership outside the religious sphere "unless they also [enjoyed] prestige for their levelheadedness, their forceful but considerate personalities, and their skill as mediators." While they did participate in chapter activities, singers were not striving for political leadership (ibid.: 158).

Henderson (1982:169-70) reports for the Kaibeto Plateau area that "a number of early leaders were Blessingway singers, but only a few also knew chantways. Informants attributed the political influence of these few chantway singers to large livestock holdings or to their employment as policemen by the BIA, not to their ceremonial knowledge." In that area between the late 1930s and 1980, about twenty councilmen have been elected; of these, five were ceremonialists and six others sons of ceremonialists (their own ceremonial knowledge, if any, not being stated). Such data led Henderson (ibid.: 170) to conclude: "While people do not specifically acknowledge the importance of ceremonial learning for selecting a leader, these facts suggest some connection. On the other hand, most ceremonialists appear to have little influence in local political matters."

Conclusion

It seems that despite all the restructuring of the last decades some link continues to exist between the political and ceremonial worlds, if not at the very top at least at the level of council delegates and chapter officers. The linkage obviously is not overwhelming nor is it predictive. However, traditional ceremonial knowledge still entails mastering a number of the skills which are as relevant in the contemporary political world as they were in the past, skills still valued by the People. Those possessing them are still accorded respect.

The evidence then, however fragmentary, suggests that before Fort Sumner ritual expertise was a prerequisite for leadership roles exemplified in positions of war leader, peace leader, and local headmen. While such expectations were slowly eroded to the point where they are now rarely visible in the top offices of the tribe, the little evidence available suggests that at the community level the expectations are still present and may lead to concrete exemplifications in the choice of council delegates and/or chapter officers.[7] How widespread this phenomenon is at present cannot be determined. However, given the historical strength of such ties, one must suspect that evidence of the formerly tight association between ceremonialism and politics will continue to be expressed at the local level, as long as values are not restructured and traditional religion is still extant. There is also the possibility that the association of the two spheres may once again become more obvious at the tribal level, through a reawakening of political interests and activism on the part of ceremonialists. Indeed, I believe that this was already happening by the middle 1970s.

References Cited

Bingham, Sam, and Janet Bingham
1976   *Navajo Chapter Government Handbook*. Rock Point, Ariz.: Rock Point Community School.

Brugge, David M.
1963   "Documentary Reference to a Navajo *Naach'id* in 1840." *Ethnohistory* 16/2:186-88.

1970   *Zarcillos Largos — Courageous Advocate of Peace*. Navajo Historical Publications Biographical Series, 2. Window Rock, Ariz.: Navajo Tribe, Research Section of Navajo Parks and Recreation.

1982   Personal communication, October 15.

Brugge, David M., and J. Lee Correll
1971   *The Story of the Navajo Treaties*. Navajo Historical Publications Documentary Series, 1. Window Rock, Ariz.: Navajo Tribe, Research Section of Navajo Parks and Recreation.

---

[7] The Tribal Court Judges' decision of April 1982 to create a Traditional Navajo Court system by establishing Peacemaker Courts in each of the six court districts opens up another possibility. Peacemakers, who will have powers to mediate and arbitrate local civil matters and who will be selected by each chapter and appointed by Navajo judges, are to be chosen for "their respect in the community and their reputation for integrity and knowledge of Navajo ways" (*Navajo Times* 1982a:1). This innovation is viewed as a revival of the old traditional custom of dispute settlement-by-persuasion using a local headman (*naat'áanii*), but one that adjusts this custom to current legal trends in arbitration and mediation, other legal concepts, and current legal problems (see *Navajo Times* 1982b:1, 1982c:10).

Carlson, Vada, and Gary Witherspoon
1968 *Black Mountain Boy: A Story of the Boyhood of John Honie.* Rough Rock, Ariz.: Rough Rock Demonstration School.

Chisholm, James
1976 Personal communication, February 16.

Correll, J. Lee
1970a *Sandoval—Traitor or Patriot?* Navajo Historical Publications Biographical Series, 1. Window Rock, Ariz.: Navajo Tribe, Research Section of Navajo Parks and Recreation.

1970b *Bai-a-lil-le: Medicine Man or Witch?* Navajo Historical Publications Biographical Series, 3. Window Rock, Ariz.: Navajo Tribe, Research Section of Navajo Parks and Recreation.

Dyk, Walter
1938 *Son of Old Man Hat.* Lincoln: University of Nebraska Press.

1947 *A Navaho Autobiography.* Viking Fund Publications in Anthropology, 8. New York: Viking Fund.

Dyk, Walter, and Ruth Dyk
1980 *Left Handed: A Navajo Autobiography.* New York: Columbia University Press.

Franciscan Fathers
1910 *An Ethnologic Dictionary of the Navaho Language.* Saint Michaels, Ariz.: Saint Michaels Press.

Henderson, Eric
1982 "Kaibeto Plateau Ceremonialists: 1860-1980." *Navajo Religion and Culture: Selected Views. Papers in Honor of Leland C. Wyman*, ed. David M. Brugge and Charlotte J. Frisbie, Museum of New Mexico Papers in Anthropology 17:164-75. Santa Fe.

Hill, W. W.
1936 *Navaho Warfare.* Yale University Publications in Anthropology, 5.

1940 "Some Aspects of Navajo Political Structure." *Plateau* 13:23-28.

Hoffman, Virginia, and Broderick H. Johnson
1970 *Navajo Biographies.* Chinle, Ariz.: Rough Rock Demonstration School.

Johnson, Broderick H. (ed.)
1969 *Denetsosie.* Chinle, Ariz.: Rough Rock Demonstration School.

1977 *Stories of Traditional Navajo Life and Culture.* Tsaile, Ariz.: Navajo Community College Press.

Kluckhohn, Clyde
1956 "A Navaho Personal Document with a Brief Paretian Analysis." *Personal Character and Cultural Milieu*, ed. Douglas Haring, pp. 513-33. 3rd revised ed. New York: Syracuse University Press.

1964 "A Navaho Politician." *Culture and Behavior: The Collected Essays of Clyde Kluckhohn*, ed. Richard Kluckhohn, pp. 182-209. 2nd printing. New York: Free Press of Glencoe.

Kluckhohn, Clyde, and Dorothea Leighton
1960   *The Navaho*. 7th printing. Cambridge: Harvard University Press.

Kluckhohn, Clyde, and Leland C. Wyman
1940   *An Introduction to Navaho Chant Practice*. Memoirs of the American Anthropological Association, 53.

Leighton, Alexander H., and Dorothea C. Leighton
1949   *Gregorio, The Hand-Trembler*. Papers of the Peabody Museum of American Archaeology and Ethnology, Harvard University, 40, no. 1.

Matthews, Washington
1890   "The Gentile System of the Navajo Indians." *Journal of American Folklore* 3:89-110.

Mitchell, Frank
1978   *Navajo Blessingway Singer: The Autobiography of Frank Mitchell, 1881-1967*, ed. Charlotte J. Frisbie and David P. McAllester. Tucson: University of Arizona Press.

Navajo Times
1982a   April 14 (vol. 24, no. 15).

1982b   April 28 (vol. 24, no. 18).

1982c   August 4 (vol. 24, no. 31).

Reichard, Gladys
1928   *Social Life of the Navajo Indians*. New York: Columbia University Contributions to Anthropology, 7.

Roberts, John M.
1951   *Three Navaho Households*. Papers of the Peabody Museum of American Archaeology and Ethnology, Harvard University, 40, no. 3.

Shepardson, Mary
1963   *Navajo Ways in Government*. American Anthropological Association, 65, no. 3, part 2, memoir 96.

1975   Personal communication, November 28.

1982   Personal communication, October 27.

1983   Personal communications, January 3 and February 18.

Shepardson, Mary, and Blodwen Hammond
1970   *The Navajo Mountain Community*. Berkeley: University of California Press.

Van Valkenburgh, Richard
1936   *Navajo Common Law I*. Museum Notes, 9, no. 4. Flagstaff: Museum of Northern Arizona.

1945   "The Government of the Navajos." *Arizona Quarterly* 1/4:63-73.

1946   "Last Powow [*sic*] of the Navajo." *The Desert Magazine* 10/1:4-7.

Vogt, Evon Z.
1951   *Navaho Veterans: A Study of Changing Values*. Papers of the Peabody Museum of American Archaeology and Ethnology, Harvard University, 41, no. 1.

Williams, Aubrey, Jr.
  1970   *Navajo Political Process*. Smithsonian Contributions to Anthropology, 9. Washington, D.C.: Smithsonian Institution.

Wyman, Leland C., and Clyde Kluckhohn
  1938   *Navaho Classification of Their Song Ceremonials*. Memoirs of the American Anthropological Association, 40.

Young, Robert W.
  1961   *The Navajo Yearbook, VIII, 1951-1961: A Decade of Progress*. Window Rock, Ariz.: Navajo Agency.

  1978   *A Political History of the Navajo Tribe*. Tsaile, Ariz.: Navajo Community College Press.

Young, Robert W., and William Morgan
  1980   *The Navajo Language*. Albuquerque: University of New Mexico Press.

Music as Symbol of Power and Status: The Courts of Mughal India

Bonnie C. Wade
University of California, Berkeley

Music, as it symbolizes the power and status of Mughal sovereigns and their Indic subjects, is the theme of this essay. In particular, I will focus on the period 1526-1707 when the Indian subcontinent experienced the reign of six great sovereigns—the "Great Mughals" Babur (r. 1526-1530), Humayan (r.-1556), Akbar (r.-1605), Jahangir (r.-1627), Shah Jahan (r.-1658), and Aurangzeb (r.-1707). During this time, the Mughals, in keeping with Islamic tradition, ordered chronicles written, and observers such as Bernier, Tavernier, and Manucci provided European accounts. Thus, we are beneficiaries of a richness in ethnographic data from this period of Indic history. David McAllester is a scholar for whom historical context and personal accounts are part of ethnography. For him, I have drawn on these chronicles for an historical ethnography of musical life in terms as personal as the chronicles permit.

In India, the Mughal reigned supreme. He had the right to appoint and to rescind the power and status of anyone in his realm. To him belonged all the land, the produce, the riches. But with him lay also the responsibilities that accompany such rights. It is not surprising, then, that the trappings of such sovereignty would include symbols of status and power, among which was music.[1] The sovereign could bestow on subordinates the symbols of power—those symbols including a flag and a kettledrum, but to him, alone, accrued the right to be heralded by the *naubat* ensemble.

While it is certain that the *naubat* ensemble was a royal ensign throughout the reigns of the great Mughals, it is more difficult to trace either instrumentarium or function of the ensemble with any consistency. In the time of Akbar, the ensemble was a very large one, requiring more than sixty players. In the chapter on "The Ensigns of Royalty" in the *Ā'īn-i-Akbarī* from that period, the instrumentarium is listed as shown below (Phillott 1977:1, 52-53).

---

[1] This essay was written in tandem with a paper for the 13th Congress of the International Musicological Society in Strasbourg, France (1982): "Playing for Power: Drum and *Naubat*, the Symbols of Might" (Wade 1982). In a manner of speaking, the present essay continues that one, and extends the discussion to the association of music with status, as well as with power.

(a) Membranophones:

18 pairs of the very large kettledrums (*kuwarga*, commonly called *damāma*)

20 or so pairs of a smaller size of kettledrum (*naqqāra*)

4 cylindrical or barrel-shaped drums (*duhul*)

(b) Idiophones:

3 pairs of cymbals (*sānj*)

(c) Aerophones: trumpet-type

4 or more long metal trumpets (*qarnā* or *karnā*) made of gold, silver, brass and other metals

some Persian trumpets

some European trumpets[2]   } *nafīr*

some Indian trumpets

2 brass trumpets in the shape of a cow's horn (*sing*)

(d) Aerophones: reed-type

a total of 9 *surnā* of the Persian kind and the Indian kind

In the list of chief musicians employed at Akbar's court only two players of these instruments are enumerated: no. 22, Shay<u>kh</u> Dawan Dhari, who performed on the *karnā*; and no. 31, Usta Shah Muhammad, who played on the *surnā*.[3] It is not clear whether these musicians played those instruments in the *naubat* ensemble.

In his account of the court of Shah Jehan, François Bernier mentions instruments which play in the *naqqāra-<u>kh</u>āna* (the "room" for the *naqqāra* or *naubat* ensemble) as "trumpets or rather hautboys and cymbals." Bernier enumerates "10 or 12 hautboys, and as many cymbals which play together. One of the hautboys, called karnā, is a fathom and a half in length, and its lower aperture cannot be less than a foot. The cymbals of brass or iron are some of them at least a fathom in diameter" (Constable 1972:260). Later in his account, and speaking of Shah Jahan's military encampment in which the *naqqāra-<u>kh</u>āna* was a tent, Bernier again enumerates trumpets and cymbals housed therein (ibid.: 363). Since Bernier appears to be less than precise in his distinction of trumpets and hautboys (double-reed aerophones), it is not possible to know of just what the ensemble consisted, beyond the trumpet *karnā* and cymbals. (I cannot imagine that *naqqāra* were absent.) It does sound from his account, however, that the size of the ensemble was severely reduced from that listed in the chronicle of Akbar. Another European, Jean-Baptiste Tavernier, observing the court of Shah Jehan, remarked in his account: "A little farther on, over the same gate, is the place where

---

[2] In the Blochmann translation of the *Ā'īn-i-Akbarī* (Phillott 1977), a footnote (vol. 1, p. 101) states that musical instruments, "as trumpets," were among the chief imports from Europe, along with broadcloth, pictures, and, after 1600, tobacco.

[3] In *Ā'īn* 30: The Imperial Musicians (Phillott 1977:682).

the drums, trumpets, and hautboys are kept. . ." (Crooke 1977: 1, 80). The instrumentarium of the *naubat* ensemble thus requires careful tracing in contemporary written sources for the Mughal period, and in iconography.

As to the functions of the *naubat* ensemble through time, it appears to have had two, one as symbol of power, the other as contributor to the musical life of the royal court (discussed later). The *naubat* ensemble as symbol of the sovereign's power I have discussed somewhat elsewhere, and I shall add only a few comments here (cf. fn. 1). Early in the Mughal empire it was the custom to have drums announce the presence of the sovereign in his audience sessions.[4] In Akbar's time and afterward, it was the *naubat* ensemble which made that announcement: "At the end [beyond the audience hall] was a great hall [*naqqāra-khāna*], where were stationed the players on instruments, and these, upon the king's [Shah Jahan's] appearing to give audience, played very loudly, to give notice that the king was already in the audience hall" (Manucci 1965: 1, 89). Tavernier wrote for the same court: ". . . the drums, trumpets, and hautboys . . . are heard some moments before the Emperor ascends his throne of justice . . . and again when the Emperor is about to rise" (Crooke 1977:80).

While it is not possible from descriptions to be certain what ensemble it was, it seems as if a *naubat*-type ensemble also functioned to announce the presence of royalty in procession beyond the boundaries of the royal encampments or fortresses. In describing the procession of the army of Shah Jahan's son, Prince Dara, Manucci commented: "Last of all was Dara on his magnificent elephant, followed by numerous elephants carrying drums, trumpets, and all manner of music, forming his retinue" (Manucci 1965:1, 263). Describing a less formal procession, the same observer related how Jahangir was capable of making light of regal pomp, in scorn of the pride and imperturbability of the great nobles.

> Sometimes he passed through the city upon his elephant, followed by many elephants, on which meat was being cooked, or wine and drinking-cups, bread, a supply of pickles, and small boxes of fruit, were carried. Others bore musicians, instruments, and drums, making a great noise. Jahangir sat eating and drinking [Manucci 1965:1, 168].

The *naubat*-type ensemble also was utilized to herald the arrival of important personages. In the *Storia do Mogor*, Manucci recounted how the Persian ambassador was welcomed with a procession:

> Aurangzeb gave orders for soldiers to be posted on both sides of the street, a league in length, through which the ambassador would pass. The principal streets were decorated with rich stuffs, both in the shops and at the windows, and the ambassador was brought through them, escorted by a number of officers, with music, drums, pipes, and trumpets. On his entering the fort, or royal palace, he was saluted by all the artillery [Manucci 1965:2, 45].

In both court chronicles and contemporary accounts can be found two other direct associations between the Mughals and music in terms of the wielding and the symbolizing of power. A ubiquitous figure in North Indian music history is the great artist Tansen, about whom Abu-l-Fazl said in the *Ā'īn-i-Akbarī*: "A singer like him has not been in India for the last thousand years" (Phillott 1977:1, 661). It is frequently noted that Tansen was from

---

[4] In the reign of Humayan (Akbar's father), the beat of drum informed people that the King was advising, and cannon announced the end of the audience period (Abu-l-Fazl 1977:1, 644). (*Akbarnāma* is written as *Akbar Nama* in the title of the translation but is written *Akbarnāma* throughout this essay.)

Gwalior, a city renowned for its great musicians through the centuries.[5] Less frequently recounted is that he was employed at the court of Ram Chand, the Rajah of Pannah. In the *Akbarnāma* Tansen's shift from Pannah to the court of Akbar is described:

> Inasmuch as the holy personality of H. M. the S͟hāhins͟hah is a congeries of degrees, spiritual and temporal, and a collection of divine and terrestrial excellences, so that when matters are discussed the master of each science imagines that the holy personality has devoted his whole attention to his particular subject, and that all his intellect has been expended on it, the knowledge which H. M. has of the niceties of music, as of other sciences, is, whether of the melodies of Persia, or the various songs of India, both as regards theory and execution unique for all time. As the fame of Tān Sen, who was the foremost of the age among the kalawants of Gwaliār came to the royal hearing, and it was reported that he meditated going into retirement and that he was spending his days in attendance on Rām Chand the Rajah of Pannah, H. M. ordered that he should be enrolled among the court-musicians. Jalāl K͟hān Qūrcī, who was a favourite servant, was sent with a gracious order to the Rajah for the purpose of bringing Tān Sen. The Rajah received the royal message and recognized the sending of the envoy as an honour, and sent back with him suitable presents of elephants of fame and valuable jewels, and he also gave Tān Sen suitable instruments and made him the cheek-mole of his gifts. In this year Tān Sen did homage and received exaltation. H. H. the S͟hāhins͟hah was pleased and poured gifts of money into the lap of his hopes. His cap of honour was exalted above all others. As he had an upright nature and an acceptable disposition he was cherished by a long service and association with H. M., and great developments were made by him in music and in compositions [Abu-l-Fazl 1977:2, 279-80].

A slightly different version appears in the *Ā'īn-i-Akbarī*:

> Rām Chand *feeling himself powerless to refuse Akbar's request*, sent his favourite, with his musical instruments and many presents to Agra, and the first time that Tānsīn performed at court, the Emperor made him a present of two lākhs of rupees. Tānsīn remained with Akbar. Most of his compositions are written in Akbar's name, and his melodies are even nowadays repeated by the people of Hindustan [Phillott 1977:2, 445; italics added].

In both chronicles the stories of Tansen are linked to the struggle to force the Raja of Pannah to "doff his cap of pride and place the ring of submission in his ear, and come into the list of tributaries" of the Mughal (Abu-l-Fazl 1977:2, 282). This was difficult, for Raja Ram Chand's forefathers had ruled over their territory for generations and had been troublesome even to Akbar's grandfather: "Among the three great Rājahs of Hindūstān whom Bābar mentions in his Memoires, the Rājas of Bhath, [Pannah] are the third" (Phillott 1977: 1, 445). Thus, the "taking" of Tansen from the court of a foe was political as well as musical

---

[5] Manucci passed through Gwalior ca. 1650 and commented: "In the town, which lies at the foot of the hill, there dwell many musicians, who gain a livelihood with their instruments . . . " (Manucci 1965:1, 69). In the late eighteenth century Gwalior began to be associated with great singers of the genre *khyāl* and that continues to the present.

play, and evidence of the involvement of music in the wielding of power.[6]

To be "worth one's weight in gold" is a saying almost synonymous with the Indic ceremony of weighing the sovereign; kings in India from as early as Ashoka (269-232 B.C.) and Harsha (600s A.D.) were party to this custom. The occasion for weighing was the sovereign's birthday, and it was a hoped-for sign of prosperity that he had gained since the previous year, even if only two pounds (Constable 1972:270). The sovereign's birthday was a time for him to bestow gifts (presumably, but not always, upon the poor) rather than receive them, and his weight provided a practical measure for gifts which would be given. The tradition had been practiced according to the birthdate in the lunar calendar, but with the introduction of Akbar's Divine Era (the solar calendar) the weighing occurred semiannually on the soveign's birthday, as it fell in both the lunar and solar calendars. On Akbar's solar birthday he was "weighed twelve times against the following articles: gold, quicksilver, silk, perfumes, copper, pewter, drugs, clarified butter, iron, rice milk, seven kinds of grain, salt; the order of these articles being determined by their costliness. . . ." On his lunar birthday he was weighed "against eight articles, viz., silver, tin, cloth, lead, fruits, mustard oil, and vegetables" (Phillott 1977:1, 277). Akbar's grandson Shah Jahan had himself weighed on each feast, first against gold and silver, and then against other articles.[7] And sons and grandsons of the sovereign were weighed once a year, as well, but it was clearly a ceremony associated with royalty.

As a reward for outstanding service and in a manner in which only a sovereign could bestow it—therefore as a symbol of power—Mughal rulers occasionally weighed a courtier against silver or some other commodity, giving them that sum in rupees. Occasionally, this honor was bestowed on musicians. Jahangir in his *Memoirs* recounted:

> Some days before this Ūstād Muhammad Nāyī (flute player), who was unequalled in his craft, was sent by my son Khurram [Shah Jehan] at my summons. I had heard some of his musical pieces (*majlis-sāz*), and he played a tune which he had composed for an ode (*ghazal*) in my name. On the 12th I ordered him to be weighed against rupees; this came to 6,300 rupees. I also gave him an elephant with a howdah, and I ordered him to ride on it and, having packed his rupees about him, to proceed to his lodging [Beveridge 1968:1, 376].

During Shah Jehan's reign, at least two musicians were rewarded in this manner: Jagnath and Dirang Khan were both weighed "in silver" and received each 4,500 rupees (Phillott 1977: 1, 682, fn. 4).

That musicians at the Mughal courts benefited from the more generalized custom of lavish gift-giving is clear from chronicles of the period. (By "more generalized" is meant the

---

[6] Tansen is mentioned in the *Memoires of Jahangir*, as well, where he is recounting childhood memories. When the *pīr* Salim Chishti was about to die, the *pīr* sent someone to Akbar with the request to have Tansen sent to him to sing. After Tansen had sung for him, the *pīr* sent for Akbar, and soon after the *pīr* died (February 1572). Salim Chishti is the *pīr* who had foretold the birth of Jahangir to the anxious Akbar who was without a son (Beveridge 1968:2, 71).

[7] Akbar's son Jahangir described the weighing which took place at the commencement of his 38th year of age: "According to custom they got ready the weighing apparatus and the scales in the house of [my mother]. At the moment appointed blessings were invoked and I sat in the scales. Each suspending rope was held by an elderly person who offered up prayers. . . . Twice a year I weigh myself against gold and silver and other metals, and against all sorts of silks and cloths, and various grains, etc., once at the beginning of the solar year and once at that of the lunar. The weight of the money of the two weighings I hand over to the different treasurers for faqirs and those in want" (Beveridge 1968:1, 77-78).

"everyday" rewarding of persons who perform well on a given occasion rather than the more specific and formalized ceremony of weighing.) An anecdote in the *Storia do Mogor* demonstrates this:

> Before speaking of the wars waged by Shahjahan and of his downfall, it is necessary to say something of his disposition. Although warlike, as he showed by his rising against his father, he was at the same time fond of music and dancing to the same degree, more or less, as his father Jahangir. His usual diversion was to listen to various instruments, to verses and poetry; and he was very fond of musicians, especially of one who was not only a graceful poet, but also a buffoon.
>
> This musician was worried by the palace gate-keepers, who are exceedingly rude to anyone who requires entrance to court. They will not permit anyone's entrance or exit without some douceur, excepting the officials, to whom they can say nothing for fear of a beating. Every time that this musician came to court the gate-keepers made him wait a long time, until he either gave them or promised them something. Anxious to rid himself of such hindrances, he composed some verses, and arrived to recite them in the presence of the king. The gate-keepers did not fail to display their accustomed insolence, detaining him until he promised to give them all that was bestowed on him this time by the king. He went in and recited in such fine style and with such graceful behaviour that the king was much delighted, and ordered for him a reward of one thousand rupees. The singer transmuted his joy into tears, raising his hands to heaven, weeping and beating his breast to show his sorrow at such a present. He said to the king with many bows that he prayed him as a favour to order him in place to receive one thousand stripes. Shahjahan smiled, and asked why he made such a request.
>
> He replied that he had promised to the gate-keepers all that he should acquire, or his majesty should make a gift of to him during the day. Thus, since they were rude, not allowing him to enter or go out without his taking out his purse and giving something, he was willing to transfer to them the thousand stripes, or even more if the king so wished. The king laughed heartily, and to satisfy him sent an order to serve out the thousand stripes to the twenty-five gate-keepers then on duty. . . . The gate-keepers got the thousand blows, while he carried off the thousand rupees, and, in addition, a horse of which the king made him a gift. . . . From that day forth the gate-keepers were very respectful to this musician, so that they might not get any more beatings [Manucci 1965:1, 182-83].

Lavish gift-giving as a general practice is an indicator of the association of music less in terms of the power of the Mughal, and more in terms of the association of music with status. Extravagant gift-giving and also the maintenance of musicians and dancers in one's employ were practiced not only by the royal households, but by numerous wealthy grandees of the Mughal empire as well. In fact, both Tavernier and Bernier remarked on the system of spending which kept anyone who wished to maintain a high status from accumulating huge sums of money. Tavernier cites an instance from the time of Aurangzeb which demonstrates the point:

> As a rule no one sees the Emperor eat except his womenkind and eunuchs, and it is very rarely that he goes to dine at the house of any of his subjects, whether

it belongs to a Prince or to one of his own relatives. While I [Tavernier] was on my last journey, Ja'far Khān, who was his Grand Wazīr, and moreover, his uncle on his wife's side, invited the Emperor to visit him and inspect the new palace which he had had built for himself. This being the greatest honour His Majesty could do him, Ja'far Khān and his wife, in testimony of their gratitude, made him a present of jewels, elephants, camels, horses, and other things, to the value of seven lakhs rupees (700,000). . . . This wife of Ja'far Khān is the most magnificent and the most liberal woman in the whole of India, and she alone expends more than all the wives and daughters of the Emperor put together; it is on this account that her family is always in debt, although her husband is practically master of the whole Empire. She had ordered a grand banquet to be prepared for the Emperor, but His Majesty, as he did not wish to dine at Ja'far Khān's house, returned to the palace, and the Princess sent after him the dishes she had destined for him. The emperor found all the dishes so much to his taste that he gave 500 rupees to the eunuch who brought them, and double that amount to the cooks [Crooke 1977:1, 310].

One of the most splendid festivals was New Year's, which was celebrated for several days around the spring solstice. On this festival gifts were given by all Ministers of State, officers, and courtiers to the sovereign; what he received on this occasion he could re-dispense or retain, as he wished.[8] In his *Memoirs,* Jahangir wrote of New Year's (March 19) 1616:

At this auspicious hour, having performed the dues of service and supplication at the throne of Almighty God, I ascended the throne of State in the public audience hall, the area of which was laid out with tents and canopies, . . . and its sides adorned with European screens, painted gold brocades, and rare cloths. The princes, Amirs, the chief courtiers, and ministers of State, and all the servants of the Court performed their congratulatory salutations. As Hāfiz Hād 'Alī, *gūyanda* (singer), was one of the ancient servants, I ordered that whatever offerings were made on the Monday by anyone in the shape of cash or goods should be given to him by way of reward [Beveridge 1968:1, 317].

That royalty and other wealthy persons in Mughal times maintained musicians and dancers in their households is well known. In the time of Akbar (who maintained the finest artists) the ruler of Malwa, Baz Bahadur, was reputed to be a good singer and to have had four hundred musicians in his service. The attitude of Abu-l-Fazl (and therefore probably of his patron) toward music and also toward Baz Bahadur's devotion to music is expressed clearly in the *Akbarnāma*:

Music and melody which the wise and farsighted have employed at times of lassitude and depression, such as arise from the press of business and the burthen of humanity, as a means of lightening the mind and of cheerfulness, were regarded by this scoundrel as a serious business, and he spent upon them all his precious hours. . . [Abu-l-Fazl 1977:2, 211].[9]

---

[8] See Wade (1982) for discussion of the gift of a *naubat* ensemble from Prince Shah Jahan to his father Jahangir on this occasion.

[9] It follows there that because of his "addiction" Baz Bahadur and his lands fell prey to Akbar's army. As a result, the ruler (former!) of Malwa is listed among the principal musicians at Akbar's court (Phillott 1977:681).

In the household of the sovereign, music and dance were patronized by the women as well as by the "official court" itself. Even in the household of the stern Aurangzeb, who moved to ban music-making, women maintained their customs. The number of women in the royal household was large, for the sovereign had several wives by political arrangements, but he also had numerous concubines, there because their families were honored to have them accepted into the ruler's harem. Each queen, princess, or other lady of quality had a household establishment for the management of her property, lands, and income:

> Ordinarily there are within the *mahal* two thousand women of different races. Each has her office or special duties, either in attendance on the king, his wives, his daughters, or his concubines. To rule and maintain order among this last class, each one is assigned her own set of rooms, and matrons are placed over them. In addition, each has usually attached to her ten or twelve women servants, who are selected from the above-named women [Manucci 1966:2, 308].

The seraglio portion of the royal residence constructed in Delhi by Shah Jehan was apparently beautiful and large. In a footnote to his translation of Bernier's *Travels*, Constable comments that the harem and other private apartments of the palace alone covered more than twice the area of the Escurial, or, in fact, of any palace in Europe:

> The Seraglio contains beautiful apartments, separated, and more or less spacious and splendid, according to the rank and income of the females. Nearly every chamber has its reservoir of running water at the door; on every side are gardens, delightful alleys, shady retreats, streams, fountains, grottoes, deep excavations that afford shelter from the sun by day, lofty divans and terraces, on which to sleep coolly at night. Within the walls of this enchanting place, in fine, no oppressive or inconvenient heat is felt [Constable 1972:267].

Since their movements beyond the seraglio were restricted, women of the royal household had relatively little daily activity, and it is not surprising that each "lady of quality" was likely to have her own musical retinue for entertainment. There were female superintendents of music and their women players; "these have about the same pay [300-500 rupees a month, the pay of the matrons mentioned above] more or less, besides the presents they receive from the princes and princesses. . ." (Manucci 1966:2, 308). Such information is rare; thus the whole of Manucci's list of superintendents is reproduced here. The word "Bae" in their names he explains as meaning "madam" or "lady" in Hindi; in the left-hand column he provides meanings of the names, given to them in the royal household.

> All of the . . . names [see Table 2] are Hindu, and ordinarily these overseers of the music are Hindus by race, who have been carried off in infancy from various villages or the houses of different rebel princes. In spite of their Hindu names, they are, however, Mahomedans. Each has under her orders about ten apprentices; and along with these apprentices they attend the queens, the princesses, and the concubines. Each one has her special rank according to her standing. The queens and the other ladies pass their time in their rooms, each with her own set of musicians. None of these musicians are allowed to sing elsewhere than in the rooms of the person to whom they are attached, except at some great festival. Then they are all assembled and ordered to sing together some piece or other in praise of, or to the honour of, the festival. All these

TABLE 2

NAMES OF THE SUPERINTENDENTS OF DANCERS AND SINGERS
WITH THEIR MEANING

Sundar Bae	Superintendent of Music
Surosh Bae	The Good Voice
Chulohla Bae	The Happy
Mirg-nain	Gazelle-eyed
La'l Bae	Ruby
Hira Bae	Diamond
Manasa Bae	Pearl
Jaliya Bae	The Net
Ras Bae	Liquor
Nain-jot Bae	Light of the Eyes
Mirg-mala Bae	Flowery, or She who Is Covered with Flowers
Gul-ru Bae	Rose-Visaged
Chanchal Bae	The Bold
Sanchal Bae	The Subtle
Dhyan Bae	The Well-Informed
Gyan Bae	The Inventive
Har Bae	Flower-Adorned
Murad Bae	The Desired
Matlab Bae	The Foreseeing
Akas Bae	The Celestial
Apsara Bae	The Seraphic
Khaldar Bae	The Freckled
Baikunth Bae	Paradise
Khushhal Bae	The Happy
Nihal Bae	The Abundant
Farah Bae (?)	The Healthy
Gulal Bae	The Rose
Kasturi Bae	Musk or Musk-Perfumed
Kar-i-sawab Bae	Taste
Basna Bae	The Pleasant-Scented
Udar-Bae (?)	The Replete
Chanchal Bae (?)	The Sufficient
Kesar Bae	Saffron

women are pretty, have a good style, and much grace in their gait, are very free in their talk and exceedingly lascivious . . . [Manucci 1966:2, 313-14].

New Year's was, of course, among the major festivals at which singing and dancing were featured. At least from Akbar's time, the festivities would commence on the day when the sun moved to Aries and would last several days. On two days much money and numerous presents were given; the *naqqāras* were beaten and singers and musicians participated (Phillott 1977:1, 286). Jahangir describes preparations for successive New Year's Festivals in his Memoires, consistently in terms something like this:

> I ordered them to decorate the porticoes of the private and public halls of the palace, as in the time of my revered father, with delicate stuffs, and to adorn them handsomely. From the first day of the Nauruz to the 19th degree of the Ram (Aries), which is the day of culmination, the people gave themselves over to enjoyment and happiness. Players and singers of all bands and castes were gathered together [Beveridge 1968:1, 48].[10]

Two generations of Mughals later, the court festivities were as constant as ever, even under Aurangzeb:

> Upon birthdays and other days of festival, above all on that of the New Year . . . the chief ladies of the court are obliged to attend at the palace to make their compliments to the queens and princesses. . . . When the ladies attend there they never go in with empty hands but always carry costly presents to be offered. They remain at the court until the end of the feast, which lasts usually six to nine days. The dancing-women and singing-women receive on these occasions handsome presents from the princesses and other great ladies. They either sing to compliment them on their birthday, or invoke on them all kinds of prosperity when congratulating them at the New Year. The ladies respond then to all the praises, which the singing-women never fail to shower on them, by full trays of gold and silver coin which they throw to them [Manucci 1966:2, 322-23].

References to other special occasions for music-making by harem musicians or others are infrequent in the chronicles of either the sovereigns or, naturally, in the writing of other male observers. In three rare glimpses we learn of particular merriment on two occasions — a marriage, and the birth of a prince. In the first instance, Abu-l-Fazl in the *Akbarnāma* relates an occasion when Akbar was (it seems, for the paragraph is deemed even by Beveridge to be "mysterious") meditating or at least absorbed in serious contemplation in his private quarters. "Suddenly there arose the noise of marriage and H. M. ordered that the music should be stopped, as a foreign sound did not suit the banquet of enlightenment" (Abu-l-Fazl 1977: 3, 1058).

In a rhapsodic passage in the *Akbarnāma*, Abu-l-Fazl describes the birth of Akbar:

> They spread the carpet of joy under the canopy of chastity and curtain of honour [under his mother], and made ready a feast of joy and exultation. The veiled ones of the pavilion, and the chaste inmates of the royal harem anointed the eye of hope with the collyrium of rejoicing and coloured the eyebrows of desire

---

[10] It is probably due to the importance of this spring solstice festival to both Hindus and Muslims and the prolonged celebration at court that the repertory of *dhamār* was so important in the repertory of court musicians.

with the indigo of merriness. They decked the ear of good tidings with the earring of success, painted the face of longing with the vermilion of pleasure, encircled the fore-arm of wish with the bracelet of purpose, and donning the anklet of splendour on the dancing foot, stepped into the theatre of delight and joy and raised the strain of praise and gratulation. . . . Rose-scented, jasmine-cheeked ones soothed the rapid dancers with camphorated sandal-wood. . . . Musicians created enchanting ecstasy, and melodious minstrels breathed forth magic strains [Abu-l-Fazl 1977:1, 57].

Manucci provides a straightforward account of the time of Aurangzeb in his *Storia do Mogor*:

When a princess is born in the *mahal* the women rejoice, and go to great expense as a mark of joy. If a prince is born, then all the court takes part in the rejoicings, which last several days, as the king may ordain. Instruments are played and music resounds; the nobles appear to offer their congratulations to the king, bringing presents, either in jewels, money, elephants, or horses [Manucci 1966:2, 320].

While references to music-making in the daily routine of the Mughals are few, they are informative. One reference in the *Akbarnāma* relates Humayan beginning a day with music, even when on military campaign:

From the close of day up to early dawn, which is the time of the arrival of the glory of heaven, there was a delightful assembly. Instructive events were described, and Mir Qalandar and other reciters and players discoursed excellent music, thereby removing the rust from his Majesty's world-adorning soul [Abu-l-Fazl 1977:1, 468].

It would appear from a commentary in the *Ā'īn-i-Akbarī* that Akbar sometimes turned night into day, holding assemblies in his private audience hall with philosophers and Sufis. Then,

about a watch before daybreak, musicians from all nations are introduced, who recreate [entertain?] the assembly with music and songs, and religious strains; and when four *gharīs* are left til morning His Majesty retires to his private apartments [Phillott 1977:1, 164; a *gharī* is 24 minutes].

Akbar's involvement with the Sufis provides a rare reference to a precise musical tradition:

Accordingly, at this time, Bakhshu Qawwal recited before him two heart-ravishing stanzas in a pleasing manner. That Syllabus of the roll of recognition (of God) displayed a countenance flashing Divine lights. Those whose vision did not extend beyond the plain outward appearance receive spiritual delight (from the singing). Much more then was the state of the internally farsighted! When H. M. returned from that wonderful condition, he gave thanksgiving to God, and filled the hope-skirt of the songster with rich coin [Abu-l-Fazl 1977: 3, 378].[11]

From Akbar's time, at least, the *naubat* ensemble (mentioned above) contributed to the regular routine of music. In the *Ā'īn-i-Akbarī* we are told: "Formerly the band played four *gharīs* before daybreak; now they play first at midnight, when the sun commences his ascent, and the second time at dawn" (Phillott 1977:1, 53). At dawn the function was not only to waken everyone (this was specifically the function of the *surnā*) but to begin the day with a concert, as well. This lasted more than three hours, and consisted of numerous specified items in an established order, described in the *Ā'īn-i-Akbarī* (Phillott 1977:1, 53).

In the reign of Aurangzeb, Bernier reported that the ensemble in the *naqqāra-khāna* played

> in concert at certain hours of the day and night . . . in the night, particularly, when in bed and afar, on my terrace this music sounds in my ears as solemn, grand, and melodious. This is not to be altogether wondered at, since it is played by persons instructed from infancy in the rules of melody, and possessing the skill of modulating and turning the harsh sounds of the hautboy and cymbal so as to produce a symphony far from disagreeable when heard at a certain distance [Constable 1972:260].

It seems fitting to end this accounting of music-making, told in honor of David P. McAllester, with a passage descriptive of the Mughal dynasty in full flower, under Shah Jehan, when the chronicles speak less of military campaigns and more of court customs, of etiquette, of wonderful goods produced in the Empire. With Shah Jehan the opulent emphasis on artistic accomplishments in architecture and the graphic arts reached its climax. The spirit of his reign is present in this description of a formal audience and the hall in which it was held:

> It is a grand hall elevated some four feet above the ground floor, and open on three sides. Thirty-two marble columns sustain as many arches, and these columns are about four feet square with their pedestals and some mouldings. . . . In the middle of this hall, and near the side overlooking the court, as in a theatre, they place the throne when the Emperor comes to give audience and administer justice. It is a small bed of the size of our camp beds, with its four columns, the canopy, the back, a bolster, and counterpane; all of which are covered with diamonds.
>
> When the Emperor takes his seat, however, they spread on the bed a cover of gold brocade, or of some other rich stuff, and he ascends it by three small steps of two feet in length. On one side of the bed there is a parasol . . . and to each column of the bed one of the Emperor's weapons is attached, to one his shield, to another his sword, next his bow, his quiver, and arrows, and other things. . . .
>
> In the court below the throne there is a space twenty feet square, surrounded by balustrades which on some occasions are covered with plates of silver, and at others with plates of gold. . . . Several nobles place themselves

---

[11] For an article which fully explains this citation, but which is based on a Sufi assembly in 1976, see Regula Qureshi (1981).

around the balustrade, and here also is placed the music, which is heard while the Emperor is in the Divan. This music is sweet and pleasant . . . [Crooke 1977: 1, 80-81].[12]

References Cited

Abu-l-Fazl
 1977 *The Akbar Nama of Abu-l-Fazl: History of the Reign of Akbar Including an Account of His Predecessors*, transl. Henry Beveridge. 3 vols. 2nd Indian reprint. (Originally published 1921.) Delhi: Ess Ess Publications.

Beveridge, Henry, ed.
 1968 *The Tūzuk-i-Jahāngīrī or Memoirs of Jahangir*, transl. Alexander Rogers [1864]. 2 vols. bound as 1. 2nd ed. (1st ed. 1909-14). Delhi: Munshiram Manoharlal.

Constable, Archibald, ed.
 1972 *Travels in the Mogul Empire (A.D. 1656-1668) by François Bernier*, transl. Irving Brock (1891). 3rd ed. New Delhi: S. Chand & Co.

Crooke, William, ed.
 1977 *Travels in India by Jean-Baptiste Tavernier (1676)*, transl. V. Ball (1886). 2 books bound as 1. New Delhi: Oriental Books Reprint Corp.

Manucci, Niccolao
 1965-67 *Storia do Mogor or Mogul India (1653-1708)*, transl. William Irvine (1907). 4 vols. Reprint, Calcutta: Editions Indian.

Phillott, D. C., ed.
 1977 *The Ā'īn-i-Akbañ by Abū 'L-Faẓl 'Allāmī*, transl. H. Blochmann (1873). Vol. 1. 3rd ed. New Delhi: Oriental Books Reprint Corp.

Qureshi, Regula
 1981 "Qawwālī: Making the Music Happen in the Sufi Assembly." *Performing Arts in India: Essays on Music, Dance and Drama,* ed. Bonnie C. Wade, pp. 118-57. Lanham, Maryland: University Press of America.

Wade, Bonnie C.
 1982 "Playing for Power: Drum and *Naubat*, the Symbols of Might." Paper given at the 13th Congress of the International Musicological Society (Strassbourg). Forthcoming in Congress Report.

---

[12] Music-making during the conducting of court business is depicted in paintings during the Mughal period. An instance of it in twentieth-century courtly India was described to me in an interview in 1978 with Shri Karan Singh, scion of the late Maharaja of Kashmir. He remembers from his childhood:

> Twice a year formal *darbār* was held and all courtiers came to bring an offering. My father sat on his throne at one end of the long rectangular hall. The Ministers sat, according to rank, and each in turn presented something. . . . At the opposite end stood a singer and the accompanists, singing while this was going on.

The Would-Be Indian

Joann W. Kealiinohomoku
Northern Arizona University
and
Cross-Cultural Dance Resources
Flagstaff

Introduction

For hundreds of years there have been white persons who viewed American Indians as "noble savages." By the teens of the twentieth century it was both fashionable and "safe" to adopt this view. Indian "threats" to white persons had become a thing of the past. Buffalo Bill and his Wild West Show were hits on both sides of the Atlantic Ocean; even Theodore Roosevelt had attended a Buffalo Bill show that featured the famous Apache warrior Geronimo. By 1910 Boy Scouts had become established in the United States, and they adopted Indian-inspired examples for camping and craft skills. The Camp Fire Girls were also established in 1910; they, too, followed an "Indian" theme for crafts and camping (Gulick 1915).

National attention to Indians seems to have climaxed in the 1920s. Congress gave universal suffrage to federally recognized United States Indians. Congress also directed the Meriam Survey to investigate Indian reservations; the devastating results created demands for reforms in government treatment of Indians. Numerous annual celebrations with Indian themes were commenced during the decade of the 1920s, attested by the golden anniversaries in the 1970s of the Gallup Indian Ceremonial, the Flagstaff All-Indian Powwow, and the "Smoki Tribe."

Groups of would-be Indians institutionalized their fantasies, and unique individuals adopted Indian ways. These continuing phenomena and the reactions toward them, by Indians and non-Indians, are the topic of this essay.

Premises

Romantics of the early part of this century used "Indian" symbols in handicrafts, kept newspaper articles about Indians, made Indian-type costumes for their children, cooked "Squawdish" and "Succotash," doted on stories about Indian maidens and love-sick braves, sang the light-opera song "Moon Deer" by Rudolf Friml, and deeply desired to understand Indian values. Some Indians endorsed this romanticized appreciation of their cultures, while others resented it. Still others were uncomfortable with the resulting paradoxes.

Kindergarten children from the 1930s through the present time believed that to sit cross-legged on the floor is "Indian style." A happy kindergarten experience is to wear a feather in a headband while toe-heeling around the classroom, one hand tapping the mouth in an aspirated "wa-wa-wa-wa." Playing Indian falls into the category of make-believe. The children, grandchildren, and great-grandchildren of those romantic folks from the early part of this century began to think that Indians were not real, or, at least, no longer extant. A few years ago my daughter was told by some non-Indian children that she was lying when she insisted that she was going to visit Indian friends. "Indians are fairytales," she was told. Many adults seem to think so, too. A Sierra Club calendar in the mid-seventies described Hopi and Navajo initiation rituals. The author of the calendar text seemed to be unaware that this beautiful calendar, designed for children, might be read by real Navajo and Hopi children.

Childcraft's annual supplement of 1980, *The Indian Book* (Childcraft Annual 1980) couched the text about currently viable Indian cultures in the past tense. The chapter about the Hopi includes instructions for making "your own kachina mask" out of two brown paper bags (ibid.: 105-07). The book concludes that Indians are "trying to keep their language, their dances and music, and a great many of the ways of their ancestors." Following this statement is a photo of a dancer, in Plains costume, captioned "A Mescalero Apache performs an old dance" (ibid.: 292). Considering the misinformation available to non-Indians, the fact that many Indians feel that their cultures are thought to be extinct is not surprising.

The myth that viable Indian cultures are dead or dying provides a rationale for some non-Indians to try to preserve Indian cultures. Many Indians perceive this as arrogant, patronizing, and based on false premises. They infer that non-Indians think that Indians do not have the wits, adaptability, and skills to protect their own cultures, even though they had the abilities initially to develop their cultures. The myth implies, also, that Indians are pawns of the white man and they are too naive and incapable of coping, to participate in the twentieth century.

Actually, many non-Indians may want to "do" Indian activities because they enjoy them. Non-Indians apparently seem to believe they must justify their actions beyond selfish enjoyment. Would-be Indians express non-Indian values when their benevolent attitude puts them in a controlling position, erodes Indian self-determination, and muddies cultural dynamics. Indians, not agreeing that "imitation is the sincerest form of flattery," feel exploited, or worse, victims of cultural rape. Further, Indians are sensitive because non-Indians do not regularly imitate other ethnic groups. Indians view this as a unique form of racism. Surely it must shock non-Indians who enthusiastically participate in "Indian" activities to learn that their actions are considered to be damaging to the persons who unwittingly serve as models.

Hills (1975) suggests that Indians might clarify their point by forming a society of Indians dedicated to preserving white culture (cf. also·Wilson 1976). Other Indians could view these activities in order to learn to appreciate white culture. In fact, I have seen Indian ritual clowns mimic non-Indian activities, but this is not known widely outside Indian circles. However, I am unaware of any cases of Indians seriously impersonating non-Indians with the notion that they are preserving those activities, or that they are promoting better understanding among Indians and non-Indians.

Indian traditions, including religious beliefs and behavior, are tribal and exclusive to the members of a given Indian group. Assimilating other groups to those traditions is contrary to maintenance of ethnic identity; as a corollary, there is no tradition of manipulating others' traditions. In contrast, white Christian societies are inclusive. They attempt to convert and assimilate outsiders; apparently they think other societies might likewise welcome assimilation. With this attitude, culture-loss is understood to be a real possibility. Persons with a world view that acknowledges culture-loss can endorse the opposite idea of preventing culture-loss. The Golden Rule of "doing unto others as you would have others do unto you" is not as appropriate a guideline as "do unto others as they would have you do unto them."

As it is, however, when a white person dances as though he or she were an Indian, the white person feels proud, while the Indian often feels resentment. Indians today encourage one another to believe that white persons cannot truly be Indians, and cannot think or behave as Indians. In contrast, when the Osage sisters Maria and Marjorie Tallchief became ballerinas, the white dance world applauded because they achieved dance assimilation in the rarified world of High Culture. Culture shock, then, exists on both sides of the blanket, so to speak. When whites dance as though they are Indians, Indians condemn them and white persons cannot understand why. Instead of being praised for having achieved dance assimilation, they are criticized as trespassers.

Theory

The differences in attitude might be explained by applying Edward T. Hall's concept of high-context and low-context (Hall 1979:49). High-context dance, for example, is embedded in a larger frame of reference that is essential to its existence. High-context dance does not exist for its own sake, and traditional Indian dance exemplifies high-context dance. In contrast, white concert dances are low-context because they can exist for their own sake. Indeed, some concert dances are comparable to the legal contract of Hall's example, in that they are supposed to be context-free. This theory fits well with the exclusive/inclusive model suggested above. If this application of Hall's high- and low-contexts and the exclusive/inclusive dichotomies is valid for comparing Indian dances with non-Indian dances, performances of Indian dances by non-Indians may never be totally acceptable to Indians unless the larger context does become extinct or unimportant.

Case Studies

Five non-Indian groups are noteworthy for their intense pretense that they are behaving as Indians. These are the Boy Scout "Koshare Dancers," the Y-Indian Guides and Y-Indian Princess Program, the "Smoki Tribe," American Indian hobbyists, and Indian clubs abroad (especially in Germany). Another category of would-be Indians includes unique individuals such as the Laubins, Reginald and Gladys, long-time concert performers of Indian dances, and M. W. Billingsley, who ran away from his Iowa home as a teenager to live with the Hopi Indians.

Indian influences are also expressed in popular culture. For example, Felipe Rose, dressed more or less as a Plains Indian, "dances up a storm while singing back-up" for the "Village People," a group that specializes in popular "macho tunes" (Goldsmith 1979:3). In June 1980, I saw a collector's card of Felipe Rose in his "Indian" dance costume, among toys outside a home on the Hopi Reservation (Can't Stop Productions, Inc., 1979). What reverse influences it may have had on some Hopi child cannot be guessed.

Steiner (1976) described the glossy use of Indian-inspired motifs by nightclub performers. Captioning a photo of ten persons dressed with full feather headdresses and long loincloths, he wrote "this talented tribe is known as the Sabreet Dancers, a night club revue combining sexual and savage fantasies so well it doesn't matter than none of the girls or guys is Indian" (ibid.: 38).

I observed an Exotic Dancer at a night club in Milwaukee, Wisconsin, in the late 1950s, who assumed a persona of an Indian maiden for her dance. She wore a feather headdress, an abbreviated buckskin skirt, and performed her version of an Indian dance in toe shoes! She told me she was a university student working her way through school, and she really enjoyed pretending to be an Indian during her performance.

DOMESTIC GROUPS

In 1969 I watched the Koshare Boy Scout dancers in performance at Indiana University. Their visible joy in performing and the enthusiastic response of the university audience were impressive, but I left the auditorium feeling uncomfortably ambivalent. The group receives glowing notices in the general press:

> In their home town . . . they are known as Buck's Brats, but around the nation they are the Koshares, a Boy Scout troop that dazzles audiences with authentic Indian dances. The remarkable man behind their success is Buck Burshears, the only leader the Koshares have had for half-a-century [Bartimus 1982b:8].

The accompanying article explains that the group was named after the "Pueblo Indian word meaning 'fun-maker'." In fact, there is no single Pueblo language, so there is no "Pueblo word," and traditional koshares are sacred clowns, not to be copied. Since the 1933 inception of the Boy Scout Koshares they have earned a $3 million Indian and Western art collection, and raised $1 million to build a clubhouse to house it. Their repertory of more than 200 Native American dances is performed in "authentic costumes handcrafted by the youth themselves" (Bartimus 1982a:D-7; 1982b:8). But on a less enthusiatic note:

> Only two years ago the Pueblo Indians became aware that the Koshare Dancers, a group of non-Indian professionals specializing in presentation of Indian dances, had rare objects belonging to the various pueblos.
> A committee was formed to regain possession of their property, and two trips were made to the Koshare headquarters, returning to the pueblos several truckloads of their arts [Arnet 1974:10].

Jimmy Little Turtle (1974:47) complained that the Koshare are the Boy Scouts who "make a mockery of Indian dances throughout the country and who get $1,000 per performance and do nothing for Indian people." (Ironically, Jimmy Little Turtle apparently felt comfortable about Indians performing dances for non-Indians. He concluded his letter by asking for "craftsmen and dancers who are free to travel to perform in shopping malls the whole year long.") Some Indians must have endorsed Burshears and his Boy Scouts, however. Bartimus assured his readers that "through his persuasion and diplomacy, Indian leaders began teaching the white boys many of their ancient rituals and dances" (Bartimus 1982a:D-7). Little Turtle anticipated that when he wrote "it seems that they are welcome at many tribal dances and then they go out and do the same for a fee" (1975:2).

That the YMCA is also interested in Indian lore is manifested by the Y-Indian Guides and Y-Indian Princess Program. The Princess Program, for fathers and their daughters, aged six to nine years, provides an opportunity for fathers and their daughters to share common interests. Each "tribe" consists of six to nine fathers and daughters, according to Richard Trenka who signed himself as a "Medicine Man," although whether he is an Indian Medicine Man or not is unclear (Trenka 1976).

In 1977 the National Congress of American Indians expressed concern with the reforms in the Princess Program manual. The reforms had been instituted by a Y-Indian task force set by the YMCA (ca. 1970) to rectify previous negative charges. "It appears," concluded the representatives of the NCAI, "that the . . . leaders who comprised the Manual Revision Committee did not have on their committee people from the Plains Indian culture on which the manual was based" (Brasch 1977:49).

Specifically, the NCAI deplores generalizations that indiscriminantly mix several Sioux tribal traditions and then incongruently intersperse key ideas from the Iroquois and Northwest Coastal tribes (ibid.: 49-50). The manual is indicted for the incorrect, sometimes blasphemous, use of Indian objects, such as the peace pipe (ibid.: 58). Sioux religious beliefs are sacred to the Sioux and "it is sacriligious for a white man to try to imitate [them]" (ibid.: 57).

The manual is faulted for not explaining the differences between social and religious dances, and for stereotyping Indian dances. NCAI cites as "gross and blatant" the idea alien to Sioux that "the daughters can end this dance by sitting cross-legged, still in the circle, and raising each hand alternately 12 times" (manual quoted in ibid.: 59). The NCAI experiences dissonance in that, although the basic dance steps described in the manual are Sioux, the manual includes un-Sioux-like choreographic instructions to the dancers to perform in a circle, with each step danced eight times in one direction and then eight times in the opposite direction (ibid.: 58). Finally, the NCAI alleges that white dancers are models and that white dancers' performances of Indian dances are "about as authentic as a basket of plastic fruit" (ibid.: 58).

Giving Indian names is likewise inappropriate "when they have no idea of the meaning of the name and they 'could be using a sacred name that has been retired and never to be used again,' (such as Crazy Horse)" (ibid.: 59). The NCAI indignantly claims that the Y-programs have exploited Indian symbols, dances, and beliefs, because "we have whites banding together in their tribes pretending they are Indian" (ibid.: 75).

The NCAI claims that the Y-programs' goal to make people knowledgeable about Indian culture is flawed by generalities, stereotypes, and disrespectful handling of objects and ideas. They question the program for turning to traditions other than their own, insisting that Y members should use their own religion to bring about togetherness of parents and children.

> You may say . . . that you are only trying to secure our religion for us so that it will not disintegrate but I believe we have been doing fine these past centuries, and we will continue to do so [Corrina Drum, quoted in Brasch ibid.: 55-56].

It wounds Indians to feel that they are singled out for what is perceived as mockery. They note that "you wouldn't have a parent/child group pretending they are Chinese or Blacks" (Webster Robbin, quoted in Brasch ibid.: 60).

> I cannot imagine any other group of people being treated the same way. . . . Can you imagine a group of non-Christian children pretending they are Catholic for an evening once every two weeks. The group of non-Christian children and their fathers taking Catholic holy names such as Jesus Christ, Saint Paul, or the Pope. Can you imagine non-Christian children taking communion, making a crucifix, or saying Hail Mary? [ibid.: 57].

Unlike the Y-Indian programs, Indian hobbyists are adults who seriously study and participate in Indian activities, especially costume-making and dance performances according to Powers in his book *This is Your Hobby—Indian Dancing* (*Powwow Trails* 1969a:42). The First National Hobbyist Powwow was held in 1969, featuring Northern and Southern style Plains dancing. "What we are trying to accomplish in a hobby Pow-wow [*sic*]; education and promoting of Indian ways, both old and new" (Nichols 1969:58; *Powwow Trails* 1969b:59).

Opinions of Indians about non-Indians who dance in powwows are varied. On the one hand, Powers advises "while non-Indian dancers are welcome on most of the reservations, they may not be at public performances. . . . Check with the powwow officials before going out on the dance floor. The general rule is to watch the religious dances, and take part in the powwows" (Powers 1966:3). On the other hand, a writer to the editor of *Indian Voices* exclaims, after saying emphatically that whites should not be permitted to dance in powwows, "if there is anything more ridiculous than white men trying to act like Indians, it might be the way most tourists dress!" (Farver 1966:11).

Classified ads in the hobbyist magazine *Powwow Trails* indicate that some readers are confident enough about their skills with Indian lore to pursue them for profit as well as pleasure: "Wanted — Indian Lore Instructor . . . Running Deer Camp for Boys . . . " (*Powwow Trails* 1966a:13). Again, "Indian Lore Counselor for well-established co-ed camp in the Adirondacks . . ." (*Powwow Trails* 1968:59). Would-be Indians can find ways from the classified ads to pursue their fantasy: "Wanted — Indian Hobbyists interested in living out as Indians this summer. Singles, groups" (*Powwow Trails* 1966b:2).

Very different from the hobbyists is the brotherhood of white businessmen from Prescott, Arizona. Incorporated as the "Smoki Tribe," a very controversial group of would-be Indians, they give an annual public performance early every August "in the dark of the moon" at the Prescott Stadium, in the performance field they call "Smoki Mesa" (Anonymous 1975a).

There are elements of secrecy about this brotherhood, known only to fully inducted members. Known facts are that the Smoki first performed in 1921 as an added feature to help boost the gate for the annual Prescott Frontier Days (Anonymous 1976b). Their first performance was a burlesque of Indian dancing, especially of the Hopi Snake Dance. However, the performance was so popular that the participants decided to devote themselves seriously to learning authentic Indian dances. They set about to dignify the endeavor by suggesting that their performances would help preserve Indian tribal dances. Toward that end they have also established a museum in Prescott for Indian artifacts. Their research about the dances and artifacts depends heavily upon publications from the Bureau of American Ethnology (Smoki People n.d.).

The organization is apparently tightly structured and there is strong control over the activities of its members when they represent the Smoki (Scholten 1976). New members must serve apprenticeships before they are fully initiated, at which time they are given a tattooed insignia on their left hands. While functioning as Smoki, they assume persona that differ from their non-Smoki lives. Professional standing is not permitted to influence status in the Smoki organization, because each member must earn his Smoki name and position. Wives of members have an informal sodality called the Smoki Squaws. They, too, have tattoos on their left hands (Smoki People ibid.).

For the past several years the group has pronounced its name with a long /i/ as in "Smokai." I surmised that they originally made a take-off on the word /moqui/, a term by which Hopi were once known by most white persons. By adding an /s/ to symbolize snakes, I projected the contrived word "Smoki," pronounced "Smokee." I justified my supposition when I was able to glance briefly at a book privately published in Prescott for the Smoki (Gillford 1971).

Their annual performance, called "Smoki Ceremonial and Snake Dance" consists of three or four dances copied from various tribes, set in vignettes. They conclude every performance with their hallmark (Anonymous 1979a), an acknowleged variation of the Hopi Snake Dance. I attended their 51st annual presentation in 1971, and was impressed by the serious demeanor, dedication, and energy of the performers. There was an admission fee to offset the expenses of renting the stadium and maintaining their museum (Anonymous

1975a). There was no commercial atmosphere—no concession stands for food or souvenirs. The audience was prohibited from making photographs during the performance. Information was explicit in both the printed program and the loudspeaker announcements that the performers were not Indians, but that white persons were performing "authentic" Indian dances (Smoki People 1971).

In an audience estimated at about five thousand persons I observed but one Indian family. I took note of the comments made by persons around me, and discovered that many persons were tourists who had been steered to the performance by the Prescott Chamber of Commerce. Despite the information to the contrary, many of them thought they had seen real Indians dancing the "authentic" Indian dances. Several of them commented about their good luck to be able to see Indians dance.

Because of their black wigs, body paint, and careful rehearsing, the dancers looked astonishingly like Indians, and performed convincingly, in my opinion. A dissonant costume feature was the fact that many moccasins fit over the feet as though they were spats instead of encasing the feet. The least successful aspects of their masquerade were the singing and drumming which, though performed with verve, were rhythmically oversimplified; the vocal qualities were also incorrect.

The Smoki Snake Dance is not an exact copy of the Hopi Snake Dance. Their understanding of the supportive myth is aberrant (Wilson 1977). The song bears no resemblance to the Hopi Snake Dance song but for the fact that it incorporates alternating slow and fast tempi; a drum accompanies the dance although the Hopi do not use a drum for their Snake Dance. Especially noticeable in 1971, the Smoki Snake Dance choreography was more elaborate than that used in the Hopi Snake Dance. The Smoki did, however, use two dance groups, the Snake Men and the Antelope Men. One set of Snake Men carried the snakes in the mouth and one hand, while a second set of men acted as "huggers" to distract the snakes and accompany the carriers, and a third set gathered the snakes after they were danced, all similar to the Hopi division of Snake Men. The Smoki performance was dignified and dramatic, as is true, certainly, of the Hopi Snake Dance.

The significant problem with the Smoki Snake Dance, as with all the Smoki dances, is that the Indians who own these dances have never given permission to the Smoki to use them. Indeed, the Indians apparently have not even been asked for permission. Concert dances in the professional theatrical world are now protected by copyright; but, as Hopi have said to me, there seems to be no way to copyright a religion, and traditional Indian dances are sanctioned by their religion. The Smoki, as the Boy Scouts, Y-Indians, hobbyists, choreographers, and night club entertainers, apparently believe that traditional performances are in the public domain, available for anyone to usurp with impunity.

This attitude is puzzling because the Smoki, as several of the other groups, justify the performance of the dances as preserving them. The conundrum is that in order to value something enough to want to preserve it, there must be appreciation; in order to appreciate something there must be understanding. The evidence is clear that the Smoki do not accept Indian values or they would not take it upon themselves to preserve Indian dances unless approved by the appropriate Indians.

Instead, their ceremonies "get more elaborate as years go by, and, not content with wrapping harmless bull snakes around in their mouths, they have added kachinas and other Hopi rituals" (Sekaquaptewa 1976:2). Indians doubt the good intentions of the Smoki; a group that genuinely wants to preserve a body of traditions should seek advice from the source instead of depending on bulletins from the Bureau of American Ethnology (Smoki People n.d.).

I have heard Indians who have not seen a Smoki performance (and few Indians have seen a Smoki performance) complain that the Smoki people are "making fun" of Indians. Having seen a Smoki performance myself, I question that allegation. Indians say that the Smoki have no respect for Indians or they would not trespass. Yet it seems that there is tremendous respect for Indians from a peculiarly non-Indian point of view. I cannot believe that 250-300 Smoki people (Anonymous 1975a) would be devoted to something they did not respect. Representatives of the Smoki told members of the Native American Club of Prescott, Arizona, that they "had nothing but respect for Indian people," and they reiterated their mission to preserve Indian cultures. The club members countered, "how dare they claim that they can preserve Indian culture . . . an annual show out of native ceremonies hurts Indian people a great deal and . . . shows disrespect" (Sepi, et al. 1976:12).

I fathom that the longevity and popularity of the Smoki derive from the fact that those who participate enjoy themselves immensely and feel rewarded in intangible ways. I suspect they also think that contemporary Indians are not as "pure" in their traditions as were those who were recorded by ethnologists in the last century; in that way they may feel less respect for contemporary Indians than for their forebears.

Smoki leaders did finally meet with Hopi leaders. It turned out to be a confrontation (Anonymous 1980a). The Hopi charged the Smoki with trespass. The Smoki claimed they had their own ritual sanctions, but they could not reveal them to the Hopi because they, the Smoki, were initiated and pledged to secrecy. The Smoki leaders said that they wished the Hopi would accept the Smokis' right to perform their dances, but if the Hopi could not accept that and wanted to try to take legal action, "so be it" (*Hopi Tribal News* 1980:1; Anonymous 1980b). In fact, then, as always, "the objections on moral grounds fell on deaf ears . . . [and] there was no legal way of telling them to stop" (Sekaquaptewa 1976:2). Apparently other rewards are greater than Indian approval.

A film was made of the Smoki performing their snake dance (Avalon Daggett Productions n.d.), so that children, who might never see a Hopi Snake Dance, would realize that the dance is not wild and savage as claimed in some accounts. The Smoki film, therefore, supposedly serves as an educational vehicle to inform American young people about a famous Indian ceremonial that cannot be filmed on the Hopi Reservation.

A postscript to this section on the Smoki: the 1981 annual performance included "Los Voladores," for which the dancers, with ropes tied to their bodies, "fly" to earth from the top of a forty foot pole. One of the Smoki dancers fell during the public performance and was severely injured. The Smoki People have given unprecedented benefit performances during the past few months to raise money to help pay the hospital bills that now exceed $200,000 (Associated Press 1982a:8).

FOREIGN GROUPS

Would-be Indians are not unique to America. Indians have captured the imagination of persons around the world:

> Interest in the American Indian may be undergoing a twentieth century resurgence in the U.S. these days, but it will have a long way to go before it catches up to Europe's fascination with the redskin.
>
> Ever since the first "savages" were hustled off and presented in full plumage in the royal courts of the sixteenth century, Europeans have been intrigued by Indians. The attraction has withstood time and "civilizing" influences [Bright 1970:8].

The most ardent of non-American would-be Indians are Germans. Interest by Germans for American Indians took fire at the end of the last century when author Karl May (a.k.a. Mai) wrote some twenty novels about the adventures of an imaginary Apache chief. May's own imagination was fed from library research, because he himself never visited America. Today there are hundreds of Western lore clubs in both West and East Germany (Anonymous 1977; Bright 1970; Minthorn 1970; Theisz 1965). Unlike American hobbyist groups that are divergent in focus and independent of one another, German groups are organized under a parent organization called IFI (International Friends of the Indian), according to Theisz (1965). They restrict their interest to the "hide period" of the Indian; that is, the late eighteenth century and most of the nineteenth century. Modern dancing and costumes are "frowned upon" (ibid.):

> The German hobbyist is more scientific in his approach to the hobby than are most Americans. He is very widely read and is on the average older than his American conterpart . . . the Indian way of life is the goal of the German hobbyist [ibid.: n.p.].

There is a group in Bad Segeberg, West Germany, that has been performing Indian theatrical plays since 1952 for the specific purpose of promoting knowledge of Indian culture, history, philosophy, and wilderness living (Anonymous 1976a:18). This fervor for American Indians has had positive feedback from Indians who have been impressed by German interest. Some Indian servicemen who were stationed in Germany have been inspired to research Indian cultures after finding themselves the subject of adulation (Theisz 1965; Ross 1981).

The first "sales mission" of the American Indian Tourism Council of Arizona was to Frankfort, West Germany, in December 1981 (Associated Press 1982b:1). Formed in 1981 by the White Mountain Apache, Navajo, Hopi, and Yavapai Apache tribes of Arizona, the purpose of the council is to "pump dollars into the Indian Economy and show people the real Indian culture" (Associated Press 1982b:1).

Some Indians feel that foreigners are sensitive to Indians, almost by definition. The editor (in 1978) of the Hopi newspaper *Qua'Töqti* did not agree, and pointed out inaccuracies and misunderstandings in the "feverish" writing about American Indians by European journalists (Sekaquaptewa 1978:6). More pungently, Henry (1975:7) recounting information from the 14th International Congress on Historical Sciences, exclaimed,

> There are today many Indians who believe "we are more understood in Europe and particularly in West Germany, than we are in our own country." And so this reporter asks: "Now do you believe they understand?" Indeed the problem of clearing out misinformation and misconception, inaccuracy and historical mythology instead of facts is even more difficult in most of the world than it is in North America.

INDIVIDUALS

This essay has discussed special interest groups that have adopted Indian identities to preserve and promote Indian traditions. There is another category of persons who assume Indian identities with similar goals. This category does not include non-Indians who were born and reared in Indian communities; it includes persons who initially had a non-Indian enculturation, who deliberately sought acculturation as Indians.

The Laubins and M. W. Billingsley are prime examples. They completely adopted Indian identities and became peculiarly vulnerable when some Indian persons did not approve of them as "Indians." Reginald Laubin began his love affair with Indians when he was a small boy. As an adult he was adopted by Chief One Bull, of the Sitting Bull Family (Bruce 1977:xi). Reasoning that his knowledge and skills at Indian dancing could bring about a better understanding of Indians, he vowed to learn everything possible about Indians and their dances (Laubin and Laubin 1977:xxxiii). He married a classmate from art school who shared his enthusiasm for Indians, and the two of them have spent almost fifty years performing concerts and writing on behalf of Indians. The capstone of their career is their 1977 book *Indian Dances of North America: Their Importance to Indian Life*. Although uneven as a scholarly work, their accounts of first-hand knowledge, experiences, and insights are valuable. Their understanding of some Indian culture areas is superior to that of other culture areas such as the Southwest. Their Indian friends may tell them "your skins may be white . . . but your hearts are Indian" (ibid.), but young Indians who do not know the Laubins are critical of the book and of them (Anonymous 1979b). They charge the authors with self-aggrandizement, cynically noting that the book proves that white persons cannot truly understand Indians or their culture. In contrast, Louis R. Bruce (1977:xi), Sioux-Mohawk, Commissioner of Indian Affairs in 1969-73, wrote enthusiastically that the Laubins are "imbued" with the "true spirit and character" of American Indian dances, and that they have been the first to present these dances on the concert stage. This was particularly noteworthy to Bruce because he is, as other Indians are, usually skeptical when non-Indians try to interpret Indian dances.

M. W. Billingsley ran away from his Iowa home in 1904, when he was fourteen years old, to see for himself the Hopi Indians and their Snake Dance. Six weeks later his father came to get him, but in 1908 "Bill" returned to Hopi and "never went home again" (Billingsley 1971:2). He was adopted into a Hopi family, and was inducted into the Snake Society (ibid.: 24-26). He became so fluent in the Hopi language, he claims he almost forgot English (Billingsley 1981). Eventually he moved to Phoenix, Arizona, and opened a trading post, became active in the Masons, and kept close touch with the Hopi, always on the lookout for ways he could be of assistance. In 1926, with the backing of the El Zoribah Masonic Temple in Phoenix, he took a group of Hopi Snake Dancers to Washington, D.C. They performed the Snake Dance for both houses of Congress to demonstrate that the ceremony was a solemn, dignified ritual, in order to persuade Congress to ignore outside pressure to outlaw that ritual (Billingsley 1971:53; cf. also photocopy of Congressional Record for 13 May 1926 in ibid.: 126). Curiously, also in 1926, the Smoki performed their version of the Snake Dance in Philadelphia at an American Legion convention held October 10-15. They especially performed for President Calvin Coolidge, who was an honorary member of the Smoki (Anonymous 1976c). Were the Smoki and American Legion trying to match Billingsley's Hopi Snake Dancers and the El Zoribah Masonic Lodge?

In order to promote understanding of the Hopi, Billingsley took a group of Hopi on tour; he lectured and they danced. In 1926 his Hopi friends built a *kiva* (a semi-subterranean combination temple/workshop/clubhouse) for him near Phoenix, where they conducted Hopi ceremonies and kiva dances in Billingsley's kiva (Billingsley ibid.: v and passim).

Billingsley continued his activities with the El Zoribah Masonic Shrine Temple. Apparently some of the white members of the lodge became "adopted Hopi" through Billingsley's auspices. There is evidence that many Hopi of Billingsley's generation either became Masons or were, in some way, affiliated with the El Zoribah Lodge. In 1970, for example, he distributed the following flier to members of that lodge:

Repeat Performance of Adopted Hopi Indians of Arizona, Inc. Adoption Ceremonial . . . 7 p.m. Saturday, December 12 - '70 . . . fill out enclosed application. Include check for $50.00 and mail to treasurer; do it now. (No annual dues.) "Come out and meet the chiefs from Reservation." Make check payable to Adopted Hopi Indians of Arizona.

Signed M. W. Billingsley
Kee Mungwee

Billingsley's memoirs, entitled *Behind the Scenes at Hopi Land*, were privately printed in 1971 with a slightly revised edition in 1974. The book is a journal/scrapbook/photo album, with numerous photos and reproductions of letters of endorsement for his work on behalf of the Hopi. It also includes a photocopy of a document signed by the Hopi men who built his kiva, sanctioning its existence.

From the 1940s through the 1970s Billingsley continued activities on behalf of the Hopi. By the 1970s those Hopi who had been his family and friends had either passed away or had begun to find it embarrassing to admit their close association with the white man who called himself "The Only Authentic White Chief of the Hopi Indians" (Billingsley 1971:iii). By 1978 a former Hopi colleague printed a disclaimer in the Hopi newspaper *Qua'Töqti* stating that he had nothing to do with a group of potential adoptees who had been turned away from a kiva in the Hopi village of Mishongnovi (Lansa 1978:2).

On 3 February 1981, I interviewed Billingsley, and experienced the uncanny feeling that I was in the presence of a Hopi. He evidenced certain characteristics I have noticed often in elderly Hopi men. He was garrulous, feisty, charming, humorous, and close-mouthed whenever talk turned to sensitive topics. Billingsley died recently at the age of ninety-three (Anonymous 1982), with Hopi memories, but few, if any, Hopi friends. Billingsley was a would-be Indian who almost made it.

INDIAN INNOVATIONS

In the United States of the 1980s, many Indians themselves became would-be Indians. For example, I am familiar with a young woman, half-white and half-Yaqui Indian, who, because she was not reared by her Indian relatives, sought to discover an Indian identity by becoming active in a large urban Indian center on the West Coast. She participates in powwows, and sprinkles her vocabulary with Siouan words. Because the Indians with whom she associates are primarily Sioux Indians, she has tried to adopt Sioux mannerisms and values. Unfortunately, many of the Sioux do not accept her. They fault her because her heritage is from the "wrong" tribe, and because she is half-white. Her distress is expressed by periods of rage alternating with periods of deep depression.

There have been numerous developments in dance and music among Indians that place them outside of the "hide period" (cf. Theisz 1965). In 1965 a girl was the first place winner in the men's division of powwow dance competition in North Dakota! (*Powwow Trails* 1965). Also in 1965, a Kickapoo Indian composer, Louis Ballard, wrote the score for the ballet *Koshare* (not to be confused with the Boy Scout group of that name). Commissioned for the Harkness Ballet Company, *Koshare* is based on a Hopi Indian legend (even though "Koshare" is not a Hopi word). It was danced by non-Indians except for the role of Spider Woman, which was danced by Marjorie Tallchief, an Osage Indian ("Smoke Signals" 1965; McCardle 1966-67). Likewise, in 1965 a dance group called the Thunderbird American Indian

Dancers opened its ranks to non-Indians. Their goal is to preserve and perpetuate American Indian culture and to "bring before the American public a picture of the Indian . . . [as a] productive member of the human race" (Powers 1965: n.p.).

In 1973, "Buffalo Bill's Wild West Show and Congress of Rough Riders of the World" was reorganized. It toured the United States and foreign countries. The producer noted that "even in countries that are anti-American the people aren't anti-cowboys-and-Indians" (Kleiner 1973). One of the performers in the show was a "Navajo Medicine Man," who, dressed as a Plains Indian, performed the Taos Pueblo Hoop Dance.

By 1975, Indian students from Bacone College in Muskogee, Oklahoma, formed a club named the Native American Intertribal Dancers to educate audiences while entertaining them, "as a step toward curing the ills of prejudice toward the Indian people" (Anonymous 1975b:3). Also in 1975, the winner of the Fancy Dress competition of a powwow held in Honolulu was an Apache youth dressed as a Plains Indian. He performed his dance on a skate board! (Lueras 1975:1).

In 1977 three Hopi demonstrated a Hopi Butterfly Dance for a group of children in Flagstaff, Arizona. Extraordinarily, their costumes did not include the traditional Butterfly Dance headdress. The dancers wore huge appendages on their backs that were shaped and painted like butterfly wings, and each had two long feathers on top of their heads as antennae! (SUNfoto 1977).

April 1978 saw a troupe of ten Hopi dancers travel to Paris as guests of the Center of American Indian Relations in Paris. After performing in France they performed in Belgium, Italy, Switzerland, and England. The Hopi were not the first group to make such a trip. Earlier, a group of Mexican Yaqui Indians and a troupe of Apaches made the same trip (Turner 1978). As mentioned previously, by 1981 the American Indian Tourism Council of Arizona was formed by four tribes in Arizona. Some members of those tribes disagree about the advisability of inviting tourists to come to their reservations (Joshevama 1982). Nevertheless, the program for attracting tourists continues.

Brown, in 1961, analyzed the way Taos Indians maintained traditional dances in context (cf. high-context, Hall 1979:47) by inventing dances for public performances (cf. low-context, Hall ibid.). By choreographing dances that are aesthetically pleasing and theatrically exciting such as the hoop dance, Taos Indians now have two basic categories of dance—"ours" and "not ours." They perform the dances that are categorized as "not ours" for off-reservation festivities (Brown 1961:33-41) in low-context situations. This survival mechanism has proved to be admirably adaptive for the preservation of Taos traditional Indian dances.

Another survival mechanism is the revival of traditional ways. Using legal sanctions, the Bear brothers, Max and Bill, founded Tantaka Wanbli Survival Program, Inc., a non-profit organization dedicated to unifying Indian nations by reviving their traditional ways (Foo 1980). An important effort of the two Sioux brothers is the revival of the Sun Dance that had been outlawed from 1904 to 1935.

Conclusion

Although many non-Indians would like to fantasize that they are Indians, their efforts cause a complicated state of affairs. For example, there is stereotyping (night club acts, popular music groups), trespass (Boy Scouts, Y-groups, Smoki), confusion of styles and sacriligious use of traditions and objects (Y-groups), unwelcome attempts to preserve cultures (Y-groups, Smoki), elaboration and tampering with choreography and music (Smoki), antiquarian purism (Germans), threat to Indians who refuse to accept white persons as good dancers (Laubins), embarrassment (Billingsley), treatment as though extinct (Sierra Club, Y-groups, Childcraft), and inappropriate selection of distinguishing features (Harkness Ballet).

But Indians themselves, trying to find or maintain their own identities, have activated important changes and complications. For example, there is identification with an alien tribe (urban Indian center member), breakdown of traditional sex roles (girl winning men's dance competition), trespass across tribal lines (Harkness Ballet), mixed dance group of Indians and non-Indians (Thunderbird American Indian Dancers), confusion of traditions (Navajo performing Taos hoop dance in Plains costume), promotion of Indian values to non-Indian audiences (Bacone College), introduction of non-Indian artifacts (powwow dancer on skateboard), change of costume to appeal to non-Indians (Hopi Butterfly Dance in Flagstaff), performance outside of the United States (Center of American Indian Relations in Paris), use of dance to bolster economy (shopping malls, tourism council), creation of new choreographies (Taos "not ours" dances), and revival (Tatanka Wanbli Survival Program, Inc.).

Evidence is lacking to show that a single Indian dance has been preserved because of white dancers, if one excepts the efforts of Billingsley on behalf of the Hopi Snake Dance. However, a possible and immeasurable spin-off from would-be Indians may be renewed energy and confidence by Indians who have reacted, even though negatively, to the enthusiasm of non-Indians. In any case, Indian dances seem to be alive with a positive prognosis for the future.

For certain, the fear that powwow dances will level distinctive Indian dances to a basic pan-Indian form seems unwarranted. There is a rich variety of Indian dances, old and new, with dynamic activities that promote both conservation and invention, to satisfy the tastes of anyone who is or would-be Indian.

References Cited

Anonymous
1975a "Dateline — Prescott." *Qua'Töqti*, August 14, p. 6.

1975b "Bacone Students Educate Non-Indians." *Qua'Töqti*, December 4, p. 3.

1976a "Indian Theater in Germany." *Wassaja*, January, p. 18.

1976b "Smoki Dance Ceremonies Planned in Prescott." *Arizona Republic*, August 5, p. B-4.

1976c "Pathways: 50 Years Ago in the SUN." *Arizona Daily SUN*, September 11, p. 2.

1977   "Indian News Notes." *Qua'Töqti*, September 15, p. 4.

1979a "Smoki People—Imitation Indians Preserving Traditions." *Qua'Töqti*, July 26, p. 1.

1979b Personal communication from several young adult Indians during discussion in lobby of Museum of the American Indian, Heye Foundation, October.

1980a Personal communication from Hopi individuals, July.

1980b "Hopis Condemn Smoki for Performing Dances." *Qua'Töqti*, September 11, p. 1.

1982   "Trading Post Operator Milo Billingsley Dies." *Arizona Republic*, July 11, p. B-1.

Arnet, Cory
1974   "The Arts: Demand Grows for Return of Indian Art Objects by Museums in U.S." *Wassaja*, August, p. 10.

Associated Press
1982a "Smoki People Plan Sun City Showing." *Arizona Daily SUN*, January 22, p. 8.

1982b "Indians Form Tourism Council." *Arizona Daily SUN*, January 28, p. 1.

Avalon Daggett Productions
n.d. "Smoki Snake Dance." Brochure. 16 mm sound motion picture, color or black and white. 12 minutes. Los Angeles.

Bartimus, Tad
1982a "50-Year Scoutmaster Leads Dancing 'Brats' to Lifelong Greatness." *Arizona Republic*, February 7, p. D-7.

1982b "Dancing Scout Troop Leaves a Lasting Impression." *Edwardsville* (Ill.) *Intelligencer*, February 22, p. 8.

Billingsley, M. W.
1970 "Repeat Performance of Adopted Hopi Indians." Flier.

1971 *Behind the Scenes in Hopi Land.* Phoenix: private printing (2nd revised edition, 1974).

1981 Personal communication, February.

Brasch, Beatty
1977 "The Y-Indian Guide and Y-Indian Princess Program." *Indian Historian* 10/3:49-60.

Bright, Barbara
1970 "Wild about the Indians: The German Love Affair with the Noble Red Man." *Six County Topics*, Region 1, April 15, p. 8.

Brown, Donald N.
1961 "The Development of Taos Dance." *Ethnomusicology* 5:33-41.

Bruce, Louis R.
1977 "Foreword" to Reginald Laubin and Gladys Laubin, *Indian Dances of North America: Their Importance to Indian Life*, pp. xi-xii. Norman: University of Oklahoma Press.

Can't Stop Productions, Inc.
1979 "Village People." Card no. 53.

Childcraft Annual
1980 *The Indian Book.* Chicago: World Book-Childcraft International.

Farver, Viola (White Water)
1966 "Indian Objects to White Dancers." *Indian Voices*, September, p. 11.

Foo, Rodney
1980 "Bringing Back the Indian Sun Dance." *Honolulu Star-Bulletin*, October 3, p. C-2.

Gillford, Wava, comp., and Bill Higgins, ed.
1971 *The Smoki People.* Prescott, Arizona: private printing.

Goldsmith, Lynn
1979 "Top Discs." *Look*, March 19, p. 3.

Gulick, Charlotte V.
1915   *A Book of Symbols for Camp Fire Girls.* New York: Camp Fire Outfitting Co.

Hall, Edward T. (interview by Kenneth Friedman)
1979   "Learning the Arabs' Silent Language." *Psychology Today* 13/3:45-54.

Henry, Jeannette
1975   "The World Congress of Historic Sciences." *Wassaja*, September 20, p. 7.

Hills, Jim
1975   "Fake Indians Again Celebrate False Ceremonies." *Wassaja*, October, p. 13.

Hopi Tribal News
1980   "Hopi Religious Leaders Meet with Smoki People." 1st edition, September, p. 1.

Joshevama, Elgean
1982   "Naht Kah-pu Hah-Kahm: Now Is Not Yet the Proper Time." Editorial, *Qua'Töqti*, May 20, p. 2.

Kleiner, Dick
1973   "Yup, It's Wild West Showtime." *Hawaii Tribune-Herald*, April 19, p. 16.

Lansa, John
1978   Letter to the Editor. *Qua'Töqti*, November 23, p. 2.

Laubin, Reginald, and Gladys Laubin
1977   *Indian Dances of North America: Their Importance to Indian Life.* Norman: University of Oklahoma Press.

Little Turtle, Jimmy
1974   "The Koshare Tribe Again." Letters, *Akwesasne Notes* 6/3:47.

1975   Letter to the Editor. *Qua'Töqti*, September 25, p. 2.

Lueras, Leonard
1975   "Indian Powwow Clearly Reflects Hawaiian Touch." *Honolulu Advertiser*, September 15, p. 1.

McCardle, Dorothy
1966-67 "News from the Washington Area." *Indian Voices*, December-January, p. 13.

Minthorn, David
1970   "Germans Create Old West Setting." *Phoenix Gazette*, October 1, p. 10.

Nichols, Joseph
1969   "Table Fees and Limited Space." Editorial, *Powwow Trails* 6/3 (June): 44, 58.

Powers, William K.
1965   "Meet the Thunderbird American Indian Dancers." *Powwow Trails* 2/3 (June).

1966   "Notes from the Moccasin Telegraph." *Powwow Trails* 3/3-4 (June-July): 3.

Powwow Trails
1965   "Last Minute News." 2/7 (December).

1966a   Classified ad. 3/1-2 (April-May): 13.

1966b   Classified ad. 3/3-4 (June-July): 2.

1968   Classified ad. 6/3 (June): 59.

1969a   Advertisement, "This Is Your Hobby—Indian Dancing by William K. Powers." 6/3 (June): 42.

1969b   Advertisement. 6/3 (June): 59.

Ross, Chuck (Lakota Sioux)
1981   Personal communication, April.

Scholten, Donald B.
1976   Personal letter, March 24.

Sekaquaptewa, Wayne
1976   "Smoki 'Ceremony' Blasphemy to Hopis." Editorial, *Qua' Töqti*, August 19, p. 2.

1978   "QT Analysis: Comments on 'Germany's Viewpoint on Hopis.'" *Qua' Töqti*, November 23, pp. 1, 6.

Sepi, Alfreda, Henrietta Tsinajinnie, and Anderson Banally [*sic*]
1976   Letter to the Editor. *Hualapai Times*, December, p. 12.

"Smoke Signals"
1965   "Indian Personalities in the News." *Indian Voices*, November, p. 9.

Smoki People
n.d.   "Smoki Ceremonials and Snake Dances Presented Annually by the Smoki People of Prescott, Arizona." Brochure, Prescott.

1971   "The Smoki People Present Their 51st Annual Ceremonials and Snake Dance." Program, August 7.

Steiner, Stan
1976   "The White Indians." Excerpted from *The Vanishing White Man* (Harper and Row). *Akwasasne Notes*, Early Spring, pp. 38-41.

SUNfoto [*sic*]
1977   "Hopi Butterfly Dance." *Arizona Daily SUN*, November 18, p. 1.

Theisz, Ronnie
1965   "Other Nations Other Powwows." *Powwow Trails* 11/5 (October).

Trenka, Richard, Medicine Man
1976   Personal letter to William B. Griffen, June 15.

Turner, Paul
1978   "It's a Long Way from Oraibi." *Arizona Daily SUN*, March 30, p. 1.

Wilson, Maggie
1976   "Courage of Convictions." *Qua' Töqti*, August 19, p. 2.

1977   "Antelope, Snake Clans in Conflict Today?" *Qua' Töqti*, July 7, p. 1.

PART IV SYMBOL AND MEANING

Sound, Danger, and Balanced Response

Marcia Herndon
Music Research Institute,
San Pablo, California

In his seminal study *Enemy Way Music* (1954), David McAllester initiates the real examination of the relationship between music and basic cultural values. In the introduction, McAllester (ibid.: 3) delineates his purpose as "an attempt to explore cultural values through an analysis of attitudes toward music and through an analysis of the music itself." This study indicates, for the Navajo, the relationship between attitudes about music and other cultural values. It provides us with a number of provocative leads and suggestions for further investigation of this fascinating interrelationship.

It is unlikely that anyone can be involved with structured sound from any culture without becoming aware of its power and its effect. Sometimes this power and effect are perceived fleetingly, as in a "moving" performance, speech, sermon, or other event. At other times, music or words leave us untouched and/or unmoved, perhaps accompanied by vague feelings of disappointment. This is so whether the perceiver is an outsider or a member of the culture whose structured sound is being displayed.

Ethnomusicologists have taken note of the power and effect of sound in numerous ways. Alan Merriam, in *The Anthropology of Music* (1964), takes a functional approach, listing such things as aesthetic enjoyment, entertainment, communication, symbolic representation, physical response, enforcing conformity to social norms, validation of social institutions and religious rituals (1964:223-24). In slightly different functional approaches, Devereux (Devereux and LaBarre 1961), applies Freudian theory to suggest that all art performs a "safety valve function," while Charles Keil (1962) distinguishes between the "solidarity function" and "release function" of music. David McAllester, in contrast, views music as an aid in inducing attitude or evoking moods. Speaking of Western music he (1960:469) notes that "we sing to put babies to sleep, make work seem lighter, to make people buy certain kinds of breakfast foods, or to ridicule our enemies."

Since these early papers and publications in this area, ethnomusicologists have continued in their efforts to deal rationally and objectively with the effect of music. It is difficult, however, to draw objective conclusions about effects which are essentially personal, cultural, and subjective responses to or interactions with structured sound, particularly music.

Perhaps the most profitable avenues which have evolved have been those emanating from cultural and individual responses to sound as it is classified by, performed by, contexturalized by, and changed by those most directly involved with it. Classifications of sound, in cognitive terms, have allowed outsider observers of a particular group to at least catch glimpses of living musical systems. These efforts have sprung directly from the implications embedded in McAllester's *Enemy Way Music.*

It is my intention in this essay to explore the interrelationship of sound, perceived danger, and the tendency toward balanced response among the Eastern Cherokee. In particular, I will examine the category of Cherokee religious music, and sound and music which is regarded as sacred and not subject to change.

Eastern Cherokee "Sacred Formulas"

In the 1820s, Sequoyah created a syllabary for the Cherokee language. His invention diffused rapidly throughout the entire Cherokee Nation, particularly within culturally conservative precincts of the pre-removal population where English was at best a little-known second language.

According to our best information, many of the Cherokee medico-magical practitioners immediately set down in writing most of their sacred formulas in the decades immediately preceding and following the Cherokee removal in 1838.

James Mooney (1891) began modern anthropological studies of Cherokee curing practices through his discovery of these written native texts, written in the Sequoyah syllabary. Mooney called these texts "Sacred Formulas." They were owned by native practitioners and formed the basis of Cherokee medico-magical philosophy and practice.

These so-called "sacred formulas," known to English-speaking Cherokee as "ceremonies," contained instructions and rituals for curing, preventing, or transmitting a myriad of culturally recognized disease entities. In addition, quite a few of these texts deal with love magic, various forms of divination, special rituals for the stickball game, for warfare and with a multitude of additional miscellaneous subjects (cf. Kilpatrick and Kilpatrick 1967).

Several major collections of these "sacred formulas" exist: James Mooney's *The Sacred Formulas of the Cherokee* (1891), Frans Olbrechts' *The Swimmer Manuscript* (Mooney and Olbrechts 1932), the publications of Frank Speck and John Witthoft (Speck and Broom 1951; Witthoft 1949; Witthoft and Hadlock 1946), the several monographs by Kilpatrick and Kilpatrick (1965, 1966, 1967), and Raymond Fogelson (1971, 1975).

In addition to these publications dealing with the sacred formulas there is a small body of tape recordings — deposited in various archives and collected mostly within the last twenty to twenty-five years — which contain some of the sung formulas.

Mooney and Olbrechts (1932) give a general pattern according to which sacred formulas are constructed. It is as follows:

1. An exclamation of warning, to attract the attention of the spirit addressed.
2. The spirit's name, sometimes its color; the place where the spirit dwells.
3. Some expression extolling its power.
4. A statement about the cause of the disease, the identity of disease-causer, or the reason for which the spirit's help is requested.
5. Some deprecatory remarks about the disease, disease-causer, or source of the problem.
6. A specific reason why the spirit being addressed is expected to cause relief or change.
7. An emphatic statement that relief has already arrived.
8. A final ending exclamation.

Although this is indeed the general structure of sacred formulas, not all of them contain each element indicated. A number of the formulas contain blanks into which the name, township, or clan of the patient or other specific items of information should be inserted.

A formula will very often be repeated four times, with a slight change each time. Thus, one may find a verse form which refers, in sequence, to earth, air, water, fire; or to North, South, East, West. This is, of course, reminiscent of some ballad forms. Accompanying these written formulas are captions, instructions concerning herbal decoctions which are to be used in conjunction with the formulas, and other necessary information.

There are not always clear separations between sung and spoken or spoken and thought formulas. At times, part of a formula may be sung and part spoken, part muttered and part sung, part muttered and part spoken, part muttered and part thought, part sung and part thought, part spoken and part thought, and so on. The totally sung versions of a formula usually have a spoken interjection at the beginning and from one to five reiterated syllables — usually *ya* or *yo* — as an ending signal, and may sometimes be prefaced by a thought prayer.

The writing of the formulas and the accompanying information tends to be idiosyncratic. Each practitioner apparently writes down just enough information to make himself or herself slightly more than a mnemonic device for retention of formulas. There is the occasional substitution of words which is deliberately done in order to prevent theft and misuse of formulas, and the more "dangerous" ones tend to be captioned with innocuous titles.

The language of these formulas is bound to form more than to content. Their efficacy is dependent, not on the meaning of the words used, but on strict adherence to wording and to form.

There are a number of archaic Cherokee word forms. Some of these are now impossible to translate. Others are simply called "referents" to generalized areas of meaning, but none are thought of as nonsense words or fillers. There is prefixing and infixing, primarily of the vowel *ah*. There is no suffixing of vowels or syllables to Cherokee words. This is because Cherokee has a vast range of emphatic suffixes which are commonly used anyway.

In addition, three other alterations from normal conversational speech are found:

1. Aphesis — the disappearance or loss of an unstressed initial vowel or syllable.
2. Syncope — the contraction of a word by omitting one or more sounds from the middle.
3. Apocope — loss or omission of the last letter, syllable, or part of a word.

The primary use of these devices seems to be to increase or to decrease, as the case may be, a word or phrase to four syllables, or occasionally to seven. In addition, texts also sometimes use "vocables" particularly when they are sung. These are symbolic referents to the most powerful spirit beings, or are employed in instances where the meaning is only for the initiate or the adept.

A number of years ago, I proposed (Herndon 1971:349-50) a continuum, among the Eastern Cherokee, from thinking to muttering to speaking to singing formulas, in which the sung form carries the greatest amount of power. Singing is undertaken in those instances where the situation is grave, or in which extreme power is necessary for other reasons. It should also be mentioned that these formulas are in ritual Cherokee, rather than any of the dialectal variations of Cherokee used in normal conversation and speech.

Within ritual Cherokee, it is of particular importance to note that the stem which means "to think" in normal Cherokee invariably means "to cause" in the ritual language. The stem "to say" is also used in a causal manner with ritual Cherokee, but with increased emphasis.

Thus, it may well be deduced that causality, whether in terms of the efficacy of the formula, or of the origin of a particular power to move, resides within thinking or saying. If the continuum of power is correct, then we may also assume that singing has even more power attached to it.

Through the medium of a ritual language which emphasizes causality, spoken Cherokee becomes a device, a bridge, and a form of communication which allows the practitioner or specialist to communicate with the spirit world, although he or she normally lives in the real world. The ritual language also allows the specialist to move into the timeless realm of that which ought to be, rather than that which is or appears to be. Thus, the sacred formulas may be viewed as a transformational device, a vehicle for communication especially constructed for dealings with the spirit world.

The manner in which structured sound is used — whether thought, muttered, spoken, or sung — is directly related to the perceived danger or gravity of a particular situation. Since perception is not only culturally defined and bounded but also subjective and relative, it would seem most productive to examine in depth those instances which *require* song.

Bruise and Snakebite

There are two occasions which demand singing: bruise and snakebite. If one proposes that singing occurs in serious conditions only, then the requirement that a formula be sung because of a bruise seems to destroy the entire hypothesis.

However, Bruise Songs are to be used, not for the simple bruises one incurs in daily life by brushing into something or hitting an arm on a table, but rather for internal damage. Bruise formulas have to do with internal bruising such as, for instance, that caused by falling down a mountain in a rockslide. These songs are also used in the case of severe gashes, amputation, excessive swelling, and concussions. With this understanding of the context, it then becomes clearer why these formulas must be sung. The danger level is high.

There are at least three separate versions, dealing with the formula for bruise. These all consist of an initial spoken statement, followed by an ending signal. For two of the formulas, the ending signal is *ya* or *yo*. For one of the formulas, the ending signal is *we hi ya*. In all four, mention is made of "wood," "rock," "earth," and "water." It is these particular references which are sung in all versions.

This correlates with a typical layperson's formula previously recorded by Kilpatrick and Kilpatrick (1964:217-18) which is translated: "I just chopped stone; I just chopped wood; I just chopped earth; I just chopped water. It will not become inflamed." The reciter of this charm symbolically transfers his or her cut to substances not subject to swelling, as is human flesh. Kilpatrick points out that the formulas for cuts are usually quite similar to those charms employed by laypeople. The shaman, however, blows on the wound or sprays the wound with chewed hickory bark in addition to using the formula.

The invocation of or comparison to "wood," "rock," "earth," and "water" is widely known, so the shaman, in singing these words, is not revealing special esoteric knowledge. He or she is merely adding expertise to a serious situation, and the sung formulas constitute only a part of the entire treatment.

Example 1. Bruise Song. (ECH II-75XD-1)

Slightly different is the second version, which I collected later. It alternates between sung and spoken sections:

> *ga no u na sta ne la di ka no gi sti* (spoken)
>
> I *a da gu ya* (4) (*da* = wood)
>
> *u so de lv sv ni wo di sho de gv yo hi* (spoken)
>
> II *na ya gu yo* (4) (*nvya* = rock)
>
> *u sv de lv swo si so* (spoken)
>
> III *ga da gu yo* (4) (*gada* = earth)
>
> *u sv de lv sv* (spoken)
>
> IV *a ma gu yo* (4) (*ama* = water)
>
> *u sv de lv sv ne wo di sv* (spoken)
>
> *yo*

The third version actually refers in the body of the formula to not swelling and not hurting. It is as follows:

> *v tla* (not)
>
> *u wo ti so i* (swell)
>
> *a da gu yo* (wood) (4)
>
> *na ya gu yo* (in the rock) (4)
>
> *ga da gu yo* (in the earth) (4)
>
> *a ma gu yo* (in the water) (4)
>
> *we hi ya* (end signal)

It should be noted that the ending signal for the third formula, *we hi yo*, is incorporated as an integral part of the first song and is repeated each time.

The sung portions of these variants of the bruise formulas all involve more or less the same text. The melodies and rhythms used, however, vary both from version to version and within repetitions of the same formula. Thus, it would appear that form is more important than melodic line, and semantic content is more important than form.

The actual singing of a bruise formula does not put the shaman into any situation necessitating the revealing of his or her information, in that the main elements — wood, rock, earth, and water — are well known. Those items of a formula which he or she may wish to retain as personal property are either spoken or thought, thus more or less assuring that material which should be private will remain so.

Whatever version is chosen, the singing of the bruise formula is done without any instrumental accompaniment. The performance requirements are directional: the song is first performed in the direction of sunrise, or East; then it is performed facing in a Northerly direction, where it is "cool"; then it is performed facing West, and then South. It is usually done in the early morning just before sunrise, and again in the evening just at sunset. It can also be done at noon, when the sun is straight above in the heavens.

The instance of snakebite is both simpler and more complex than the instance of singing for bruises or internal injuries. The major concern with a snakebite is its tendency to swell, and the necessity to draw out the poison. If the snakebite is attended to immediately, tobacco juice is thought to be good in drawing out the poison. If some time has passed, a basswood or cottonwood bark poultice is used. These remedies are employed in addition to the standard snakebite kit, available at any drug store, which is carried by many people in the North Carolina mountains today. It is important to note here that we are not discussing a system which ignores chemical and physical remedies, invoking external aid from the spirit world alone. Rather, in most instances, one sees a combination of therapeutic efforts being made. This is particularly true in dangerous or life-threatening situations.

The snakebite song ceremony is intended to assist in drawing poison out of the flesh. The song is sung four times and water is splashed on the afflicted area. The snakebite formula itself is quite simple. The first line—*a ma gu yo*—is translated "a germ that lives in running water." An alternate version is *a ma gu hi*. The second line is *ama gu a ne hi*, or "they live in water." The third line is *ama gu a ne sgo yi*, or "you don't see where they live." Each line is repeated four times, and the formula is ended with five repetitions of *ya—ya, ya, ya, ya, yaaaa*.

The song is as follows:

Example 2. Snakebite Song.   (ECH II-75XD-1)

135

Kilpatrick and Kilpatrick (1970), in *Notebook of a Cherokee Shaman*, give a different formula for snakebite:

yv da hu haw (4) (*ivy:da:du:ha?* = "over there has them, he")

sami (4)

gha (4)

ut si na wa, hv ni ga

(relief, it. You have just come to strike it)

The first line is sung four times; the second and third line are onomatopoetic statements of the slithering of a reptile and the rattling of a rattlesnake; the fourth line is spoken. Whereas the first snakebite remedy indicated uses basswood or cottonwood in preference to other herbs or applications, the second snakebite formula uses tobacco sprayed upon the site of the bite, and the jawbones of a rattlesnake waved over the body.

In addition, there are a number of conjurations for dreams of being snake-bitten. Mooney and Olbrechts (1932:175-78, 197-98) cite two good examples of this kind of conjuration. It is important to note that the possibility of dreaming of snakebite is almost as serious as being bitten by a snake. Both instances require immediate action; however, in the case of dreams, singing is *not* required.

Thus, we are dealing with two states of awareness in talking about the waking, actual world and the world of dreaming. The two are interconnected; each can have an effect on the other. This distinction between the waking state and the sleeping state should be considered in connection with the red and white states mentioned in Cherokee literature, which deal with a state of readiness for battle, aggression, and hostility (the red condition); and a state of acceptance of peace, calm, and tranquility (the white state).

Transformation from one state to another is effected by means of ceremonial and ritual activity. Ritual formulas are used to affect the realm of the abstract, and are accompanied by physical actions designed to affect the realm of the concrete.

Similarly, snakebite song formulas, whether intended to cover actual snakebite cases or those which have been dreamed about, are accompanied by the application of physical, concrete means—such as poultices or herbal decoctions. Here, too, the ritual formula is intended to deal with cause, while physical effects are handled through pragmatic means.

Conclusion

The proposition that the sung form of a Cherokee ritual formula carries the greatest amount of power seems to be verified in those instances requiring singing. Both bruise and snakebite are situations of great perceived danger; both instances can be life-threatening.

It is a truism within anthropology that everyday situations require everyday response, and danger demands "magical" or otherwise special response. For the Cherokee, while all ritual formulas are a means of transformation from one state of mind to another, a second set of factors must be considered. The transformation itself must be placed along a performance continuum—from thinking to muttering to speaking to singing—in response to the amount of gravity or danger involved in the particular situation.

While it is highly unusual for most Cherokee ritual formulas to be sung, the possibility remains. So, too, it is conceivable that a dream of snakebite, for example, if it appeared in epidemic proportions, might require singing.

In all instances, with the exception of very serious situations already by definition requiring singing, flexibility is maintained within the sphere of the ritual formulas. Balanced response is always demanded. The power of sound to evoke or to induce, as noted by McAllester (1960:469) for Western music, is an integral part of the cognition and strategy of the Cherokee shaman.

The sung formulas are regarded as conduits and/or bridges. They are the means by which a transformation or a translation of circumstance is attempted. They are traditional, sometimes idiosyncratic, retained through time only if proven efficacious, and highly symbolic. They evoke, invoke, command, and incite. Written in ritual Cherokee and thus indicating a departure from the realm of the normal or usual, they bridge the chasm between rationality and irrationality, sacred and secular, sleep and wakefulness, that which is and that which ought to be, aggression and peace, and the imperfection and disharmony which is a lie about the reality of the peace and harmony of the universe.

References Cited

Devereux, George, and Weston LaBarre
  1961   "Art and Mythology." *Studying Personality Cross-Culturally*, ed. Bert Kaplan, pp. 361-403. Evanston: Row, Peterson.

Fogelson, Raymond
  1971   "The Cherokee Ballgame Cycle: An Ethnographer's View." *Ethnomusicology* 15:327-38.

  1975   "An Analysis of Cherokee Sorcery and Witchcraft." *Four Centuries of Southern Indians*, ed. Charles Hudson, pp. 113-31. Athens: University of Georgia Press.

Herndon, Marcia
  1971   "The Cherokee Ballgame Cycle: An Ethnomusicologist's View." *Ethnomusicology* 15:339-52.

Keil, Charles
  1962   "Sociomusicology." Unpublished manuscript.

Kilpatrick, Jack F., and Anna G. Kilpatrick
  1964   *Friends of Thunder*. Dallas: Southern Methodist University Press.

  1965   *Walk in Your Soul: Love Incantations of the Oklahoma Cherokees*. Dallas: Southern Methodist University Press.

  1966   "Eastern Cherokee Folk Tales Reconstructed from the Field Notes of Frans M. Olbrechts." *Bureau of American Ethnology Bulletin* 196:379-447.

  1967   *Run toward the Nightland: Magic of the Oklahoma Cherokees*. Dallas: Southern Methodist University Press.

  1970   "Notebook of a Cherokee Shaman." *Smithsonian Contributions to Anthropology* 2/6:83-125.

McAllester, David P.
  1954   *Enemy Way Music*. Papers of the Peabody Museum of American Archaeology and Ethnology, Harvard University, 41/3.

1960 "The Role of Music in Western Apache Culture." *Selected Papers of the Fifth International Congress of Anthropological and Ethnological Sciences*, ed. Anthony F. C. Wallace, pp. 468-72.

Merriam, Alan P.
1964 *The Anthropology of Music*. Evanston: Northwestern University Press.

Mooney, James
1891 "The Sacred Formulas of the Cherokees." *Seventh Annual Report of the Bureau of American Ethnology*, pp. 301-97.

Mooney, James, and Frans M. Olbrechts
1932 "The Swimmer Manuscript: Cherokee Sacred Formulas and Medicinal Prescriptions." *Bureau of American Ethnology Bulletin* 99:1-319.

Speck, Frank, and Leonard Broom
1951 *Cherokee Dance and Drama*. Berkeley: University of California Press.

Witthoft, John
1949 *Green Corn Ceremonialism in the Eastern Woodlands*. Occasional Paper from the Museum of Anthropology of the University of Michigan, no. 13. Ann Arbor: University of Michigan Press.

Witthoft, John, and Wendell Hadlock
1946 "Cherokee-Iroquois Little People." *Journal of American Folklore* 59:413-20.

Text and Context in Lakota Music

William K. Powers
Rutgers University

In Native American Humanities it is an error to consider a
text . . . out of its cultural context, for the context is what
gives it its Native American meaning [McAllester 1980:3].

Texts

In this essay I am concerned with the music of Yuwipi, a contemporary curing ritual
of the Oglala (Sioux) and other Lakota-speakers who live mainly on the Pine Ridge and other
reservations in South Dakota. In particular I am interested in examining Yuwipi song texts
and the various contexts in which these songs are learned and performed.

My interest in Yuwipi, and Lakota culture in general, predates my interest in anthropology
and ethnomusicology by at least twenty years. Although in 1966 and 1967 I was fortunate
to have been able to work closely with the Oglala Yuwipi man, George Plenty Wolf of the
Red Cloud Community, Pine Ridge,[1] it was not until 1971 that I truly was able to think about
the relationship between music and culture. This understanding was partly if not entirely inspired
by David P. McAllester who, in 1971, arranged for me to attend Wesleyan University as a
master's candidate in anthropology. I arrived as an intellectual half-breed — part student and
part informant, the latter a result of having spent each of my summers at Pine Ridge since
the age of thirteen. I had learned to live Oglala culture, but it was not until much later that
I realized there was any benefit in *studying* it. I worked my way through Wesleyan by teaching
a practicum on Plains Indian music and dance in partnership with the late Navajo specialist
and *bon vivant* Douglas ("Doogie") Mitchell. During this time there were numerous visiting
artists at Wesleyan, and McAllester was able to bring to campus an Oglala singer of great
reputation, William Horn Cloud, who was not only the chief singer for George Plenty Wolf,
but a good friend of mine. Needless to say, my master's thesis was launched.

In the summer of 1971 with departmental support I returned to Pine Ridge for the
purpose of writing the thesis "Yuwipi Music in Cultural Context" (Powers 1972). Ten years
later, the major part of this research was published (Powers 1982). However, there were still
some problems, mainly ones concerned with translation, that were not resolved. These
problems, which I now clearly see as problems of context, stemmed from the following:

---

[1] I am grateful to the American Philosophical Society for its generous support in 1966 and 1967, and to the National
Endowment for the Humanities for its generous support of later research.

Yuwipi songs originate with the medicine man, or Yuwipi man as he is locally known, in a Vision Quest. In the Lakota belief system, spirits—humans, animals, birds, and so forth—appear to the initiate and teach him things about the spiritual world during a one-to-four day fast on an isolated hill. Part of what the medicine man learns are prayers and songs that are to be employed in various rituals such as the Sweat Lodge, Sun Dance, and Yuwipi. Later on, the Yuwipi man teaches these songs to one or more men who serve as his lead singers at the Yuwipi meetings. Actually, only one singer need be present during the ritual to lead the songs but, more frequently than not, three or four singers are present to help the common people in attendance sing the sequence of songs.

During the course of the meeting, which is held in a darkened room, all of the participants sing along with the Yuwipi man and his lead singers. The darkness tends to give the ceremony a sense of timelessness, and also creates an impression of closeness. The drum beats, played on small tambourine drums held by each of the singers, are magnified, and the voices blend loudly in the small enclosure of a room. In the Plenty Wolf variation, everyone sings a sequence of seventeen songs, each song marking important phases of the meeting in which the spirits are invited to the gathering and prayers are offered. The patient to be cured addresses the spirits about his or her illness, they decide on the best form of curing, and finally the patient is cured, often by the direct "touch" of the spirit on those parts of the body which are troublesome. Later the spirits are given tobacco offerings, and after they leave the adepts participate in communal smoking of the sacred pipe and a ritual feast comprised of traditional foods, particularly a stew made from the meat of a small puppy. Throughout the entire ceremony, the Yuwipi man serves as the medium; the spirits are addressed through him, and he responds on their behalf.

All of the Yuwipi songs sung during the ceremony, except perhaps an occasional dance song (sung for the benefit of the spirits who like to dance) are, even by Lakota standards, esoteric. Only the initiates understand them fully, and the initiates are usually those men who have actually gone on the Vision Quest, have actually learned these types of songs in visions, and have returned to be advised by other *wicaša wakan* (sacred persons) as to the meaning of their visions and ordeals. But even among those who have sought visions, it is likely that only those men who "walk with the pipe"—that is, who elect to become medicine men—are likely to comprehend completely the meaning of the song texts. The adepts—the common people, as they are called—of course sing these songs with all due respect and reverence, but in fact most of them have only a cursory knowledge of what the texts actually signify. For the followers of Yuwipi, and this would include even the singers who lead the songs and who have been privy to the Yuwipi man's lengthy exegeses of them, know little about the actual experiences in which the Yuwipi men first learned the songs, and what, in fact, the words really mean. Despite the fact that each Yuwipi man explains his visionary experience(s) called the *Hanbloglaka* (dream talk), the texts still are often incomprehensible to most.

In this regard, the followers of Yuwipi are not unlike adepts everywhere who join in singing hymns and repeating endless litanies that make reference to the world of spirits without fully comprehending the meanings. For all of them, it is the act of participation in the rituals that is important, the act of saying prayers and singing songs that makes the interlude sacred. Interpretations, and this would include every possible type of dogma, definition, and etymology as well as the layer upon layer of belief and ritual into which religious ideas are embedded, are reserved for the religious specialists of all religions. And it is partly this act of discrimination between shaman and common person that gives strength and credibility to religion. If everyone *understood the meanings* of the sacred texts and the sacred lore, things would be less sacred. Perhaps things would not be sacred at all. Without the hierarchy of the shamans and other interpreters of the sacred, religion would not exist.

But let me return to text and context. The point that I want to make is that given the visionary as well as empirical context in which Yuwipi songs—and this would hold for other sacred and secular song too—are learned and performed, one must consider that these songs exist in a number of related contexts rather than a single one. There is never a single cultural context, only configurations of contexts that constantly shift and rearrange themselves situationally. If it is, as McAllester states (in the opening epigram), context that makes meaning particularistic—in this case more Lakota than anything else—then it is not one context but the continuous process of manipulating an infinite number of contexts in a culturally relevant way that makes people know who they are as well as who they are not. Therefore, to say that a Yuwipi song is sacred because it is performed or learned in a sacred context, i.e., on a Vision Quest, or in a Yuwipi ritual is only part of the explanation. There are other contexts in which Yuwipi songs are learned and performed, and often the meanings of Yuwipi songs shift as the contexts change even though the texts do not, or rarely, change at all.

Before examining the various kinds of contexts in which we find Yuwipi songs, let me begin with the text. Here I shall use one Yuwipi song as an example. By doing so I do not wish to imply that there is anything particularly special about this song. It happens to be the opening song of the George Plenty Wolf ritual and, as I shall demonstrate later, has been sung at other rituals by other specialists also—clearly a contradiction in Lakota terms which regard this song as having been taught only once by the spirits to one mortal, that mortal being Plenty Wolf.

The Lakota texts to the song are as follows:

1. *Kola leci lecun ye*
2. *Kola leci lecun ye*
3. *Kola leci lecun ye*
4. *Hecanaun kin taku yacin k'un he hecetu kte*
5. *Hocoka wanji ogna iyotake cin Wakantanka cekiya yo*
6. *Hecanun kin taku yacin k'un hecetu kte*

In lines 1-3, the words may be translated to mean "Friend, do this here." The word *kola* (friend—male address term for another male) stems from an old word having the connotation of "comrade" or someone who can be relied upon to come to the rescue during combat. A *kola* would be expected to lay down his life for someone with whom he mutually shares this form of address. Today, however, the simple gloss carries a wider semantic range of friend, pal, and buddy. *Leci* means "here," "in the general vicinity of the speaker." *Lecun* means "to do this" and *ye* is an enclitic of entreaty.

Lines 4 and 6 translate "If you do it, whatever you want will be so." *Hecanun kin*, "if you do that"; *taku yacin*, "something you want"; *k'un* is the past definite article (i.e., the phrase *taku yacin k'un he* means "something that we agreed upon in the past you want"); *hecetu*, "to be so, to be right, to be appropriate"; *kte*, enclitic designating the future tense.

Line 5: *Hocoka* is a term used to indicate the interior of a camp circle in the old days. Everything inside the camp circle was considered (or hoped) to be safe. Metaphorically extended, everything outside the camp circle was dangerous, inhabited by enemies. *Wanji* means "one," and here "someone"; *ogna* means "inside"; *iyotake* means "to sit," and *cin*, a form of the definite article which in this case marks a noun clause, i.e., "the one who is sitting inside the camp circle." *Wakantanka* is conventionally glossed as Great Spirit, or Great Mystery, and I have pleaded elsewhere that it should not be glossed at all (Powers 1977). The term is employed by missionaries to signify "god." *Cekiya* means "to pray to" and *yo* is an imperative enclitic used by males only.

If we were to simply translate the song text freely, we would arrive at something like:

1. Friend, do this here.
2. Friend, do this here.
3. Friend, do this here.
4. If you do it, whatever you want will be so.
5. The one sitting in the center of the camp—pray to Wakantanka!
6. If you do it, whatever you want will be so.

Once translated however, if we are to understand what it all means, we should begin by asking some obvious and fundamental questions such as: Friend, do *what* over here (wherever that is!); If you do what (?), what is it that you want to be accomplished? And who is the one sitting in the center of the camp (*wherever* that is!). Who is being commanded (by whom) to pray to Wakantanka? Part of what meaning means requires relating these texts to a larger framework, or context if you will, that links these texts to the remainder of Lakota belief, ritual, and society at large.

Contexts

In an earlier paper (Powers 1980) I demonstrated that from an ethnotheoretical perspective, the Oglala verbalize about learning, composing, and performing in such a way as to differentiate between sacred and secular categories (although these categories, it should be noted, are western inventions; the Lakota categories simply conform to them—or we conform to theirs, depending on one's point of view). In the sacred sphere, the Oglala learn (*unspeic'iye*, "to cause one's self to know") whereas in the secular sphere the Oglala "catch" a song (*olowan oyuspe*, "to catch [as a ball] a song"). When a person learns (*unspeic'iye*) a song, however, it is never clear *from whom* the song is learned, unless of course, the source is explained. Hence, a Yuwipi man, in this case, may learn a song from a spirit—say, an animal or bird—and a singer may learn a song from a Yuwipi man. It is only after the nature of the learning process or situation is made clear that one can really translate the texts; depending on the source or context, the meaning of the song may, and frequently does, vary.

For example, in the song texts cited above, when the Yuwipi man sings the song, he is reciting verbatim song texts that were dictated to him by a spirit in his vision(s). In the first three lines, the spirit is addressing the Yuwipi man (during the course of the vision) as "friend," and the spirit is telling him to "do this" (that is, perform the Yuwipi ritual) "here" (that is, where the ritual is *currently* being held). Stated another way, the visionary "here" is the empirical "there" because the spirit is speaking to the Yuwipi man in some conceptually far off place (say, on a hill top in the West, where the spirit [read: body] of the Yuwipi man has been transported by supraempirical beings or forces). A better exegesis, but a poorer translation would be something like: (The spirit said to me:) "Friend, do this" (Yuwipi ceremony) "over here" (where we're gathered now).

Lines 4 and 6 then become more obvious. If the Yuwipi man performs the Yuwipi ritual properly as he is doing at the moment, whatever *he wants* will come to pass. But what *he wants* changes from one meeting to the next, because all Yuwipi meetings have different kinds of objectives and these objectives are determined by those persons sponsoring the Yuwipi,

not by the Yuwipi man himself. The purposes of the Yuwipi are many: praying for the sick —
someone present at the meeting or someone confined to a hospital bed; praying that family
problems may be sorted out and peace restored between loved ones; prayers for safety of
a relative who is leaving the reservation to go away to college, or on relocation, or into the
military. Hence, whatever *you* want is essentially whatever *the people who attend the meetings
want*. *You* is appropriate, however, because it is only through the mediation of the Yuwipi
man that the adepts's prayers can be offered (and, with hope, answered) by *Wakantanka* and
all that is represented in the ethereal world: the spirits of humans, animals, birds, as well
as inanimate phenomena. The Yuwipi man sings and prays to the spirits, while the people
pray through him and through his intercession their prayers are answered.

In line 5 an understanding of Lakota history, ritual, and belief is required to clarify
the reference to the camp circle and the person sitting inside it. Here the person is from one
point of view the Yuwipi man himself. But from another, each of the adepts attending the
Yuwipi are momentarily, at least for the duration of the meeting, "sitting inside the camp
circle." The camp circle (*hocoka*) is a metaphor, or perhaps metametaphor referring to olden
times before the establishment of the reservation when the Oglala camped in circles, and
sometimes concentric circles. The *hocoka* refers to the area inside the outer perimeter of tipis. It
was (and is) contrasted with *hookawinh*, "the edge," or *outside* the camp circle. As a metaphor,
both terms are equated respectively with safe and dangerous, good and bad, friend and enemy,
and so forth. In the context of the Yuwipi ritual, however, the rather common room or house
that serves as the meeting place is through the songs, prayers, and intervention of the Yuwipi
man and spirits who come to him to help him, symbolically transformed into a "camp circle."

Inside the darkened room, the central part of the room is delineated from the outer part
by a string of tobacco offerings that circumscribe what the Lakota call the *makakagapi*, roughly
translated as "mellowed earth" or, simply, "altar." The Yuwipi man for most of the ritual sits
or stands in the center of this delineated space while the common people sit outside the space
with their backs against the wall. The walls of the house or room are another kind of delineator
that separates everyone from the "real" or secular world outside. And for the hour or two that
the Yuwipi lasts, everything inside the room is "old time," and everything outside is modern. It
should be noted, however, that these distinctions are analogic; the Oglala do not talk directly
about sacred and profane, or inside and outside, as if they were French academicians of L'Année
Sociologique. But the analogy is clear: the major difference between their perceptions of the
ritual and that of anthropologists is that the Oglala are *engaged* in the songs and prayers as part
of religious action. They are not detached and analytical about their behaviors.

In this larger and richer context, the song texts clearly become an attenuation of a
moving experience, one that has led a common man to ultimately become a medicine man,
a Yuwipi man who "walks with the pipe" in order that his people may live long life
together. Implicit is the hope and belief that this life will be a Lakota one even though it
is certainly understood that the Indian people live as an enclave in what they regard as a "white
man's world" in which they occasionally interact. The larger context of the entire opening
song then might be extended to mean something like the following:

Yuwipi man speaking: When they put me on the hill, I had a vision. In this
vision the voice of a man (or woman, or, animal or bird) came to me and
addressed me "friend." The voice told me to do this ceremony in a darkened
room — just like it is here tonight. "If you do it" the voice said, then all of the
things that those people who rely on you want and need will come true: they
will live with their relations for a long time. The voice said to me: "You — you

who choose to sit in the center of the camp circle—the center of the universe—You! Pray to Wakantanka! You *must* pray to Wakantanka in order for all those things to come true. If you do—if you pray to Wakantanka—whatever each of the people who comes to this Yuwipi meeting requires will come true.

It should be made clear here that the only person who understands *all* of the meanings of the songs is the Yuwipi man himself. If asked by another Oglala (or anthropologist), the Yuwipi man is quite capable of explaining the meanings of what is otherwise an abbreviated version of a very significant visionary experience. But the Yuwipi man does not explain each line of text to his adepts during the course of the Yuwipi because, as I stated before, it is the action, the participation, in Yuwipi that makes it significant. Without explanation, then, the songs become very personal to each of the persons attending the ritual. The texts are open to interpretation by each of the adepts in attendance if they choose, but the beauty of Yuwipi song, like any religious song or prayer, is that it is essentially meaningful because all people can inject their own sense of meaning into the text. The song texts are meaningful because they have no meaning, except in a very personal sense.

But of course, by virtue of the fact that the songs are known to have been learned in a vision, they are regarded as being sacred, and the meeting in which the songs are sung is regarded by convention as providing a sacred context. But the meaning is quite different when the context shifts from the perspective of the Yuwipi man who has lived through the experience of the composition to, say, that of one of the singers to whom he teaches the song, or to one of the adepts who simply sings a set of texts learned not through a conscious process but by absorbing the songs as they are sung over and over. As the texts become further removed from the source of their inspiration, the original (and perhaps subsequent) Vision Quests, the meanings change, even to the extent that there may be no agreement between the Yuwipi man and his adepts as to the significance of the text, unless of course there is consultation among them.

Learning the song from the Yuwipi man, as the singers do, as opposed to absorbing the texts through repetition in the meetings, are two quite different processes. In the first case, the singers usually learn the songs outside the context of the ritual. Therefore it is quite clear to them that the words are those of the Yuwipi man and of the spirits who visit him during the Vision Quest. The singers may be told about the conditions under which the songs were learned, and will accept the significance on the basis of pure faith in the integrity of the Yuwipi man. But in the second case, when presented with the textual material as part of the ritual in which an adept finds himself a participant, it is likely that the individual will begin to interpret the texts in a way that is meaningful to him alone. That is, *the individual*, not the Yuwipi man, becomes the "friend" in the text. Here the context shifts so that it is the Yuwipi man who addresses the adept as friend rather than the spirit addressing the Yuwipi man as such. Furthermore, "doing this over here" has an existential meaning for the adept, where it has an abstract, futuristic sense to the Yuwipi man. To the adept, "whatever you want will be so" is a personal statement; it is an expression of the individual who attends the Yuwipi, not a collective representation of the community to which the benefits of such a meeting accrue. Finally, the "one sitting in the camp circle" is likely to refer as much to the adept as it is to the Yuwipi man. During the Yuwipi meeting, once the altar has been built, and in analytical terms the profane dwelling is transformed into sacred space, everyone in attendance is seated, metaphorically, in a place of safety, goodness and, most importantly, Indianness. Outside, things are dangerous, hostile, and non-Indian.

One might say that even more contexts can be layered upon these already stated. For example, the Yuwipi song texts may be sung outside the ritual context, in a rehearsal gathering of the singers. The texts may even be—although this is rare—recorded, in which case the sacred texts can be played on a record player under the most secular of occasions. Logically, one might assume that the number of contexts that can be imposed on the singing of these texts is infinite, and with each context there is a rearrangement or entirely new construction of meaning subject to interpretation.

Finally, Yuwipi songs, like other sacred and secular songs, are very likely to travel from one meeting to the next even though, by Oglala standards, these songs are the property of the individual Yuwipi man who has learned them in the Vision Quest. This is because the singers often control the singing during the meeting. One singer may sing for more than one Yuwipi man, and in so doing he (or they) may occasionally introduce the songs learned by one Yuwipi man into the ritual of another. Since songs like the one analyzed here are often one of a category of, say, opening songs, it is very likely that, given the relatively few singers who participate in these meetings, songs from one ritual specialist wind up in the meeting of another. In my participation in Yuwipi, I have never heard a Yuwipi man make reference to "foreign" songs, and it may concluded that all songs learned in visons by all Yuwipi men are sacred. Therefore the intrusion of one's into another's is not of critical importance to the Oglala (although I have known anthropologists to fret about it).

In such cases when these intrusive songs become part of the ritual, one can only ask "What do they mean?"—to the Yuwipi man, the singers, and the adepts? Certainly their significance can be measured only in private rather than public terms. In this case, these songs simply become part of a larger corpus of sacred songs that seem to fit into the general category of privately significant but publicly acceptable religious songs, part of what may be regarded as a tribal analog of ecumenicism.

The act of making sense out of nonsense, then, is a creative act (quite opposed to the formalist's preoccupation with making nonsense out of sense). It is no wonder that arguments often ensue over the appropriateness of the meaning of the text—not only between anthropologists, but between the native singers and adepts. It is more correct to say that everyone has a greater possibility of being right than being wrong, because ultimately the meaning of the text is largely dependent on personal experience and interpretation. The range of variation, of course, is contingent upon cultural relevance; it is unlikely that any personal narrative about the meaning of a Yuwipi song is entirely arbitrary. But, again, there is a wide range of variation in such interpretations, some of which sometimes give the impression that the adepts (or anthropologists) simply do not understand the *true* meaning.

As I show here, even the interpretation of one song can be greatly varied from one context to the next. But this song represents only one out of seventeen songs sung in the Plenty Wolf Yuwipi variant, and this variant represents one of perhaps several dozen Yuwipi men at the present time functioning at Pine Ridge as well as the Rosebud and Cheyenne River reservations and other Lakota reservations. Each set of appropriate songs is again a new challenge to interpretation, with hundreds of adepts seeking meaning in hundreds of songs that are being composed through the visionary experience every day. Any analysis of these song texts, and this would probably hold for any viable genre of song, must begin with an understanding of the creative nature of learning and performing both religious and secular texts.

To find the right meaning, then, requires not only translating the text, but understanding the limitless number of contexts in which the same texts are likely to be sung and listened to. The creative use of song is an extension of the creative use of culture, and the variability of Yuwipi text and context is clearly an indication that Lakota culture persists as a viable part of American society, one filled with its own Lakota meaning.

References Cited

McAllester, David P.
1980   "'The War God's Horse Song,' An Exegesis in Native American Humanities." *Music of the North American Indians*, ed. Charlotte Heth. *Selected Reports in Ethnomusicology* 3/2:1-22. Los Angeles: University of California Press.

Powers, William K.
1972   "Yuwipi Music in Cultural Context." M.A. thesis, Wesleyan University, Department of Anthropology.

1977   *Oglala Religion*. Lincoln: University of Nebraska Press.

1980   "Oglala Song Terminology." *Music of the North American Indians*, ed. Charlotte Heth. *Selected Reports in Ethnomusicology* 3/2:23-41. Los Angeles: University of California Press.

1982   *Yuwipi: Vision and Experience in Oglala Ritual*. Lincoln: University of Nebraska Press.

Sound as a Symbolic System: The Kaluli Drum

Steven Feld
Departments of
Music and Anthropology
University of Texas, Austin

How do sounds actively communicate and embody deeply felt sentiments? This question should be at the core of an ethnographic and social scientific concern with music, yet ethnomusicology is just beginning to untangle issues of the musical sign, the relations between symbolic form and social meaning, and the performance of sounds as communicative action. In this essay[1] I wish to contribute an empirical example of how one class of sounds is socially structured to convey meaning. In doing so I will also try to raise issues that are generally relevant to the theory of musical meaning. By concentrating on the invention, performance, and understanding of drumming among the Kaluli people of Papua New Guinea I will show that while sounds overtly communicate through and about pattern, they may be socially organized to do far more by modulating special categories of sentiment and action when they are brought forth and properly contexted by features of staging and performance.

There are two opening contexts — one anthropological, the other musical — which form the present arena in which Papua New Guinea drums are ideologically situated. First is the social reduction of a sound to its visual source. Museums are filled with drums from Papua New Guinea; books and catalogs of "primitive art" are filled with their images. These celebrate shape, carving, and decoration, often indulging in superlatives about delicate lines, glistening colors, and intricate designs. But what is the consequence for sound? What do we know from these visual displays about the real life of the drum, which is its sound in performance? Unfortunately, all too little. At this point the sounds of Papua New Guinea drums are rarely heard by outsiders who discourse about them; the sounds have become secondary to their source and the instruments are primarily objects for our visual contemplation.

[1] This essay is based on field research undertaken in 1976-77 and 1982. For their concern that I properly understand the meaning of Kaluli drumming, I am deeply grateful to several Bosavi drummers and intellectuals: Gaima, Gigio, Seli, Sili, Gobo, Ganigi, Jubi, Kulu, and especially Gaso. I am also grateful to the organizations that supported this research: the Institute of Papua New Guinea Studies, the Archives of Traditional Music at Indiana University, the National Endowment for the Arts, and the University of Pennsylvania Research Foundation. Oral versions of this material have been presented at the 1979 annual meeting of the Society for Ethnomusicology; the Center for Studies in Ethnomusicology, Columbia University (1981); the Philadelphia Anthropological Society (1982); and the Goroka Ethnomusicology Conference (1982). Thoughtful questions at these occasions have led to a number of improvements; many thanks and no blame to those who posed them.

Musicologically there is a deeper problem. The axiom of much work has been: when a sound is not complex in the material aspects of its acoustic organization, assume that its social meaning is essentially shallow. Musical meaning, in this view, is "in the notes" and not "in the world." The melodic, metric, and timbral organization of sounds are taken as *prima facie* indexes of the social significance of musical action. For Papua New Guinea drums, the consequences of such a view are considerable. Writers of general books, articles, and record jacket notes have assumed a kind of minimalism regarding the meaning of these sounds. Such assumptions rest simply on external auditory grounds: singular timbres, isometric patterns, solo or group performances in or out of synchrony with singers, lack of use in large multi-part percussion ensembles.

Without engaging in further polemic about the form and implication of these closures I hope to reopen the issues by addressing this question: how and why can an acoustically simple phenomenon *only* be understood through recourse to complex social facts? Treating the Kaluli drum sound as a symbolic system, rich both in the particulars of its situated meaning and in the general scheme of how Kaluli make sense of their world, we might also come around to the realization that acoustic organizations are always, at a prior level, socially organized.

My discussion will proceed, as did my fieldwork, from detached visual observation to linguistic and musical participation, beginning with the artifact and its social life, moving to its sound shape out of context, then to its magical construction, finally culminating in its performance and evocative response. First, something about the people and their place.

The Kaluli are one of four subgroups (culturally identical but differentiated by slight dialect variations) who collectively refer to themselves as *Bosavi kalu*, "Bosavi people."[2] They number some twelve hundred and live on about five hundred square miles of tropical forest lands just north of the slopes of Mt. Bosavi on the Great Papuan Plateau in the Southern Highlands of Papua New Guinea. They reside in longhouse communities separated from each other by an hour's walk along forest trails. Each community is made up of members of two or three named patrilineal descent groups, comprising about fifteen families or, in all, some sixty to eighty people. Kaluli people are swidden horticulturalists whose staple food is sago; they also maintain large gardens and hunt small game, wild pigs, and birds in the surrounding primary forest.

Traditional ceremonial life in Bosavi was prolific. In addition to one major ceremony of local invention, several other ceremonies, incorporated from the Lake Kutubu area to the east, the Kamula area to the south, and the Lake Campbell area to the west, gained great popularity. While Kaluli musical activity is primarily vocal, mussel shell, seed pod, and crayfish claw rattles are used as accompaniment for various ceremonies. It is in this instrumental and ceremonial context that drums have made their way into Kaluli ceremonial life, coming from the south side of Mt. Bosavi in the last one hundred years. They are played in several settings, principally as a late afternoon prelude to an all-night ceremony.

The Artifact

The Kaluli drum is single-headed and conical, just short of three feet long, and generally measures about five inches across each opening. It is always decorated by a set of carved ridges above the open end, and painted with natural red, white, and black substances.

---

[2] For a general ethnography of the Kaluli, focusing on ceremonial action, see E. L. Schieffelin (1976).

Kaluli call it *ilib,* which is also the term for "treehole," "chest" (of the body), or "resonant chamber." All drum parts are named with human body part terms; most important here are the inner terms *uš, dagan,* and *megɔf. Us* is the term for "egg," "nut," "phlegm"; it is also extended to mean "batteries," "film," and "tape." In essence it denotes an outer shell covering a living inner substance. This is the term used to describe the upper portion of the drum's inside chamber, below the "head." *Dagan* is "voice" or "throat"; this is the area just above the open *megɔf* or "mouth" end of the drum. To produce sound from its "body" (*domo*), a drum must resound from its "head," resonate in the "inner chest," and speak from its "voice" through a "mouth."

Drums are made by, owned, cared for, passed on, and played by Kaluli men. No special status is attached to these activities, given the generally egalitarian nature of Kaluli social life. Drums are not considered "secret" or "sacred" like flutes, bullroarers, or *garamuts* (slit drums) elsewhere in Papua New Guinea; they do not figure in initiation or otherwise in male-female relations. While Kaluli women do not touch the drums or know about drum construction or magic, drums are kept in open view for all to see in the longhouse. Additionally, there are no ritualized taboos about drums, and men do not go to elaborate or deceitful ends to hide them from women (cf. with cases cited in Gourlay 1975 for examples of how social stratification and initiation in Papua New Guinea highly correlate with the "secretness" of instrumental usage).

The Sound

Aside from these initial observations, the most striking impression that quickly develops about Kaluli drums derives from the sound. The drum pulse is regular and isometric, beating about 135 times per minute of play. The pitch is singular, a low frequency complex with a clear separation of the sound of the slap and the sound of the main pitch, the slap being the fundamental frequency (usually in the area of *CC* or 65 Hz) and the main audible pitch the first overtone one octave higher (in the area of *C* or 130 Hz). Additionally, the second overtone (in the area of *G,* or 196 Hz) and the third overtone (in the area of *c* or 261 Hz) are quite prominent. The 4th, 5th, 6th, and 7th overtones are also relatively strong; there is no rapid falloff until this point. The resultant auditory sensation is a shifting figure and ground, with strong sense images of the octaves at C, and the inner 5th at G (cf. Fig. 1, p. 150).

The pulsation is regular, neither a slow throb nor a rapid warble. The envelope shape of each pulse is marked by a sharp and definite attack with no hesitation, a brief but full body sustain, and a long decay with no trailing effect. First listening confirms the idea that each pulse continues to and overlaps the next; there are no discrete sound breaks or silences in between one pulse and the next. A slight reverberation from angling the drum toward the house floor is also apparent, but the general sensation of resonance — a thick, densely textured overlapping pulse — is not primarily an echo effect. Rather it derives directly from the instrumental materials and the prescribed manner of playing. The dynamics are held constant at one level once the drum pulsing begins. At five feet from a player the drum is one of the loudest sounds Kaluli make or hear; at about 80 decibels on the A scale (up to 85 with two or more players) it is easily two to three times louder than a normal face-to-face conversation. In summary, the immediately salient acoustic features of drumming are the intensity and regularity of pulsation, the denseness of the sound as a continual overlapping throb, and the layering quality of the pitches, with clear octaves and the inner 5th constantly shifting figure and ground.

Figure 1
Spectrogram with Overtones for Three Seconds of Drumming

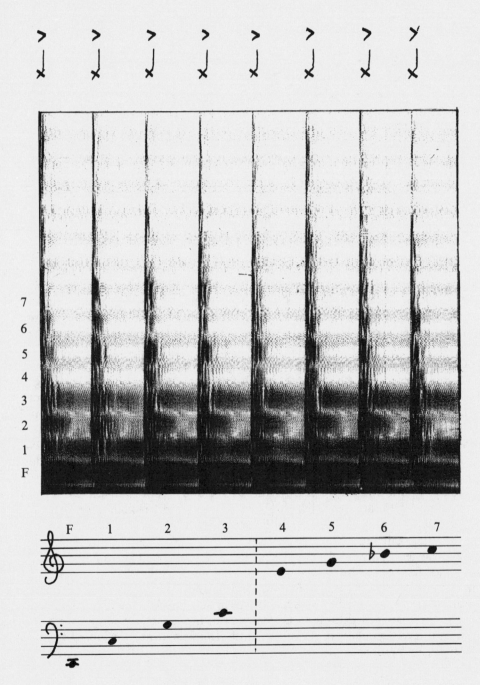

x = 135 M.M.

Construction

These quick visual, social, and acoustic observations did not begin to acquire cultural meaning for me until I learned about the process of constructing a drum, a process through which magical mediation imparts sonic pattern to the material object and infuses it with aesthetic power. If pursued in a linear manner (which is rarely the case), it takes about six days to make a drum.

On the first day a *dona* tree (a magnolia, *Elmirillia papuana*) is cut and a four foot long section is chosen, soaked in water, and prepared for hollowing. While four or five other tree types are occasionally used, *dona* is preferred by most Kaluli drummers due to its lightness and resonant qualities.

On the second day the soaking log is removed from water and one end is hollowed in about two feet in length and two or three inches in diameter. Traditionally this was done by a combination of burning, scraping with bamboo, and sanding with rough leaves. Today machetes and small knives are also used. Once one end is successfully hollowed, the same process begins at the other end. When completed, a ridge about two inches thick remains between the two hollowed sections. Again the drum is left to soak overnight.

On the third day the actual working on the drum is halted and a hunting party is convened to capture a *tibodai* bird. This may take several days. Once the bird is caught the feathers are plucked and placed inside the drum while the inside surfaces are further smoothed and widened. Then, in the most dramatic aspect of the process, the throat and tongue of the bird are placed on the bridge that separates the two hollowed areas. The bridge is cut through from top to bottom while a magical saying (which I am not permitted to reveal here) is softly recited by the maker. Before discussing the significance of this action, this is what happens in the next few days.

First, the openings are shaped, the ends of the drum are scaled down to their final size, and work is oriented toward preparing the drum for its first sound test. A *yobo* (large anglehead lizard, *Goniocephalus* sp.) is hunted and skinned. While certain other lizards and snakes occasionally provide skins for drumheads, most Kaluli like the *yobo* best because it is not too thick and responds well to heat in tuning. The rim of the drum is prepared with a gluey latex from tree bark and the stretched skin is placed around the rim and tied down with cane. It is then dried in the sun or by a low fire; fresh ashes are often spread over the head to heat it evenly.

Next, four lumps of beeswax are placed on the head, centered, and shaped. They are designated *kol* but metaphorically referred to as *seida gasa kɛlɛn id*, "bush dog ear shit." When these are attached another saying is softly recited so that the head of the drum will assimilate the quality of a *seida gasa himu* or "bush dog heart." The beeswax bumps are thus empowered to throb and pulse like the heart of a bush dog on the chase.

Sound tests then may take several hours. The *kol* are shaped and reshaped, heated and reheated; the head is "fed" chewed ginger or cordyline leaf by players spitting these substances into the open end of the drum. This keeps the inner side of the head moist while the outside is tightening from heat. Simultaneously the drum is played, listened to, and commented upon. If the sound "hardens" (*halaido domeib*[3]) the final day will be devoted to carving the ridges at the mouth end, sanding and refining the inner and outer surfaces, and painting. If the sound does not "harden" then another skin will be sought and the testing

---

[3] The metaphor of "hardness" in Kaluli language and aesthetics is treated more fully in Feld and B. B. Schieffelin (1982).

process will begin again. If several skins are unsuccessful the drum shell will be discarded.

While the final visual decorative processes are important in the overall appearance of the drum, it is worth noting here that a drum can be washed and painted in a matter of two hours. In the construction process it is the determination of the proper sound that takes precedence over all visual dimensions of the instrument. The painting materials — *sowan*, a white ground clay; *bin*, an orange-red substance from the seed pods of *Bixa orellana*; and *tig* or *asɔn*, black from tree resins (or more recently, burnt rubber) — are all easily obtainable and it is only necessary to paint a drum right before a ceremonial performance.

Now back to the significance of *tibodai*. This bird is the Crested Pitohui (*Pitohui cristatus*), more commonly known as the Papuan Bellbird. The name derives from the way this shy little bird calls from tree perches with a continuous throbbing sound. Jared Diamond (1972:293-94), a prominent observer of Papua New Guinea birds, writes:

> The song consists of a long series of identical notes which are initially all on the same pitch at equal time intervals. The pitch lies approximately an octave above middle C. One of the two remarkable features of the song is the length. One song which I timed and which seemed to be of average length lasted 175 seconds without interruption. . . . The other and more remarkable quality is the unusual throbbing. . . . Although the song is muted and not loud it carries for long distances of up to a half mile. . . .

These qualities, equal pulsation at the same pitch, extraordinary length and consistency, throbbing quality, and resonant carrying power, are in fact the most desired acoustic properties of the drum. Thus, breaking through the voice of the drum with the voice of *tibodai* is a process that insures the drum its basic sonic character. But what is the significance of choosing a bird as the mediator of human instrumental sound?

Kaluli classify birds both morphologically (based on similarities of beaks and feet) as well as by families of sound. The sound classification is more widely shared, and relates salient taxonomic categories to myths about the origin of sounds as well as congruent taboos and magical sayings. Additionally, in the tropical forest sound is the principal means through which Kaluli recognize birds.[4] They hunt by sound (mimicing the calls), relate to the cycle of daily and seasonal time by the cycle of bird calls and migrations, reckon space by acoustic indications of distance where one cannot see through the forest, and generally associate birds with the sounds they hear around them. In part, the reason for this is that birds are also *ane mama*, "gone reflections," spirits of the dead. Thus categories of bird sound are also categories of spirit-human vocalization.

There are seven sound groups:

those who say their name (*ene wi salan*)
those who make a lot of noise (*mada ganafodan*)
those who only sound (*imilisi ganalan*)
those who speak the Bosavi language (*Bosavi to salan*)
those who whistle (*holan*)
those who weep (*yɛlan*)
those who sing (*gisalo molan*).

Tibodai is in two of these groups, those who say their names and those who whistle. The

---

[4] An elaborated treatment of bird sound vis-à-vis taxonomy and symbolism is found in Feld (1982:71-85).

"says its name" classification relates the name *tibodai* to the onomatopoeia in *tibo tibo tibo tibo*, a vocal representation of the pulsating song. The "whistle" classification is more significant. Birds with whistling voices are considered a special category of spirits, and their sounds are often associated with spirits of dead children. Thus we have the notion that bird sounds are not only natural indicators of the Bosavi avifauna; they are equally considered communications from the dead to each other and to the living. As such, bird sounds and sound categories are powerful mediators; they link sonic patterns with social ethos and emotion.

Play and Performance

Drumming is generally performed for four or five hours as a late-afternoon prelude to an all-night, major ceremony. This type of performance is called *ilib kuwɔ* (literally, "cut drums"). One to five costumed dancers perform continuously. They are usually organized in two groups, one at each end of the longhouse, 60 feet apart. They first play in place, bobbing up and down as they perform. Once the sound has "hardened" (that is, has begun to pulsate strongly), they may crisscross down the corridor and switch positions, then return to their own starting points. When a drum sound becomes "unhard" the player stops immediately and begins to rework the beeswax bumps. In this activity the actual performance of the drum is no different from the exercise of tuning it.

Indeed, if there is a striking fact about how Kaluli handle their drums, it is that they spend as much if not more time tuning and figeting with them than actually performing *ilib kuwɔ*. It is the continual reworking of the *kol* on the head and the "feeding" of ginger or cordyline that is most important here. When queried about this "feeding," Kaluli often responded that like a child, whose language is "unhard," the drum must be fed so that its sound will "harden." As in the realms of maturation and language acquisition, *halaido*, "hardness," is a basic prerequisite of dramatic evocation.

In performance too, Kaluli cannot stand still when they tune or practice drumming. They bob up and down, sway to the side and always remain in motion. Drumming must be a full bodily sensation, never just the slap of the wrist or palm onto the skin surface. The drum is usually held in the left hand; as the body moves up and down, the left hand pumps the drum so that it both angles down to the floor and meets the right hand which is swinging in a pendular movement. The right hand hits the *kol* squarely against the thick parts of the upper palm and lower portion of the third and fourth fingers. There is just the slightest flex of the wrist. When teaching me to drum and dance, Kaluli always stressed that I should feel the pulsing sensation in my upper arms and chest, not just in the lower hands and fingers.

This movement complex is related to both a conceptualization of dance and the nature of the costume worn for drumming. Like other expressive modalities (weeping, poetics, song), dance originates with a bird, *wɔkwele*, the Giant Cuckoodove (*Reinwardtoena reinwardtsi*). Cuckoodoves nest in rock gorges near waterfalls, and their calls are a two part *wɔk-wu*, heard above the sounds of water. In motion the bird bounces up and down in place, stable on the first syllable (*wɔk*), bouncing up on the higher outward syllable (*wu*). Kaluli dancers must move up and down like *wɔkwele* in front of a waterfall. In the rear of their costumes are palm streamers that spring from the waist to the shoulders and then fall down to their ankles. In movement these streamers (*fasela*) make a *shhh* sound like a waterfall as the dancers move up and down creating their flow. The dancer's voice (or, in this case, drum) sounds above the continual *shhh* of the waterfall, like a *wɔkwele* in a rock gorge (cf. Fig. 2, p. 154).

Figure 2. Kaluli Dancer with Drum.

These features of motion and costume sound enhance the purpose of drumming, drawing the audience into a nostalgic, sentimental, and reflective mood by filling the house with an intense continuous sound. Like ceremonial songs which are aimed at making audience members so sad that they are moved to tears, drumming, while technically a "warmup" to an evening ceremony, occasionally provokes people in the same way.

Kaluli say that this process of evocation is dependent upon the "hardening" of the drum sound in performance. Once the drummers "harden" the sound and begin a long stretch of continuous pulsation, Kaluli are apt to remark: *dagano halaidɛsege, kalu yɛlimeib-kɛ!*, "the voice having hardened, people will really weep!" "Hardening" then is the locus of aesthetic tension. Concretely, it is the moment when the throbbing drum voice is no longer heard as a bird voice calling *tibo tibo*, but is now heard, on the "inside" reflection, as a dead child calling *dowo dowo*, "father, father." This is the point when Kaluli listeners are completely absorbed by the sound, reflecting on its inner meaning rather than its outer form. It is this "hardening" that moves listeners to thoughts of deceased children and to tears.

One reason why the sound is so absorbing is that the texture of multiple drums creates a sonic environment in the longhouse where figure and ground constantly shift. Kaluli understand the concept of unison but have no term for unison sound-making, and indeed find it unnatural precisely in its dissimilarity to all of the sounds in their forest environment. Comparing their own organizations of sound to the dense textures of waterfalls and forest birds, Kaluli only produce vocal and instrumental sounds that are canonic. Their term for this patterning is *dulugu ganalan*, "lift up over sounding." Sound in the Kaluli universe is never linear, with one part discretely following behind another; parts are always layered so that they "lift up over" one another, and this is the prominent feature of drumming.

This concern with "hardening" in evocation also surrounds the process of talking about drumming. Drums must "talk"; a wobbly or punctuated nonresounding drum is said to be *towɔ mɔtolan*, "not talking words"; it is *halaidoma*, "unhard." When it is "talking" (*tolan*) it is saying *dowo*, "father," and the sound is "hard" in both the linguistic and aesthetic senses of that metaphor.

Similarly, aesthetic evaluation concentrates on the "hardness" of the drum sound as it "carries" (*ɛbɛlan*). This verb is usually used to describe water motion that is visually evident at one place but then flows out of sight. This carrying property extends to indicate continual auditory sensation and feeling beyond the production of a sound. Sound is "hard" when it stays in your head and forces its presence on your feelings.

Like the construction of drum sound in its material and cultural senses, play and performance aim to crystallize a core set of Kaluli sensibilities about sound and persuasion. Substances are not only infused with meaning; an arena is created for those meanings to be actively performed and communally reconfirmed.

Adding the Metaphors

Claude Lévi-Strauss argues that one way to approach the complexities of human activity is to abstract key symbols from their experiential contexts and recast them onto a vertical, paradigmatic axis so that they can be observed like a cultural table of contents. Looking at the layers of the drum story, the links between sound and meaning can be initially addressed this way, as a constellation of basic Kaluli metaphors.

1. The drum is a body. The hard decorated outside covers the substantive living, resounding, breathing, inside. Sound must be formulated from head to voice before it can forcefully burst onto the scene.

2. The drum voice is a *tibodai* bird voice. The qualities of pulsing, throbbing, carrying, and continuous sound are those selected and arranged as meaningful. Starting from a punctual *bo . . . bo . . .* it swells into an intense *tibo tibo tibo tibo tibo*, with each sound, like the double syllable name, overlapping the next.

3. The drum pulse is the heart of a bush dog. It pounds out the chase, intensifying until the catch is made.

4. The drum speaks like a child. Like Kaluli children, drums must be "fed" prechewed food so that their language "hardens" to a well-formed and grammatical pattern. Drum voices mature from the onomatopoeia of bird language to the hardness of human words, ultimately saying *dowo dowo dowo dowo*, calling for "father."

5. The drum pulse must "flow." Like water, which can flow beyond perceptual immediacy but remain in a mental map, sound must "stay with you" once it perceptually ends. Drum sound is forceful when it transcends the event and remains in your head, continuing to flow.

6. The drum pulse is not discrete. The sound carries in layers of canonic density, whether one drum or several are playing. There are no sound breaks, and parts are not isolable segments that follow one behind the other. They are compact sounds which "lift up over" each other and layer as figure and ground.

7. The drum sound is not what it appears to be. It has multiple reflections, insides and outsides. Like the whole world, which has a visible realm and a reflection realm, one the deeper reality of the other, the drum voice has an inside, which is the voice of a *tibodai* bird. But birds are also reflections of the dead, and inside the *tibodai* bird voice is the voice of a dead child, the voice of a reflected spirit gone from the visible. So too with the sound. Outside the strongest perceptual image, the octaves produced by the fundamental, 1st and 3rd overtones, there is an inside sound, the musical 5th produced by the strong second overtone. Like the drum/bird/child figure-ground, the drum sound shifts focus so that its "inside" can be heard.

8. The drum sound must "harden." A Kaluli origin myth tells how the world was once mushy and soft; *alin* the Goura Pigeon and *odɛn* the Scrub Turkey stamped on the ground to "harden" it. Like the necessity for physical hardness, so too in social life: children, language, and evocative performance must "harden." Children avoid eating soft substances until their bodies and language "harden." A "hard man" is one who is strong, assertive, and not a witch. A song that does not "harden" — has no climaxing structure in the poetics and performance — will not move a person to tears. Like a body, a child, language, or song, drum sound must be shaped from substance to meaningful form.

The overlapping significances of these eight metaphoric constructs shape the grounds upon which drum sound can be said to have a situated meaning that is socially created and shared by those who understand—in part tacitly—its dimensions. Yet of all the ways these constructs can be grouped, one significant issue is the extent to which we are dealing with metaphors specific to drums, or interpretive constructs that Kaluli apply to *all* sounds and the grounds upon which they are meaningful. While images of the body, child, and bush dog heart are specific here, the notions of "flow," "hardness," "inner" reflections from outer substances, and "lift up over" density are general axioms that are essential to the interpretation of all communicative expression in the visual, verbal, musical, or choreographic modes for Kaluli. But in some ways the center of it all—the single most important fact about the drum sound, and the single most important trope for all Kaluli aesthetic action—is bird mediation.

Had we started with the dance we would have been led to bird mediation in the up/down movement and the image of a *wɔkwele* at a waterfall. Had we concentrated on costuming, we would have been led to bird mediation in the symbolism of color (Feld 1982:66-71). Had we begun with the larger sonic setting for drum performances in audience cheering and response, we would have been led to bird mediation in the way women's cheering is inspired by and patterned after the calls of the Superb Bird of Paradise. Had we begun with staging, we would have been led to bird mediation in the concept of lighting the longhouse so that light splashes through the hall like the forest, lighting the birds that come and go and perch on their travels. Each feature of performance, context, staging, and sound leads back to this central notion: through the mediating scheme of bird transformation, Kaluli expressive behaviors are metaphorically empowered to communicate social ethos and emotion. In other codes (weeping, poetics, speaking, song) this mediation is grounded in concrete models provided by myths. In this case, drum sound, the mediation is grounded in concrete action during construction—action whose efficacy is confirmed in magical spells.

Why birds? Precisely because their symbolic dualism creates imaginative possibilities for the mind, and their constant presence creates a continual reminder that Kaluli are part of forest world that "talks" to them. Since Kaluli dead reappear in the treetops as birds, all bird sound is at once both indicative of the avifauna and communication from those who have gone *ɔbɛ mise*, "in the form of birds." Bird sound, like drum sound, is filled with an "inside," a deeper layer of meaning in sound. The voice of a child, dead and abandoned, inside a bird voice, inside a drum pulse, emerges as the inner reality of drumming, an emotional reality that resides not only on the inside of the sound but at the inside of what it means to be Kaluli and be moved by evocative performance.

Analysis and Synthesis/Sound and Meaning

Electronic musicians and structural anthropologists seem to have two things in common: a powerful belief that the proof of analysis is in synthesis, and an understanding that coherences often demonstrate their existence through reversals, fractures, oppositions, and transformations (rather than linear form or action). Neither principle is foreign to Kaluli.

In a cycle of stories Kaluli celebrate the exploits of a fellow named Newelɛsu and his cross-cousin, Dosali. Newelɛsu is a klutz, a trickster, boisterous and immodest, with little control of his appetites. Dosali is the opposite: cool, collected, always in command of his energies. A persistent theme in these stories is Newelɛsu's desire to take a wife, and the ways he consistently loses control, invokes wrong or inappropriate strategies, and is left panting on the sidelines, envying his cross-cousin's slick moves.

Once, at a ceremony, Newelɛsu is taken by the beauty of Dosali in full costume, drumming *ilib kuwɔ* to a cheering and enthusiastic crowd in the longhouse. He realizes that a potential consequence of such powerful evocation is at the center of his own desires: causing a woman to lose her heart to a man, leading to elopement and marriage. The possibility is thrilling, and he decides to perform at the next ceremony. But he is carried away: in his fervor he gets confused and ends up cutting down the wrong tree. Finding it too difficult to hunt a *tibodai* he simply snares a kingfisher from his garden and sacrifices its voice. Being too tired to get up early to catch an anglehead lizard he decides that any old snake will do. And so on, down to the very last aspect of his costume and the painting for the drum. The result, predictably, is disastrous: his drum sounds *donk donk donk donk*, the pulse does not "harden," no one is the least bit moved, and the performance is sham. Once again, no control, no evocative power, no woman.

While this story reconfirms the importance Kaluli attach to detail and to the ability to turn substance into communicative form, it also states something deeper about life: understanding how to make, listen to, and feel the force of drum sound runs right to the core of knowing how to be Kaluli. Newelɛsu, like a character straight out of Beckett, is both profoundly funny and sad because his mistakes are so obvious and the action of making them so existentially salient. In the end, when we come through analysis to synthesis, it is clear that drumming is not superfluous action in which Kaluli need make no emotional investment. Rather it is purposive action, for which Kaluli are called upon to engage personally. To participate is to interpret drum sound by animating the most basic Kaluli aesthetic strategies: find the "inside" of the "layers," observe the "hardening," and feel the "flow."

Aside from the specific means Kaluli utilize to interpret the message of drumming, it seems there are other implications here for the study of musical meaning. What drummers make and what listeners hear is acoustic pattern; Kaluli attend to the sound of drumming to find, both aurally and socially, outer and inner layers of structure. But meaning is more than pattern alone, more than a mirror image of structure. For Kaluli, meaning resides in the knowledge that a sound is always more than it appears to be; that pattern is a clue to finding the "inside," or the "inner reflection."

Meaning then, in a communicative sense, is dependent on interpretive action, action which is the alignment of cultural knowledge and epistemology with the experience of sound. Meaning does not reside "in the notes" because the way the notes are formed, listened to, and interpreted derives from prior social imposition. Hearers of Kaluli sound share a logic for ordering their experiences. That logic (hear sound as mediated, hear mediation as a bird, hear bird sound as a spirit voice), in its most general form (all things have an inside and the inside is a reflection from the spirit realm), is called into play every time Kaluli listen to or produce musical sound. What is essential, then, is not that we have a motivated and somewhat iconic correspondence between the character of *tibodai* sound and the character of drum sound. Rather, it is that Kaluli have invented an interpretive logic for hearing that correspondence and deciding what it is about once it is acoustically perceived. Sounds actively communicate and embody deeply felt sentiments for Kaluli because their listeners know they must be prepared to find the "inside," and because they know "reflections" are socially real.

References Cited

Diamond, Jared M.
1972 *Avifauna of the Eastern Highlands of New Guinea.* Cambridge, Mass.: Nuttall Ornithological Club.

Feld, Steven
1982   *Sound and Sentiment: Birds, Weeping, Poetics, and Song in Kaluli Expression.* Philadelphia: University of Pennsylvania Press.

Feld, Steven, and Bambi B. Schieffelin
1982   "Hard Words: The Functional Basis for Kaluli Discourse." *Analyzing Discourse: Text and Talk*, ed. Deborah Tannen, pp. 351-71. Washington, D.C.: Georgetown University Press.

Gourlay, K. A.
1975   *Sound Producing Instruments in Traditional Society: A Study of Esoteric Instruments and Their Role in Male-Female Relations.* Canberra: Australian National University Press.

Schieffelin, Edward L.
1976   *The Sorrow of the Lonely and the Burning of the Dancers.* New York: St. Martins Press.

PART V

THE ART AND THE ARTS

Leaf-Music Among the Salasaca of Highland Ecuador

Joseph B. Casagrande
University of Illinois
and
David K. Stigberg
University of Illinois

Introduction

Blowing across a blade of grass stretched tightly between the thumbs may well be a universal way of making noise or even rudimentary music (Sachs 1940:38).[1] However, there are many other ways that grasses and leaves are used as sound-producing instruments in various parts of the world, and these instruments are often capable of music of considerable intricacy. A kind of free kazoo (*mirliton, näselhäutchen*) fashioned from a leaf has been reported from the Solomon Islands and is perhaps more widely known (Sachs 1928:108), and leaves are also used as sound-modifiers covering the apertures of flutes in several African cultures (cf. De Hen 1960:202-03). More complicated are the oscillating ribbon reeds, not of grass but of cedar bark and other materials, enclosed between two pieces of bark or wood, found in British Columbia and elsewhere in North America (Galpin 1903:129-30; Izikowitz 1935:253-54). In a still more elaborate form of ribbon reed, a long narrow leaf or blade of grass is coiled in a spiral to form a trumpet-like cone, and the sound is produced by blowing into the flattened narrower aperture, causing an inner membrane and sometimes a separate inserted blade to vibrate; such instruments have been documented in various parts of South America (Izikowitz 1935:252-54), in Hawaii (Roberts 1926:44-45), Samoa (Moyle 1974:57, 69), and New Zealand (Andersen 1934:292-94). Finally, there are the traditions of Central and Eastern Europe, in which the instrument — a pear, lilac, or other leaf, and in a particularly widespread form, a piece of the inner bark from a birch tree — is blown across while held against the lips. The music of these instruments is often complex, as can be heard on recordings from Rumania,[2] but apart from a single study (Schrammek 1961), no serious attention has

[1] The authors wish to express their gratitude to Rudi and Francisca Masaquiza for consultantship in the preparation of this essay, and to Gary Apfelstadt for the illustration of *hojas de capulí* (Fig. 4). All photographs are by Joseph Casagrande.

     Dr. Joseph B. Casagrande, Department of Anthropology, died while this essay was still in preparation. Norman E. Whitten, Jr., Department of Anthropology, assisted David Stigberg, School of Music, in completing it from the late Joseph Casagrande's notes.

[2] These recordings include *The Folk Music of Rumania*, Columbia KL-5799; *Rumanian Songs and Dances*, Ethnic Folkways FE 4387; and *Music from Rumania*, Argo ZFB 41.

been afforded any of these European performance practices. Elsewhere in the world, the music of leaves has seldom been described.

Among the population of Salasaca pampa in Central Andean Ecuador, there exists a tradition of music-making with cherry leaves, *hojas de capulí* (*Prunus serotina Ehrh*[3]). For a number of years, the late Joseph B. Casagrande was engaged in research in the Ecuadorian highlands and, beginning in 1968, collected several recordings of music performed on these instruments in Salasaca. Our purpose here is simply to document this practice, to indicate something of its importance, and to describe the music that is representative of at least one contemporary stylistic orientation of the performance tradition itself.

There has been some notice of the musical use of leaves in Ecuador. Four citations are gathered together in Carvalho Neto's *Diccionario del folklore ecuatoriano* (1964:94), all for northern Ecuador, and all for leaves in ensembles known as *bandas mochas*. Three of these references are for ensembles of Afro-Ecuadorian musicians, in Chota (Carchi Province) and Ibarra (Imbabura). These *bandas mochas* include men playing orange or banana leaves, aerophones made from calabash or gourd shells (*calabazas*, *puros*), and various other instruments, and would seem to be modeled after the military bands of European derivation that are a characteristic feature of highland musical life. However, the remaining reference in Carvalho Neto is for Checa, in Pichincha Province slightly to the south, and does not include an ethnic specification. It describes a *banda mocha* with *rondador* (panpipes), flute, guitar, and *hojas de capulí*.[4]

The expression *banda mocha* is not employed by performing musicians in Salasaca (though some know of the phrase), but one traditional practice does involve the playing of leaves along with flutes and drums in large ensembles. It is possible that the practices we have seen in Salasaca and others have reported from northern Ecuador are representative of a larger number of interrelated performance traditions in the Ecuadorian Andes. Nevertheless, Salasacan musicians emphasize the importance of performance with *hojas de capulí* in their community, and are quite tentative regarding the existence of such practices among the surrounding populations. While this may be dismissed as merely a matter of local pride, it may also indicate a focus on music-making with *hojas de capulí* that is distinctly Salasacan.[5]

---

[3] According to Gade (1975:161), "*capulí* is a 'bird cherry' that was probably introduced from Mexico after the Conquest. Its name corresponds to the Nahuatl word *capulquauitl* and Acosta (1962:185) noted seeing *capulí* 'only in Mexico and in no other country.' It has no pre-Conquest associations in Peru and there is no archaeological or documentary evidence of its presence in the Central Andes before the sixteenth century."

[4] The descriptions from Chota are from Festa (1909:307-08), and Costales Samaniego and Peñaherrera de Costales (1958:214), given almost in their entirety in Carvalho Neto (1964:94); the observations of a *banda mocha* in Ibarra are Carvalho Neto's own, and that for Checa is from unpublished field research, by Ligia Osorio S., in 1961.

[5] Performance of a *banda mocha*, available on the recording *In Praise of Oxalá and Other Gods: Black Music of South America*, Nonesuch H-72036, is very similar in style to the music performed with leaves in Salasaca, and in fact this piece, entitled "Oigame Juanita," is known to Salasacan musicians. Regarding the general use of leaves as musical instruments in Ecuador, in the first volume of what will eventually be a comprehensive study of Ecuadorian instruments, Coba Andrade (1981:100) states that "tanto los indios como los negros utilizan hojas de los arboles frutales con las cuales entonan sus canciones"; presumably more details will appear in a subsequent volume. Finally, it should be noted that both Norman Whitten and William Belzner of the University of Illinois report their observations of the musical use of leaves, among coastal lowland as well as highland populations in Ecuador.

Salasaca

Salasacapampa, as the 4236 (in 1979; see Carrasco A. 1982:25, 104) native Quichua-speaking Salasaca call their territory, is located about 14 kilometers southeast of the city of Ambato, in Tungurahua Province of Central Ecuador. Although slightly nucleated around the old plaza and the new one where a well-known cooperative of handicrafts is located, the basic settlement pattern is dispersed and, except for the strong commercial emphasis on woven tapestries as an ethnic art, the people are primarily subsistence-oriented horticulturalists skilled in working marginal land. Additional cash income is derived from wage labor work on the coast and Upper Amazonia, making and selling fiber and rope, and general catch-as-catch-can jobs near or far from their homeland. Sources of income for particular individuals range from bullbaiting at local fiestas to operating small stores in their own homes and the renting out of costumes for fiestas.

The Salasacan people form a "bounded" community, although its precise boundaries or formal demarcation are often hazy. There are a number of features that set Salasacapampa off from the surrounding area: Quichua spoken as a first language, almost no intermarriage between Salasacans and neighboring mestizos, and a hostile, protective stance of their territory vis-à-vis all outsiders (cf. Scheller 1972, Carrasco A. 1982). Long a *comuna*, indigenous commune, Salasaca became its own parish of Pelileo Canton in 1972 in order to obtain pavement for the Ambato-Baños section of the Ambato-Puyo highway which runs through their territory. Nonetheless, the Salasaca maintain local autonomy and hegemony over their parish and have their own political officials in charge of their own territory. In addition, with the coming of the modern world, Salasacans gained their own cemetery, releasing them even more from dependence upon neighboring mestizos.

Salasacan dress, combined with their own distinctive dialect of Quichua, clearly sets them off as a distinct native culture of modern and historic Ecuador. Typical of the Salasaca are their black ponchos and heavy white felt hats made in the neighboring community of Pelileo. The men wear white shirts and short trousers that come just below the knee, both made of a kind of rough cotton cloth. Men also wear a scarf-like woolen cloth called a *vara y media* typically of a purple-reddish color that comes from a dye made from cochineal, an insect propagated by the Salasaca themselves. Women wear the same hats as men and typically wear white, colorfully embroidered blouses and black skirts (*ancas*) wound around the waist and wrapped by one or more woven belts (*fajas*). Most Salasacan women wear several strands of beads around their necks of which the finest are made of real coral and imported Italian faience porcelain beads that are highly prized. Gold or coral-colored glass beads are also worn, as are bracelets of the same material. Both sexes typically go barefoot, although nowadays many younger and middle age people wear shoes. Salasacan women wear their hair braided but unlike some other groups including the Otavaleños, the Canaris, and the Saraguros in the far south, the Salasacan men do not do likewise, preferring instead a rather distinctive "long cut." Although Western style dress, including sweaters, trousers, and "alpine" style short-brimmed felt hats and mass-made shirts, is now worn, especially by younger men, everyone in Salasacapampa has available for special occasions a full set of Salasacan clothing.

That the Salasaca have maintained in fairly vigorous form a good deal of their "traditional" culture also set them off from their mestizo neighbors and from a great many "Indian" communities. The Salasaca still observe a full annual fiesta cycle of seven or eight major celebrations (Carrasco A. 1982). Each of these is sponsored by a *prioste* and a rather elaborate retinue of sustainers and helpers. Internal government is still very largely in the hands of *alcaldes*—appointed annually by the local priests (ibid.). They meet quite regularly and constitute an effective decision-making group. Many other traditional ways still persist, including cuisine, folk medicine, and the like.

It is within this broader context that Salasacan music should be set. Again, as contrasted with many other indigenous or one-time indigenous communities, music still flourishes as part of Salasacan traditional culture. It figures significantly in the observances at all major fiestas that are essentially community-wide in nature. Although they may be localized, both with respect to the residence of the *prioste* responsible for a particular fiesta and where that celebration actually occurs, people are free to come from throughout Salasacan territory. Music is also an important part of the ceremonies at a marriage which essentially involve a set of elements including public observance of the changed status of the newly married couple, feasting and drinking, and musical performances.

Other than leaves, there are a variety of musical instruments traditionally established among the Salasaca. There are several flutes, including a transverse *flauta*, and at least two varieties of whistle flutes, the three-hole *pingullo* and the smaller, six-hole *pijuano* (*pifano*). The *rondador* (panpipes) of varying sizes and numbers of tubes so common elsewhere in Ecuador is rather rare in Salasaca. There are a number of drums with and without snares, called, depending on size and context, *caja*, *tambor*, and *bombo*. Among the various string instruments introduced by the Spanish, the violin has achieved virtual indigenous status, having been assimilated into traditional musical performances and commonly played by native musicians. The harp and guitar, on the other hand, although common elsewhere in Ecuador, are not prevalent in Salasaca (see Figs. 1 and 2).

There are at least two major dimensions of contrast in Salasacan musical performances. One contrast is essentially that between indigenous, Runa (Quichua for "people," "human") and Spanish-derived or "mestizo" music. Another contrast is between various occasions in which musical performances occur. Here, a basic distinction is between the more elaborate calendrical festivals where brass bands of mestizo musicians (Fig. 3) are invariably employed as against other less formal occasions such as the ceremonies that accompany marriages. Leaf-music essentially occupies a third category. It is often performed as a kind of recreational music, casually and spontaneously, in impromptu duets or by an individual young man while simply walking about the community. One informant gave an almost lyrical account of young boys going out in the evenings playing flutes and looking for girls with whom they might spend the night, and then pursuing them again the next day playing *hojas de capulí*. Here, leaf-playing was associated with youth, love-making, and gaity, and our informant, a married man of thirty-five, talked about such episodes with a palpable touch of nostalgic enjoyment.

Much of the music played on the more typically Salasacan instruments, including *hojas de capulí*, is described as being *muy antigua*, "very old," and is thought of as distinctively Salasacan as against the constant assault via transistor radios, 45-rpm records, and now even television sets, of popular music from a variety of Ecuadorian, Latin American, and even foreign sources. Nevertheless, it must be stressed that Salasacans today do make use of this material in their music-making with *hojas de capulí*. At the same time, older members of the community bewail the fact that with the proliferation of radios and record players, the performance of leaf-music is much less common than in former years. There is no gainsaying, however, that leaf-music is still a well-known if not actively practiced tradition. Virtually every adolescent has heard leaf-music and is familiar with it, and most boys in their mid-teens have a least attempted, often with little success, to learn this rather difficult art.

Figure 1. *Pingullo* and Drum.

Figure 2. Salasacan *Danzante* with Flute and Drum Ensemble.

Figure 3. Mestizo Band in Fiesta Procession.

Musical Analysis

Following is an analysis of five *tonos* or *tonadas*, played on *hojas de capulí*, recorded by Casagrande in Salasaca in 1968.[6] The style of these performances is consistent with others we have heard, and, according to judgments obtained from Salasacan musicians, is representative of traditional practice. However, while some informants did comment on the antiquity of the pieces themselves, their origin has not been determined. In fact, it is certain that at least some of these pieces are not peculiar to Salasaca, but are widely known in the Ecuadorian highlands. Furthermore, it is quite possible that any or all of them are not traditional in origin, but rather popular compositions based on traditional highland styles; this is indeed suggested by internal evidence, and also by the pieces' very titles: "Indio Ecuatoriano," "Cosecha de Cebada," "Taita Salasaca," "Empeñando Sombredito," and "Imbabura de Mi Vida." As we have noted, Salasacan players of *hojas de capulí* commonly make use of music of extra-local origin in their performances, and commercial recordings of popular music and of traditional highland music in folkloristic renderings by professional musicians, are available to them in the radio broadcasts that have become an important part of life in Salasaca. The performances examined here very well may be adaptations of this kind of material.

The *hoja de capulí* (Fig. 4) becomes a musical instrument and is played roughly as follows. A leaf of suitable size, perhaps 11 to 15 centimeters long and 3 to 4 centimeters wide, is picked and then folded longitudinally, not along the central spine but close to one edge, roughly 1 centimeter from fold to edge at the widest point. The leaf is placed against the mouth, fold inward, with the narrower side above and pressed against the upper lip. The musician then blows, air escaping through a channel between upper lip and leaf, causing a section of the leaf to vibrate and thus produce a sustained tone (Fig. 5). Many musicians stretch the leaf against the mouth with the fingers of one hand, but the more accomplished among them are able to play the instrument with the mouth alone. Once the technique of sound production is mastered, it is a relatively simple matter to alter pitch with small adjustments of the lips and within the oral cavity. Controlling pitch, however, is something else again, and demands considerable proficiency.[7]

The *hoja de capulí* produces a high, clear, loud tone, and the skilled musician, as evidenced by the recording analyzed here, is capable of truly virtuosic performance with the instrument. Pitches can be changed quickly and with precision, with a range of articulation from glissandos to rapid staccato sequences. Dynamic variety is limited, but does occur. The most immediately striking feature of these performances, however, is their high tessitura, overall exhibiting a range from about *b'* to *b'''*. While the typical range for an individual performer in these pieces is approximately an 11th, a player in one piece has to negotiate the range of a minor 13th, from *b'* to *g'''*.

The performances to be examined are duets, played by two musicians with *hojas de capulí*. These duets are polyphonic, generally with a clear division of roles between an upper,

---

[6] *Tono* and *tonada* are both terms used by Salasacan musicians in reference to these pieces. They are terms with various meanings in Ecuador and elsewhere in Latin America, but they are often used, as they would seem to be here, as general designations for pieces of instrumental music, and for the music or melody, as opposed to the text, of vocal genres as well. See Carvalho Neto (1964:399).

[7] A similar technique seems to be involved in the playing of instruments made from the inner bark of birch trees described by Schrammek (1961), and it is likely to be that employed in the playing of tree leaves in other European practices as well.

dominant melody, and a lower, subordinate accompaniment. Duet performance with *hojas de capulí* is well established in Salasaca, but it is only one of several practices. Solo performance with leaves and other melodic instruments, often with percussion accompaniment, is also characteristic, but performances for large mixed ensembles of leaves, flutes, and drums have also been described there. We have collected solo versions of some of the performances analyzed below, and they agree in essential detail with the melodies of these duets. The accompanying part, of course, adds a dimension lacking in the solo performances, and may also shed light on musical conceptions relevant to performance of the melodies themselves.

Generally, these performances are quite homogeneous in style, and common to them is a set of distinctive features that is shared among many Andean musical traditions. These features are by far most familiar in music from the highlands of Peru, but they are much more widely characteristic, found in music of the Andes from Columbia through Bolivia, to northern Argentina and Chile.

"Indio Ecuatoriano" (transcribed below as Ex. 1) is the simplest in structure of the five pieces, but is otherwise representative. For the sake of clarity, the transcription omits some details, particularly of a rhythmic nature, not essential to the analysis that follows.

Figure 4. *Hojas de capulí.*

Figure 5. Musician with *hoja de capulí.*

In all of the performances, the regular metric organization is firmly established and maintained throughout except, typically, at final cadences, and in some examples at important structural divisions. Four of the five pieces exhibit the basic ternary rhythm of "Indio Ecuatoriano," in 3/8 or 6/8, with a range of tempo from ♩. = 58, roughly, in "Indio Ecuatoriano," to ♩. = 90 in "Taita Salasaca" (Ex. 7). The fifth piece, "Empeñando Sombredito," is particularly lively and somewhat different in rhythmic organization. Transcribed below in 3/4 (Ex. 8), it displays constant eighth-note activity, with ♩ = 162.

Example 1. "Indio Ecuatoriano."

The organization of phrases (shown above) is also generally characteristic. In fact, not only the repetition of short phrases in pairs, but also the particular binary design exhibited by "Indio Ecuatoriano" is found, albeit irregularly, in all of these pieces. The internal proportions of this periodic structure vary considerably, with the contrast in the second half sometimes limited to a few opening notes (see the opening period of "Imbabura de Mi Vida," Ex. 9). Both the general and specific organizational features described here are found in other music of the Ecuadorian highlands, and in Andean traditions elsewhere as well.[8]

In the performance of "Indio Ecuatoriano" the opening period is simply repeated, stated six times altogether. Almost throughout, the upper part is repeated with little variation. Variation in the lower part is somewhat more substantial, as the beginning of the third statement of the binary period (Ex. 2) illustrates. More significant, however, is the cadential change that marks the end of the performance (Ex. 3):

---

[8] These characteristics, along with melodic features yet to be described, are exhibited in much of the material transcribed in the publications of the Ecuadorian musicologist Segundo Luis Moreno (1930, 1949, 1957, 1972); see also the "Apendice Musical" in Costales Samaniego and Peñaherrera de Costales (1968: 447-96). Raoul and Marguerite d'Harcourt's study (1925) contains music with similar characteristics from Peru and Bolivia as well as Ecuador; examples of more recent collections of Peruvian material are provided by Holzmann (1966, 1967). Finally, Vega (1944:125-52) contains a general discussion of these characteristics as they are found in the larger Andean region.

Example 2. Excerpt from "Indio Ecuatoriano."

Example 3. Excerpt from "Indio Ecuatoriano."

Phrases with melodies exhibiting the anhemitonic-pentatonic framework so characteristic of Andean styles are predominant in all the performances. However, the presence of a structurally important sixth pitch (F#) in phrase B^a of "Indio Ecuatoriano" and in an identical, harmonically suggestive context in two other pieces ("Cosecha de Cebada," Ex. 6, and "Taita Salasaca," Ex. 7) should be noted, and the same pitch occurs prominently in the lower part of "Indio Ecuatoriano" as well. Further important departures from this pentatonic norm, as will be shown, are found in other performances.

When the basic pitch material of the essentially pentatonic melodies in these pieces is ordered according to their principal cadences, two contrasting arrangements are the result. These correspond to two of the pentatonic modes in Raoul and Marguerite d'Harcourt's pioneering classification of Andean melody, in *La Musique des Incas et ses survivances* (1925:131-54), but it is important to note that apart from the significant differences in cadence, the tonal emphases of the pentatonic passages in all of these pieces are quite similar. The two contrasting scales are given below, in descending form, corresponding to the characteristically descending melodies from which they have been abstracted. In all pieces, principal cadences are found at the bottom of the melodies' overall range. The two scales are represented by two pieces each; the third scale given below, found in one piece, combines elements of both types:

Example 4. "Contrasting Scales Used in Five Pieces."

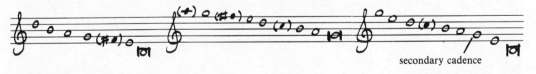

secondary cadence

"Indio Ecuatoriano"   "Empeñando Sombredito"   "Taita Salasaca"
"Cosecha de Cebada"   "Imbabura de Mi Vida"

While melodies with the second scalar configuration are widely found in Andean traditions, the first type, with its distinctive cadential leap down a perfect 4th, in "Indio Ecuatoriano," and the still more distinctive leap of a minor 6th (in the sequence *e ' - g ' - b*), in "Cosecha de Cebada" (Ex. 6) and "Taita Salasaca" (Ex. 7) may be more narrowly Ecuadorian in occurrence. The d'Harcourts (1925:137) observed that this scale was "très employé in Équateur," and a large amount of music from the Ecuadorian highlands, collected in this source as well as elsewhere, exhibits this cadence along with other features found in the performances for *hojas de capulí*.

The following example, found in Moreno (1972:184), is typical. This piece, from the Province of Azuay, south of Salasaca, is an example of a *danzante*, a musical genre associated with dancers known by the same name who are an important institution in the ceremonial life of many communities in highland Ecuador, including Salasaca itself.[9] The fact that, along with other characteristics, *danzantes* also share the ternary meter of these duets, although they are typically faster in tempo, is worthy of note. (To facilitate comparison, the example is transcribed a minor 3rd below the original):

Example 5. A *Danzante*.

The lower part in these duets plays an accompanimental role. At the beginnings of pieces, and at internal structural divisions, its entrance seems to be cued by the upper part, it is briefly tacet in several passages, and is generally less active. There is, however, more variation in recurring passages in the lower part, and often evidence of uncertainty of pitch. While this may indicate a technical or musical deficiency, it also suggests that the musical responsibilities of this performer are less strictly or concretely defined than those of the performer of the melodies themselves.

Nevertheless, there are regularities in the accompanying part. The fact that, with some exceptions, the lower part essentially shares the pentatonic orientation of the principal melodic lines themselves is significant. At the same time, however, while there is a good amount of independent melodic activity in the lower part, its movement is also rather clearly dictated by harmonic considerations. This is indicated by the general predilection for pitches a 3rd below stressed pitches in the upper part, but it is also manifest in an especially striking characteristic, namely the primary and secondary emphases on E and G, respectively, quite consistently in triadic configurations with pitches in the melodic line, in the accompanying parts of all performances.

There are other features of these performances with harmonic implications; we have noted the F# in the suggestive sequence D-F#-A in "Indio Ecuatoriano," and more harmonically provocative passages in other pieces remain to be illustrated. But it is the accompanimental stress on G and E that is most pervasive and least ambiguous, and this is a harmonic characteristic that links these pieces with a widespread practice, one found in popular music based on Andean styles but also in many traditional contexts as well: the performance of melodies similar to those seen here, pentatonic in framework, and bimodal in effect with a

---

[9] Several other examples of *danzantes* are found in Moreno's various publications. Discussions of the *danzante* — as dancer and as music — are found in Carvalho Neto (1964:183-86), and in Costales Samaniego and Peñaherrera de Costales (1968:161-77). For *danzantes* in Salasaca, see Costales Samaniego and Peñaherrera de Costales (1959:88-108), Scheller (1972), Carrasco A. (1982).

constant oscillation between tonal centers a minor 3rd apart, and with harmonizations dominated by movement between the two triads, one major and the other minor, constructed on these two scale degrees.[10]

However, it is one thing to indicate the existence of such phenomena, but quite another to determine their significance, and the nature and dimensions of the harmonic conceptions upon which these performances depend are not at all clear. In this regard, it should be noted that while the violin has been adopted in Salasaca, harps, guitars, and other instruments of European derivation with chordal capability are not to this day characteristic of local musical life. Compounding the difficulty for understanding not only harmony but other aspects of these performances as well, is the question of their sources. As we have noted, they are quite likely to be adaptations of music of extra-local origin. It is best to regard these performances as composites, reflecting traditional Salasacan musical conceptions along with others of diverse and uncertain origin, mingled in ways that make them extremely difficult to disentangle.

These are problems that should be borne in mind through the course of the following brief discussion of the remaining pieces. All of these pieces are multisectional and, most important, display a complexity of tonal organization not found in "Indio Ecuatoriano."

"Cosecha de Cebada" (Ex. 6) is a case in point. It begins with a binary period, AAB^{a}B^a, that is, in effect, an expanded version of "Indio Ecuatoriano." It then continues, however, with a contrasting structural unit, and ultimately exhibits the overall ternary scheme: AAB^{a}B^a C AAB^{a}B^a. The transcription shows each of these sections; A and B^a are given as they are performed at their first appearance and it is to be understood that they vary somewhat as they are repeated.[11]

Section C in "Cosecha de Cebada" is of particular interest. It is based on a single figure, outlining an E-minor triad, and its melody concludes dramatically on the highest pitch of the piece's entire range. Not only does section C contrast in tonal emphasis with the rest of the piece; it is different in its essential character, seemingly unstable and unable to stand alone, without the balance or closure of the binary period that precedes and follows it. It is therefore the apparent functional differentiation of the structural elements of "Cosecha de Cebada," rather than the ternary form itself, that makes it a significantly more complex piece than "Indio Ecuatoriano."

The remaining pieces exhibit still greater structural complexity. "Taita Salasaca" begins with a binary period (AAB^{a}B^a) as in "Indio Ecuatoriano" and "Cosecha de Cebada." This is followed by a contrasting section (C), like that of "Cosecha," based on a single triadic figure; here, the triad outlined is B minor rather than E minor, marking a significant harmonic departure from the opening section. Furthermore, this contrasting section is transitional in function, leading to a third section, a period of slightly different structure than we have seen thus far (DD'). Finally, this section in turn is followed by a restatement of the opening material, at the beginning slightly but significantly varied. The overall ternary scheme can be diagrammed as follows, with section C enclosed in parentheses to indicate its transitional

---

[10] The bimodality so often characteristic of Andean melody has been noted by several commentators; discussions that include some attention to harmony as well can be found in Sas (1935), Vega (1944:156-64, 170-75), Aretz (1952:30-38), and Pagaza Galdo (1961:77-85). It is unfortunate that polyphonic and harmonic aspects of these musical styles, in view of their importance to the practice of many of these traditions today, have been given so little serious attention. These are subjects given only cursory examination by Moreno, in but one of his major studies of the music of highland Ecuador (1930:203-10).

[11] The final cadence of "Cosecha de Cebada," not shown in the transcription, is identical to that of "Indio Ecuatoriano."

Example 6. "Cosecha de Cebada."

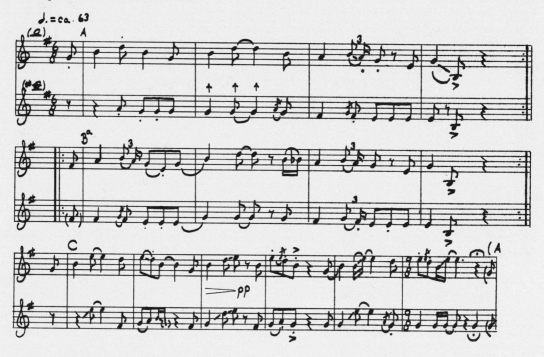

function: AAB^aB^{a′} (C) DD′ A′AB^aB^a. The entire structure, with some variation in its pattern of repetitions and recurrences, is stated three times.

(There are a number of points to be made concerning the following transcription. First, the rhythm of the opening three-note figure, which appears throughout "Taita Salasaca," actually varies considerably, often with pronounced stress on the second note, and closer to ♪♪♪ or even ♫♩ than to the equal eighth notes of the transcription. Second, the section chromaticism of the lower part in section DD′ is misleading. These pitches may reflect indecision on the performer's part. The passage is performed differently at each recurrence, until, for the final statement of DD′, the pitch *g′* is simply repeated to accompany the entire passage. Third, it might be noted that the "Lydian" scale segment in the melody of this section is reflective of a widespread Andean tendency, one noted by the d'Harcourts (1925:143-45) and several later researchers.)

"Empeñando Sombredito" (Ex. 8) is structurally similar to "Taita Salasaca" (Ex. 7), but still somewhat more complex. As in "Taita Salasaca" (and "Cosecha de Cebada"), a passage static in harmony, a reiterated figure outlining a single (E minor) triad, follows an opening binary period (AAB^aB^a). Interestingly, however, "Empeñando" then continues with a restatement of phrases from the opening period, transposed up a perfect 4th (A⁴A⁴), followed in turn by a restatement of B^aB^a at the original tonal level.[12] The resulting scheme is a kind

---

[12] It is of some interest that while the melody of phrases A⁴A⁴ is for the most part a note-for-note transposition of phrases AA, the accompaniment differs in one respect, harmonizing with the pitch *e″* where a literal transposition would call for *f″* (see measures 3 and 7 in sections AA and A⁴A⁴ in the transcription). Occasionally, but only occasionally, is the pentatonic scale adhered to in the parallel passage in the opening section, with an accompanying pitch of *b′* instead of *c″* (see section AA, measure 7).

Example 7. "Taita Salasaca."

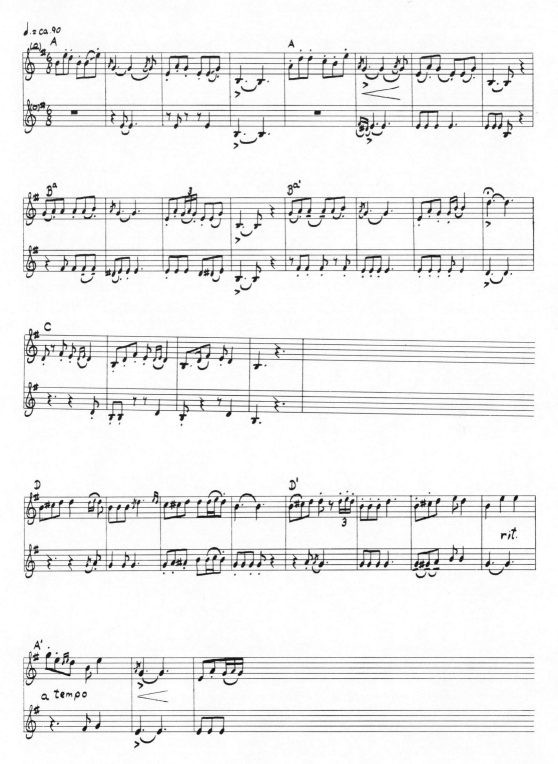

Example 8. "Empeñando Sombredito."

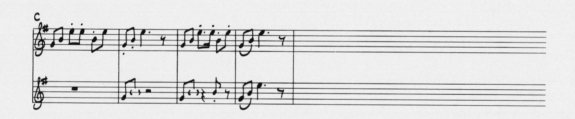

Example 9. "Imbabura de Mi Vida."

of rounded binary form, AAB^{a}B^a (C) A^{4}A^{4}B^{a}B^a, although the entire performance exhibits a considerably more irregular pattern.[13]

AAB^{a}B^a (C) A^{4}A^{4}B^a AB^{a}B^a (C) A^{4}A^{4}B^{a}B^a AA (C) B^{a}B^{a}B^{a}B^a

The last piece, "Imbabura de Mi Vida" (Ex. 9), greatly resembles "Empeñando Sombredito" in structure. As in "Empeñando," an opening period with the characteristic movement between tonal centers a minor 3rd apart is followed by a tonally static passage; here, a single note, e'', is repeated, accompanied by the notes e' and g'. This is followed by contrasting phrases, not transpositions of the opening material, and diatonic rather than pentatonic but tonally centered on C and thus representing a harmonic departure identical to that found in "Empeñando Sombredito." In the continuation, this rounded binary structure, AAB^{a}B^a (C) DE^{d}B^{a}B^a, with less irregularity than that of "Empeñando Sombredito," is stated four times.

Conclusion

These pieces performed by Salasacan musicians with *hojas de capulí* display many characteristics found widely among Andean musical styles: typically descending melodic lines; binary periods made up of short, repeated phrases and phrase segments; the pervasive use of anhemitonic-pentatonic scales; an emphasis on tonal centers separated by a minor 3rd; polyphony in which the 3rd is the favored harmonic interval. Three pieces, with their distinctive cadential leaps of a descending 4th and minor 6th, may represent a more strictly Ecuadorian practice. We have also noted that the moderate to lively triple meter all these pieces display, while by no means an exclusively Ecuadorian characteristic, is commonly found and may be especially important in the traditions of highland Ecuador.[14]

Beyond this, we have tried to indicate something of the structural complexity of these pieces, and especially the structural role that tonal organization and harmony perform in them. These are features that may be reflective, directly or indirectly, of extra-local and perhaps popular influences. Should this be the case, these performances may represent a level of involvement with non-indigenous musical styles, with popular music and commercial media, that must be understood in its totality. The possibility of such a holistic, dynamic perspective raises issues about Andean musical styles that scholarship in the region has thus far largely failed to explore (Béhague 1982). Very similar in style to the performances of *hoja de capulí*, these pieces were performed, interestingly, by a band of European instruments, with trumpet, trombone, saxophone, sarrusophone, clarinet, cymbals, snare drum, and bass drum. In any event, the importance of such bands in the Ecuadorian highlands, and the hiring of these bands in Salasaca in particular, may have stylistic relevance for the performances examined here. The repeated-note passage in "Imbabura de Mi Vida," and the triadic figures that generally pervade these melodies, would suggest such an influence. Also, the performances of military bands would constitute a source, although one among many, for the structural complexity and harmonic features of these performances as well.

---

[13] It must be said that the suggestive alternation of cadential pitches g' and e' in the accompaniment of the opening period is not observed with any consistency in the performance.

[14] Along with the many *danzantes* displaying this rhythmic organization printed in Moreno's publications, special note should be made of *danzante* melodies collected in Lican, and transcribed in Carvalho Neto (1962:26-27).

References Cited

Acosta, J.
1962   *Historia natural y moral de las Indias.* 2nd ed. Mexico: Fondo de Cultura Económica. (Originally published 1590.)

Andersen, Johannes C.
1934   *Maori Music with Its Polynesian Background.* New Plymouth, New Zealand: Thos. Avery. Reprint, New York: AMS Press, 1978.

Aretz, Isabel
1952   *El folklore musical Argentino.* Buenos Aires: Ricordi.

Béhague, Gerard
1982   "Ecuadorian, Peruvian, and Brazilian Ethnomusicology: A General View." *Latin American Music Review* 3/1:17-35.

Carrasco A., Eulalia
1982   *La organización social y el alcalde.* Quito: Mundo Andino.

Carvalho Neto, Paulo de
1962   *Folklore de Licán y Sicalpa: Contribución.* Publicaciones Especiales, no. 1. Quito: Instituto Ecuatoriano de Folklore.

1964   *Diccionario del folklore ecuatoriano.* Quito: Editorial Casa de la Cultura Ecuatoriana.

Coba Andrade, Carlos Alberto G.
1981   *Instrumentos musicales populares registrados en el Ecuador.* Otavalo, Ecuador: Instituto Otavaleño de Antropología.

Costales Samaniego, Alfredo, and Piedad Peñaherrera de Costales
1958   *Yunga Ñan, o historia cultural y social del campesinado de la Provincia de Bolivar.* Llacta, Año III, vols. 5-6.

1959   *Los Salasacas: Investigación y Elaboración.* Llacta, Año IV, vol. 8.

1968   *El quisihuar o el árbol de dios.* Vol. 2. Quito: Instituto Ecuatoriano de Antropología y Geografía.

De Hen, Ferdinand J.
1960   "Beitrag zur Kenntnis der Musikinstrumente aus Belgisch Kongo und Ruanda-Urundi." Inaugural dissertation, Faculty of Philosophy, University of Cologne.

d'Harcourt, Raoul & Marguerite
1925   *La Musique des Incas et ses survivances.* Paris: Paul Geuthner.

Festa, E.
1909   *Nel Darien e Nell'Ecuador: Diario di Viaggio di un Naturalista.* Torino: Unione Tip, Editrice Torinese.

Gade, Daniel W.
1975   *Plants, Man and the Land in the Vilcanota Valley of Peru.* The Hague: W. Junk. (Vol. 6 in the series *Biogeographica*, ed. J. Schmithusen.)

Galpin, Francis W.
1903 "The Whistles and Reed Instruments of the American Indians of the North-West Coast." *Proceedings of the Musical Association*, 29th session, 1902-03, pp. 115-38. London: Novello and Co.

Holzmann, Rodolfo
1966 *Panorama de la música tradicional del Perú.* Lima: Casa Mozart.

1967 *Cancionero Andino Sur.* Lima: Casa Mozart.

Izikowitz, Karl Gustav
1935 *Musical and Other Sound Instruments of the South American Indians.* Göteborg: Elanders.

Moreno, Segundo Luis
1930 "La música en el Ecuador." *El Ecuador en cien años de independencia*, ed. J. Gonzálo Orellana, Tomo II, pp. 187-275. Quito: Imprenta de la Escuela de Artes y Oficios.

1949 *Música y danzas autóctonas del Ecuador.* Quito: Editorial "Fray Jodoco Ricke."

1957 *La música de los Incas.* Quito: Editorial Casa de la Cultura.

1972 *Historia de la música en el Ecuador.* Quito: Casa de la Cultura Ecuatoriana.

Moyle, Richard
1974 "Samoan Musical Instruments." *Ethnomusicology* 18/1:57-74.

Pagaza Galdo, Consuelo
1961 "El Yaraví." *Folklore Americano* 8-9:75-141.

Roberts, Helen H.
1926 *Ancient Hawaiian Music.* Bernice P. Bishop Museum Bulletin, no. 29. Reprint, New York: Dover, 1967.

Sachs, Curt
1928 *Geist und Werden de Musikinstrumente.* Berlin: D. Reimer. Reprint, Hilversum: F. A. M. Knuf, 1965.

1940 *The History of Musical Instruments.* New York: W. W. Norton.

Sas, Andrés
1935 "Ensayo sobre la música Inca." *Boletín Latino-Americano de Música* 1:71-77.

Scheller, Ulf
1972 *El mundo de los Salasacas.* Guayaquil: Fundacion Antropologica Ecuatoriana.

Schrammek, Winfried
1961 "Birkenblattblasen." *Festschrift Heinrich Besseler zum Sechzigsten Geburtstag*, pp. 7-14. Leipzig: Deutscher Verlag für Musik.

Vega, Carlos
1944 *Panorama de la música popular Argentina.* Buenos Aires: Editorial Losada.

Unity of the Arts
in the
Aesthetics of Kpelle Performance

Ruth M. Stone
Indiana University

Scholars of the arts have debated extensively concerning the alleged presence or absence of aesthetic concepts among various world peoples. Since Alan P. Merriam's assertion (1964) that the Basongye of Zaire did not possess an aesthetic that is verbalized in the way that Westerners verbalize about art, others have shown evidence of vocabularies and rules of aesthetic critique. In Africa, these have included two researchers who have worked in the Guinea Coast region of Liberia—Warren L. d'Azevedo (1966) and Robert F. Thompson (1973). The literature provides evidence, then, of people other than Westerners who possess aesthetic value systems and articulate these systems. The intent of the present essay[1] is to articulate elements of the Kpelle system of aesthetics and to emphasize the processual means by which aesthetics are created, sustained, and changed.

The material upon which this discussion is based was researched in the Bong County area of Central Liberia, particularly in the Kwala-wola-lá chiefdom.[2] A fuller discussion of

---

[1] I have worked on several versions of this essay since presenting a draft of it at the annual meeting of the Society for Ethnomusicology in Austin, Texas in 1977. Since that time, I have profited from discussion with students and colleagues and have considerably revised the original text. I would like to acknowledge particularly the comments of the late Alan P. Merriam, Kent Maynard, John Johnson, Judith Hanna, and Verlon Stone. The research for this work was carried out in 1975-76 under a joint doctoral dissertation grant from Fulbright-Hays and the Social Science Research Council. I alone, however, bear the responsibility for the ideas set forth here.

[2] The following summary of Kpelle orthography is adapted from that developed at the Kpelle Literacy Center, Totota, Liberia (Welmers and Spehr 1956):

     ′   high tone; when it appears on the stem of a word, it governs until another tone mark appears.

     `   low tone; when it appears on the stem of a word it governs until another tone mark appears.

     ^   high-low compound tone; high tone on the first syllable, except when the tone mark appears on the last syllable of a word. In that case, the high-low occurs on that single syllable.

  gb   *g* and *b* said together.

  kp   *k* and *p* said together.

  ŋ   as in si*ng*.

  y   *y* and *g* sound somewhat like "ch" in German "ach."

  ɓ   like a *b* but with air going in rather than out when lips are closed (b is the upper case).

  ẹ   as in b*e*t.

  ọ   as in c*au*ght, but shorter.

the musical ethnography has been presented elsewhere (Stone 1982). Briefly, however, the Kpelle constitute a slash-and-burn group of rice cultivators who are increasingly participating in cash crops. The political organization of autonomous chiefdoms and patrilineal descent groups is strongly influenced by the pan-tribal Poro and Sande associations to which most adult men and women respectively belong (Gibbs 1965:199-240).

Performing groups, such as the two I studied intensively, are characterized by a hierarchical arrangement of roles with a performance chief (*pêle-kaloŋ*) presiding over the group and serving as intermediary to other entities. Typical ensembles incorporate singers, dancers, and instrumentalists, the latter playing the master drum (*fêli*) and the supporting drum (*gbùŋ-gbùŋ*).

Data gathering for this study included extensive feedback interviews in which Kpelle people watched videotaped recordings of performances and offered verbal assessment and comment. Largely undirected in the beginning and more directed later on, these interviews were tape-recorded and transcribed prior to analysis. Thus, my conclusions derived in large part from verbalization by Kpelle people about Kpelle artistic communication. Some insights, however, were inferences I have made based on my day-to-day experience of nuances which were never explicitly stated but which form, nevertheless, important underpinnings of Kpelle aesthetics and which I attempted to verify through further questioning and experimentation.

Artistic communication centers in complex events known as *pêle* where a constellation of singing, dancing, speaking, and costume display create focal interaction. Artistic communication is not, however, confined to these delineated times and spaces. Rather, it enters into the most mundane and ordinary situations of everyday life and can occur as a speaker incorporates a proverb to bring home a point to his or her listener. Artistic communication permeates all Kpelle life, only reaching its most concentrated saturation in the locus of *pêle*, the music performance event.

In the course of looking at the aesthetic evaluation of music, I cannot help but be impressed by the interrelation of what many Westerners consider to be separate art forms. Many of the terms utilized to analyze aesthetic elements of music apply equally to verbal and plastic expression. One central and, probably, most basic concept that distinguishes artistic from non-artistic communication is summed up in the term *sâŋ*. Expression with *sâŋ* is artistic; that without it is not. Expression containing *sâŋ* is, first of all, multifaceted in character. Performance of this kind might be termed "thick performance" in an extension of Clifford Geertz's (1973:6-7) term "thick description." This thickness is manifested in various ways in the diverse art forms. In sculpture, the carver exposes a number of planes rather than hewing a single surface. In tie-dyed cloth, the artisan displays ever enlarging concentric circles. In speech, a woman argues to a friend that children cannot be expected to be any different than what they have been taught by their parents, saying,

If you hear a song from that town child's
Ba wule da mẹni taa loloŋ lá, gẹ ni daai

mouth, then it is the song of that town.
tí su wule ká tí.

Literally, the word for proverb in Kpelle is *sâŋ* but, as I am proceeding to show, *sâŋ* is much broader in meaning than a proverb as ordinarily conceived.

In music, sound, timbre and rhythm as well as textual ideas are performed with multiple presentations as the ideal. In response to questioning, one performer commented:

Singing involves many, many *sâŋ* and the meanings are many.
Wule tooǫ ɓa sâŋ tée tée nyaŋ zu-kûlai tamaai.

He referred to multiple sound-patterns with variations, contrasting timbres, and textual proverbs, all presenting various faces of core concepts.

An entire essay could be devoted to the ways multifacetedness is expressed in music performance. A chorus, for example, ideally responds not in unison, singing the same part, but as a group combining many interlocking ostinato parts. At every turn, it seems, elements are fractured and broken up, only to be recombined into the artistic whole to be created. The ideal is to bring maximum diversity into a controlled unitary creation.

In dance, this faceting is particularly striking. Dancers segment their movement patterns—dancing a short time, pausing, dancing again, pausing, and dancing yet again. The audience expects such segmenting and delights in it. Each part may be only slightly varied from the earlier. Differences, however, are noted and admired.

The faceted interaction should be contrasted, not only to non-artistic and ordinary interaction but also to ritual communication, both of which are more continuous and less variable. Thus a dancer in the *kǫli-gón-són* event which exhibits ritual elements is expressly forbidden from segmenting dance in the way that is so admired in ordinary events. None of the movements to mark the pauses is evident, and the dance continues uninterrupted until the dancer simply departs from the dance arena.

The Kpelle ideal in terms of faceting can be summed up by a performer's comment:

We take one Kpelle word [in performance] and keep turning,
Kwá Kpęlę-woo tǫnǫ siye, kú bène péne,

turning it, as many as five times.
e seri lǫ́ǫlu.

In this case the choice of five times is merely to indicate numerous times.

A very clear example of how such faceting denotes aesthetically pleasing or displeasing communication occurred in a performance by an epic storyteller-singer. He included in his rendition of the Wǫi epic a particular episode wherein the central character and culture hero, Wǫi, banishes one of his wives for being unfaithful. Wǫi moves her to the edge of the village where, at the fork of the road, she must use her voice to carve bowls for her male clients. When a man comes to get a bowl, her magical voice is full of *sâŋ* as the multifaceted sound patterns depict the variegated strokes of her work. Each word indicates through onomatopoeia the different sounds.

Large inside, large, large, large.
Bóŋkai kpolôŋ, kpolôŋ, kpolôŋ, kpolôŋ.

Large, large, large, large, flat.
Kpolôŋ, kpolôŋ, kpolôŋ, kpolôŋ, fę́ę-laa.

Small, small, shiny black, shiny black, flat.   (7 times)
Kóro, kóro, mǫ̀nǫ, mǫ̀nǫ, fę́ę-laa.

Small, small, bowl inside.
Kóro, kóro, kalû bóŋkai.

Bowl shiny black, shiny black.
Kalû mònǫ, mònǫ.

As payment for the bowls, the male clients go to bed with Wọi's wife and the sound is then portrayed by the storyteller:

A vikiŋ, a vikiŋ, a vikiŋ, a vikiŋ.

Later a woman client appears and Wọi's wife shows her obvious distaste of carving for a female. She uses only one word to depict the carving sound, omitting *sâŋ* in marked contrast to her work for the male clientele:

Ugly, ugly, ugly, ugly, ugly, ugly,
Kpíti, kpíti, kpíti, kpíti, kpíti, kpíti,

Ugly, bowl, ugly.
Kpíti, kalû, kpíti [Stone 1982:62].

The audience reinforces such an interpretation by laughing aloud at the way this latter example of carving is executed. The opposition of the two performances with *sâŋ* present in the former and absent in the latter is very clear to the participants. The highlighting of such an opposition becomes the pivot for humor in this case.

In addition to the quality of multifacetedness, communication with *sâŋ* exhibits, according to Kpelle consideration, the characteristic of being subject to multiple interpretations. That is, people do not maintain that a single explanation is the proper one. Rather, in the case of a verbal *sâŋ* or proverb, conversations ensue as individuals delight in debating the many possible meanings. One such phrase that a number of singers use is,

I am a swaying thing,
ŋá kẹ́ a duŋ-kpúŋ-tàŋ-kpaŋ,

If I strike a tree its dew doesn't fall,
ŋa sòǫ wúru ma nẹŋ fá pú,

If a tree strikes me my dew falls.
Wúru a sòǫ mâ nẹŋ kẹ́ lí a pú [Stone 1982:73].

Audiences may argue as to whether the individual depicted as swaying is weak-willed, lazy, or impulsive. They may also speculate about particular people they know who may be referred to by the singer.

Communication in performances frequently involves allusion by singers, drummers, or others to performance names, *pêle-laa*, many of which embody *sâŋ* and are subject to multiple interpretations. Soloists particularly insert these names, manipulating them to enhance or degrade the status of participants. Performance names of one well-known male singer included Leŋ-kpei-tuna (False-rain), Kpǫlǫ-mú-tumu (Snake-of-the-thicket), and Mǫ́yiŋpẹlẹẹ-kolo (Insect-of-the-small-rice). The exact qualities that each name implies often spark lively discussion.

While the quality of *sâŋ* implies multifacetedness and multiple interpretation, it also implies subtleness and indirectness of communication. For example, a singer may describe sadness through an extended image such as the following:

> Our fellow young women, I raised my eyes to the sky,
> *Kú ɓarâa kpèla-pẹ̀lẹẹ, ŋá ŋei tẹ́*
>
> I lowered them.
> *ŋelei sú, ŋá nyèŋ.*
>
> My tears fell *gata-gata* like corn
> *Ŋẹi yá è pù gata-gata yệ gbài-*
>
> from an old corn farm.
> *kpàŋ-sú-gbài* [Stone 1982:61].

Here teardrops are metaphorically depicted as corn kernels falling from the ears in a deserted field. Layering elusive images serves to enrich the possible connotations. In another example, a singer performs the phrase,

> Come cut the log in the road so that I may pass.
> *Pá i perei kọọi tee ŋa tẹẹ.*

The singer is not literally requesting a tree to be cut, but rather is hinting that a token gift of liquor or other substance is required for the performance to proceed with full vigor.

Indirectness may take another form as one observes the process of communication or the creation of *sâŋ* through time. Participants employ intermediaries to create artistic communication. They layer through time the people who are part of the communication process. For example, an audience member who makes a speech evaluating the performance speaks and the master of ceremonies (*posîa*) repeats and relays the speech, phrase by phrase. While such repetition is unnecessary for basic understanding, the relaying enhances the aesthetic status of the communication.

A man may also pay a token gift to a singer so that she will insert a secret name of his lover into her song. As such, the mention of the name in the song will form communication with the lover, carried out through the agent of the singer. Such relay carries high aesthetic value.

The creation of communication that carries the quality of *sâŋ* cannot be examined as a whole without specific attention to the factor of time. *Sâŋ* is not simply an object to be identified and labeled without reference to the process by which it is structured by people. As Anthony Giddens (1979:3) admonishes, " . . . we must grasp the time-space relations inherent in the constitution of all social interaction." The very flow of interaction that leads to the creation of *sâŋ* is essential to its definition. If we take the singer who requests that the "log be cut" so that the performance can proceed, the understanding of the sequence of events leading to the particular phrase is essential. If this request for a pause is sung at an improper time, the creation of *sâŋ* is not accomplished in the same way it would be if the performance had proceeded far enough for the patron to evaluate properly the quality of the singer and the audience's support of that person. Timing is of the essence to the very being of *sâŋ*. We cannot understand the meaning of the phrase without knowing something of the time context in which it is executed.

At one performance I attended, the playing had just begun and musicians were still adjusting their parts one to another when a member of the audience stepped forward and asked the *posîa* (master of ceremonies) to stop the music so that he might offer a speech. The speech would have contained the quality of *sâŋ* and been, in verbal terms, a performance much like the music was a performance. The master of ceremonies declined, however, explaining to the would-be speaker, "*Goo káa ma*" (It is pregnant). In others words, the performance was at a critical point and should not be disturbed. The speaker's timing had proved incorrect. In this case, the *posîa*'s comment could not be properly understood or interpreted without reference to the temporal dimension of the interaction. Examined outside of the time dimension, the situation would be rendered rather meaningless. Many performers demonstrate artistic flair by capitalizing on the proper moment for performance saturated with *sâŋ*. Those who attain renown as gifted dancers, orators, master drummers, or solo singers all know how to synchronize the performance of *sâŋ* with other streams of interaction. They know when to insert *sâŋ* for the maximum effect and appreciation. For *sâŋ* is only meaningful in context and the context changes from moment to moment in a complex performance event. Split-second timing becomes essential.

Not all participants are equally entitled to communicate *sâŋ*. Those entitled to employ and manipulate *sâŋ* are the high status performers, balanced by the other performers. The vocal soloist (*wule-tóo-nuu*), for example, is entitled and expected to create *sâŋ* and is balanced by his or her counterpart, the supporting soloist (*tomo-soŋ-nûu*) who performs little that is considered *sâŋ*. This part-counterpart relationship is analogous to that of the master drummer (*fẹli-yale-nuu*) and the supporting drummer (*gbùŋ-gbùŋ-tua-nûu*). The master drummer employs *sâŋ* against a continuous non-*sâŋ* pattern of the *gbùŋ-gbùŋ* (two-headed, stick-beaten, cylindrical drum).

From a broader perspective this also holds true for the chorus which, in relation to the other participants, serves as the counterpart. Simultaneously, however, the chorus is internally constituted with its own internal part-counterpart relationship. Within the chorus are the *mûu-siye-ɓelai* (owl-raising-people). These individuals perform *sâŋ* in counterpart to the non-*sâŋ* of the rest of the chorus. In this case, the patterns are ostinato patterns. They are seldom heard at the beginning of an event but proliferate as the interaction achieves synchrony and meshes.

In summary, the Kpelle aesthetic as embodied in a system of *sâŋ* applies to plastic as well as oral arts. It centers on the manipulation of interaction to create multifaceted, multi-interpretable, and subtly indirect communication. *Sâŋ* may be evident in everyday life, but reaches saturation in performance events where it is much more dense and layered. The hierarchical concept of social organization that prevails influences the artistic creation since certain individuals are given greater license in its creation. These are the solo performers who achieve high status within the event, whether or not the status transfers into everyday social relations. What d'Azevedo (1973:149) has said of the Gola woodcarver can be reiterated for the Kpelle artisan: "He is, to a considerable extent, the conscious recreator of his own status; for he manipulates the symbolic content of his role through the continual reenactment of the private drama of spiritual guidance." While individual creativity is exhibited in the creation of *saŋ*, this must be contrasted to that which is either mundane or ritual. The mundane is unadorned, and ritual must be continuous as well as communal in key features. *Sâŋ* presents an alternative to the eternal and exists, therefore, in delicate balance to it.

References Cited

d'Azevedo, Warren L.
  1966   *The Artist Archetype in Gola Culture.* Reno: University of Nevada.

  1973   "Mask Makers and Myth in Western Liberia." *Primitive Art and Society*, ed. Anthony Forge, pp. 512-38. London: Oxford University Press.

Geertz, Clifford
  1973   *The Interpretation of Cultures.* New York: Basic Books.

Gibbs, James L., Jr.
  1965   "The Kpelle of Liberia." *Peoples of Africa*, ed. James L. Gibbs, Jr., pp. 199-240. New York: Holt, Rinehart and Winston.

Giddens, Anthony
  1979   *Central Problems in Social Theory.* Berkeley: University of California Press.

Merriam, Alan P.
  1964   *The Anthropology of Music.* Evanston: Northwestern University Press.

Stone, Ruth M.
  1982   *Let the Inside Be Sweet: The Interpretation of Music Event among the Kpelle of Liberia.* Bloomington: Indiana University Press.

Thompson, Robert F.
  1973   "Yoruba Artistic Criticism." *The Traditional Artist in African Societies*, ed. Warren L. d'Azevedo, pp. 19-61. Bloomington: Indiana University Press.

Welmers, William E., and Otto Spehr
  1956   *Spoken Kpelle.* Totota, Liberia: Kpelle Literacy Center.

Crossing the Sensory Domains
in
Native American Aesthetics

Barbara Tedlock
Tufts University

Within the extant literature on Native American plastic and performing arts there exists a small but growing subfield known as ethnoaesthetics which attempts to interpret the artistry and aesthetics of a people from an "inside" perspective.[1] To date, this inherently interdisciplinary field includes ethnographic semiotics, performance approaches, reenactment, and indigenous statements concerning the creation, experience, and criticism of the arts. The pioneering texts in this field were single genre studies, with the earliest work concerning the plastic rather than the performing arts. Two outstanding examples from this period include Ruth Bunzel's monograph (1929) on Pueblo pottery and Lila O'Neale's (1932) on Yurok-Karok basketry. The first discussion of the ethnoaesthetics of a performing art appeared twenty years later in David McAllester's monographs on Navajo (1954) and Apache (1960) song. Recent notable works on the ethnoaesthetics of single genres within Native American plastic and performing arts include Nelson Graburn's (1972, 1976) work on Eskimo soapstone sculptures, in which he carefully documents and compares the aesthetic judgments of the native connoisseur with those of the non-native connoisseur; Charlotte Frisbie's (1967) discussion of Navajo perceptions of beauty in songs of the girl's puberty ceremony; Joann Kealiinohomoku's (1967) article on the aesthetics of Hopi dance; Claire Farrer's (1979b) paper on Mescalero Apache body-painting; and Leanne Hinton's (1980) chapter on the aesthetics of Havasupai voice quality and sung vocables.

Although Native American artists have not limited their own artistic activities to a single sensory dimension, the scholars who have studied these arts have usually focused on either the visual or the musical arts.[2] This unfortunate scholarly tendency reflects European and American cultural patterns, including university specialization, rather than native reality. Three happy exceptions to this tendency in art scholarship are Dina and Joel Sherzer's (1976) work with the Kuna of Panama, and Gary Witherspoon's (1977) and David and Susan

---

[1] For brief reviews of the field of ethnoaesthetics see Dark 1967, Farrer 1979a, and Silver 1979. The majority of the ethnographic work within the field has been produced by researchers working in African and Afro-American plastic and performing arts. Some excellent studies in this area include d'Azevedo 1958, 1973; Schneider 1956, 1966; Sieber 1971; Bohannan 1961; Thompson 1966, 1973, 1974; Armstrong 1971, 1975, 1981; Fernandez 1971; Kaeppler 1971, 1978; Chernoff 1979; Memel-Fote 1968; Warren and Andrews 1977; Price and Price 1980; Vogel 1980.

[2] Even such an excellent scholar as Bill Holm, who has specifically mentioned in print that the most skillful Kwakiutl carvers are the best dancers and song composers (1965:93) has, so far, failed to bring a similar balance into his own scholarly publication on Kwakiutl arts.

McAllester's (1980) with the Navajo of Arizona. In all cases they displayed the contrast and interplay between the spatial and temporal communicative streams within Native American traditions. The Sherzers viewed Kuna *molas* (sewn appliqué shirts and blouses) from a semiotic perspective within the social and cultural context as parts of clothing, ritual, ethnic, economic, and artistic systems. They then compared the *molas* (a woman's art form), with formal oratory (a man's art form) finding that verbal art in Kuna culture is in the realm of deep meaning, expressing the basic themes and problems of Kuna life including religion, history, magic, and social control, while visual art is superficial and decorative, involving no deep meaning or need for interpretation or explanation.

In a more ambitious ethnographic semiotics, Witherspoon (1977) analyzed Navajo sandpainting, jewelry, songs, textiles, language, intellectual style, and behavior, finding that the dominant theme or pattern of Navajo aesthetics is based on the single underlying principle of dynamic symmetry. David and Susan McAllester's (1980) recent contribution to the field of ethnoaesthetics is a dual act of reenactment of the Navajo aesthetic. In this sometimes misunderstood (Liffman 1981), genre-breaking book, the McAllesters both document the degree to which their own ears and eyes have been modified by their many years of contact with Navajo culture, and force the hearer/looker to experience their understanding of that culture. Here the Navajo aesthetic, which Witherspoon so elegantly analyzed, is recreated by acts of restrained translation combined with a startling array of traditional and unconventional ethnographic photographs. David McAllester, by keeping the original Navajo word order in English, an order he says is "one of the linguistic clues to Navajo thinking" (1980:17), forces the English reader who expects smooth literary translations to slow down and puzzle out these syntactically awkward house-blessing texts. Likewise, Susan McAllester, through her startling juxtaposition of photographs which portray with equal reverence Navajo traditionalism and Navajo acculturation, shocks and slows down the viewer who desires either social commentary on Navajo poverty or else romantic pictures of strictly traditional hogans. Her forceful visual demand is simply for direct visual experience of Navajoness without value judgments. Through these dual acts of ethnographic realism, an unusual eye/ear rhythm is set in motion that demands synaesthetic thinking on the part of the hearer/looker.

My own research in ethnoaesthetics, which took years to reach the level of synaesthetic understanding, began within the more traditional single-genre paradigm as a study of Zuni kachina (ancestor deity) songs, with special attention to the processes of composition, editing, rehearsal, performance, cueing, aesthetics, and criticism.[3] Zuni Pueblo, which is located in western New Mexico, currently has a population of approximately 7000 people. The inhabitants, who are all Zuni speakers, are well known for their remarkable silver and turquoise jewelry and their Sha'lako ceremony at which kachinas bless six to eight new homes in the village each year.[4] The reporting and analysis of my musical work at Zuni, which was based on 48 hours of taped formal interviews concerning 116 taped kachina songs and many hours of participant-observation at Zuni, was the basis of my M.A. thesis at Wesleyan University (Tedlock 1973). None of the song tapes used in this analysis were single-voice, out-of-

[3] My research at Zuni Pueblo was undertaken with the permission of the head of the Zuni civil government, Robert Lewis. Both the fieldwork and the library research involved in producing this essay were supported, on separate occasions, by grants from the National Endowment for the Humanities, the Wenner-Gren Foundation for Anthropological Research, and a Weatherhead Fellowship from the School of American Research. I am most grateful to all of the people and institutions which made this project possible.

[4] Still by far the best description of a Zuni Sha'lako ceremony is Edmund Wilson's (1956:3-48).

context studio performances, but instead were all multivoiced live performances taped by Zuni song composers and performers at Zuni Pueblo between 1966 and 1972. The making, replaying, and discussion of such performance tapes is now common practice at Zuni.

By beginning with the performance of these texts (the singing) rather than with the text itself (the song, including both linguistic and musical notation), I have found that important contextual and metacommunicative issues such as time, place, manner, framing, or keying of the performance, as well as composition, rehearsal, interpretation, and evaluation of the performance, are emphasized. Decentering the song text reveals the emergent quality of performance and allows participants, performers, and audiences to take center stage, both within formal, elaborate, public performances and within the informal, spontaneous, optional performances of everyday life. By 1978, in an advanced seminar at the School of American Research, organized by Charlotte Frisbie (1980) and with David McAllester in attendance, I presented a paper on Zuni Kachina Society singing which focused on this type of performance-centered approach to ethnomusicology (Tedlock 1980). Also by this date I had begun to realize that the other-than-sound qualities of these performances were not a completely separate system but also needed to be taken into account in order to understand even a tiny fraction of Zuni aesthetics.

My first breakthrough in the area of Zuni aesthetics, or more precisely Zuni meta-aesthetics, came when my husband and I traveled with a small group of Zunis to Shongopavi on Second Mesa in order to view the Sio Calako, the Hopi version of the Zuni Shaꞌlako dance.[5] I was stunned when, after what I felt had been a beautiful first set, the Zunis remarked that the dancers' costumes looked old, dirty, even dingy, and that they were disappointed because they could not hear the song lyrics clearly. An elderly Zuni said: "They sing like wind blowing in a cave, they make that mumbling sound [*umumukꞌana*]. You can always pick out a Zuni by the way he sings — he'll have to make it clear — those guys mumble."[6] His wife said she was frightened and wanted to go back to the car. She described the performance to me as *attanni*, "muffled, old, fearful," and contrasted it with kachina costumes and vocal style at Zuni, which she considered *tsoꞌya*, "clear, new, beautiful." It was not until later that I realized that this contrast between *attanni* and *tsoꞌya* was not simply what Francis Hsu (1979:522-23) would call an example of neutral ethnocentrism, but that these two terms were important meta-aesthetic categories that had application within Zuni culture itself. Briefly stated, *tsoꞌya* may be glossed "multicolored, chromatic (in the musical sense), clear, bright, sharp, new, dynamic, varied and beautiful"; while *attanni* may be glossed "powerful, taboo, dark, muffled, shaggy, old, static and fearful."[7] I have arrived at these glosses over several years of discussion and analysis of Zuni visual and auditory data.

---

[5] For early descriptions of the Sio Calako (Zuni Shaꞌlako) at Hopi, see Fewkes 1897 and 1903.

[6] The orthography used for this and other Zuni words and phrases is a practical one in which the vowels (a, e, i, o, u) should be given their continental values; double vowels (aa, ee, ii, oo, uu) should be held longer than single ones; most consonants should be pronounced as in English, except that *p* and *t* are unaspirated, *lh* should be pronounced simultaneously, and *ts* is like the *ts* in English "bats." The glottal stop ꞌ is like the *tt* in the Scottish pronunciation of "bottle." Double consonants (cch, hh, kk, ll, llh, mm, nn, pp, ss, ssh, tt, tts, ww, yyꞌꞌ) are held a bit longer than single ones. Stress is always on the first syllable except where indicated differently.

[7] The Zuni word *attanni* is neither the proper term for the English concept "ugly" — which best translates into Zuni as *yaza* — nor is it the contrary of *tsoꞌya*, which is *kwaꞌ tsoꞌya* or "not multicolored, not clear, not beautiful," and so forth.

In the visual domain of the natural world, Zunis apply the term *tso¹ya* to the rainbow, the last stages of a New Mexico sunset, the collared lizard, the mallard drake, and the Rocky Mountain swallowtail butterfly—each of which has several bright, highly saturated hues. The rainbow, as Zunis see it, consists of the colors red, yellow, and blue-green, which they usually do not allow to blend into one another in their painting of it. Each of these colors is shown as a uniform, highly saturated hue, usually separated from the next hue by a thick black outline or else carefully painted so as not to blend into the neighboring color. Turning to the sunset, the very last stage of certain sunsets is *tso¹ya* when a clearly delimited turquoise suddenly appears among the red, purple, and yellow streaks. The collared lizard is considered *tso¹ya* because of the red and yellow iridescent (*shukkutuliya*) areas outlined in black on the collar of this otherwise totally green lizard. The drake mallard, unlike the female, has an iridescent green head and white collar and outer tail feathers, in addition to sharing with the female a violet speculum or wing patch bordered with black and white. This complex banding, combined with iridescent green, white, and violet, is what marks the male mallard as *tso¹ya*. The female, in contrast, is merely *k¹okshi*, "attractive or good," since she lacks the green head and complex banding of neck and outer tail feathers. The wings of the Rocky Mountain swallowtail butterfly are bordered by a series of yellow spots heavily outlined in black; on the lower wing, the series is paralleled by black-bordered zones of iridescent blue, with the final zone occupied instead by a red spot. By way of contrast, the principal natural referents of the term *attanni* are the crow and the black bear.

Shifting to the auditory domain of the natural world, only those bird calls with a maximally varied tonality are considered *tso¹ya*. Among the seventy-four species of birds which Zunis recognize (Ladd 1963), the great majority of calls are described as *we¹¹acchoy*, "shouting," or *k¹oye*, "crying"; only six birds are said to be able to *tena¹u*, "sing": the western meadowlark, sage thrasher, mockingbird, canyon wren, lark sparrow, and mourning dove. These six birds all have songs which have been described by ornithologists as "continuous," "pleasing," "vibrant," and "varied." The western meadowlark has a "variable song of seven to ten notes, flutelike," also described by naturalists as a "bubbling medley of rich, flutelike phrases" (Wetmore 1964:300). The sage thrasher's song is "a clear, ecstatic warbled phrase, with low trills" (Peterson 1961:227), and the mockingbird's song is "a long continued succession of notes and phrases of great variety" (ibid.: 224). Researchers have described mockingbirds as having the ability to imitate other birds so expertly that only electronic analysis can detect the difference; a mocker can change its tune eighty-seven times in seven minutes and repeat each tune several times. The canyon wren is the star vocalist of the western gorges, with its "wild and lovely song" consisting of "a silvery cascade of descending notes followed by an upward flourish which is so powerful that it can be heard a quarter of a mile away" (Wetmore 1964:320). The lark sparrow ranks among the finest sparrow vocalists; its song is a sweet mingling of rich notes with various trills and buzzes. In the auditory domain, then, the Zuni apply the term *tso¹ya* to bird songs with a succession of clear rich notes and long phrases of great variety, often containing trills, buzzes, and other embellishments. The only bird call Zunis consistently describe as *attanni* is the muffled hoot of the owl.

In the visual domain of the cultural world, *tso¹ya* describes flower bouquets, jewelry, pottery, beadwork, the costumes of the Zuni Olla Maidens, kachina dance costumes, the arrangement of kachinas in the dance line, and the interior decoration of Sha¹lako houses, all of which display a great variety of textures, forms, and colors. Zunis do not apply their term *tso¹ya* to any individual flower—for example a single red rose or even to a bouquet of red roses—but rather to a bouquet of mixed flowers consisting of at least four different species and colors, including white. There is one exception to this rule, which is a mythic flower whose composite head contains individual red, yellow, white, and blue-green petals. This flower is painted on the masks of the Salimopiya kachinas who officiate both at Sha'lako and at the Kachina Society initiation. As one Zuni remarked to Ruth Bunzel back in 1928, "The children do not mind being whipped by the Salimopiya. They are such pretty dancers" (Bunzel 1932:980).

The *tso'ya* visual aesthetic is displayed over and over again within Zuni culture. The costumes of kachinas are multitextured and multicolored; they can include cotton and woolen textiles, hanks of red and green or multicolored yarn, artificial flowers, butterflies, bees, birds, popcorn, chili, feathers, entire duck heads, skins and furs of various animals, evergreen branches, cottonwood sticks, silver and turquoise jewelry, leather and shell bandoliers. Entire dance lines are judged as *tso'ya* at Zuni when the line of forty or more identically costumed dancers includes two or three men who choose to be individualists (*samayashe''a*) and to impersonate other, different kachinas. Whenever this occurs, the dance leader places an individualist asymmetrically in the dance line rather than centering him (cf. Fig. 1, p. 192) and if there is more than one individualist he places one of them unevenly—for example, fifth and twelfth—in line rather than either bunching them together or evenly spacing them along the entire line: "Just so it'll look good." Thus, although the dancers in a particular kachina dance line may not be *tso'ya* when considered individually, the addition of one or more individualists may produce the *tso'ya* evaluation for the line as a whole. A contrasting pattern can be seen in the Nahalisho dance line, which is usually judged as *tso'ya* by Zuni audiences and performers, but this time because each dancer has individually distinct clothing and his mask is painted differently. As one Zuni dancer put it: "They are *tso'ya* because some of the designs are really artistic, including things like deer heads, corn, butterflies, flowers, parrots, the rainbow, pottery designs, and each Nahalisho dresses differently from each other one."

In the Zuni singing groups known as the Olla Maidens (two voluntary associations consisting of approximately ten women each who travel the powwow circuit singing Zuni kachina songs), each woman, like the male Nahalisho kachina dancers, displays the *tso'ya* aesthetic individually in her multilayered, multicolored traditional clothing. No two women dress exactly alike, though each one wears a traditional black manta, white buckskin moccasins and leggings, a red sash, and a large quantity of very expensive turquoise jewelry. Their polyester, rayon, and cotton blouses and capes consist of bright, highly saturated hues of nearly "da-glo" intensity, with shining silk and rayon ribbon trimmings; no two women wear the same blouse, underskirt, or cape. Each woman also balances a water jar (olla) on her head which usually has the traditional deer-and-medallion design (Kenagy 1978). This overall pottery design is judged *tso'ya* by most Zunis because of the deer motif, placed in full profile underneath a Rocky Mountain swallowtail butterfly motif which is represented in straight-on bilateral symmetrical form (cf. Fig. 2, p. 192). Bunzel (1932) found this design element to be a relatively frequent one on Zuni ollas, identified by two separate women in different years as the "deer house" (*na'lan k'yakwenne*), and I have found that it is considered *tso'ya* primarily because the swallowtail butterfly itself is judged *tso'ya*.

In the culturally produced auditory domain, *tso'ya* describes newly composed kachina songs when the text is rich in allegorical meaning, is sung clearly, and when the basically diatonic melody has a stepped construction beginning low and ending high, plus containing short chromatic sequences of semitones. Generally speaking, for an entire song to qualify as *tso'ya* it must contain two very different melodies, one in the verse (A) or "coming out" (*kwayinanne*) section and another in the chorus (B) "talking about" (*shilhnanne*) section of the song. Each of these two melodies has its own tonality, set of tones, and tonal relations; a third melody, known as the "strong part" (*i'ts'umme*) and containing short sequences of

Figure 1. Zuni Mountain Sheep Dance with One Deer Individualist. Painting by Zuni artist Patone Cheyatie, done in 1928. Photograph taken by the author at the School of American Research, Santa Fe.

Figure 2. Zuni Water Jar with the "Deer House," the House consisting of a Rocky Mountain Swallowtail Butterfly. Photograph taken by the author at the School of American Research, Santa Fe.

chromatic runs, is grafted onto the very end of each of the traditional five sections of the song (AABBA). As one Zuni critic and song composer put it:

> The most *tso'ya* part of songs is in the last *kwayinanne* [A]. It's always like that. They sing better on the last *kwayinanne* than on the first one. Well, you'll realize that when they do the last part, just watch the mudheads [clowns who accompany the dancers]. I guess it gets to them, and they start dancing with them [the kachinas], giving the deer cry. They get excited on the last part.

In parallel fashion, the song text should consist of two vastly different levels of meaning which are linked by a particularly striking image or metaphor.

In the visual domain of culture, *attanni* is a quality of the shaggy, dark, matted hair and costumes of ogres, and of crudely naturalistic designs painted on kiva walls as well as on certain types of ceremonial pottery. In auditory culture, the *attanni* aesthetic occurs in traditional songs of the medicine societies (of which there are fourteen), which have relatively simple texts and melodies totally lacking in chromaticism; the sound of rattles blurs the perception of both words and melody. The songs of the medicine societies are typically through-composed in a chain pattern A [*kwayinanne*] B [*shilhnanne*] A B A B A B . . . , contain but one simple melody repeated in A and B, and are lacking altogether in a "strong part" (*i'ts'umme*) or third melody.

The *attanni* aesthetic ultimately belongs to an ancient heritage that Zunis share with Native Americans in general — namely, that of shamanism and specifically bear possession. In fact, Zunis freely recognize the expression of this aesthetic among neighboring peoples; thus it is not a defining feature of their own ethnic self-identity. The *tso'ya* aesthetic, on the other hand, is a crucial identity marker, acting (according to different versions of the creation myth) to mark the separation of the macaw from the raven subclan of the Picchiikwe clan (Stevenson 1904:40); a dual division or moiety system separating Zunis into "summer" and "winter" people (Cushing 1896:385); and to separate Zunis from non-Zunis (Parsons 1923:141; Benedict 1935:1:258; Tedlock 1972:265-66). According to these various creation myths, when the sun's spokesman placed two eggs in a sacred basket of meal and requested the people to choose an egg, they chose the beautiful (*tso'ya*), spotted blue egg rather than the plain or "dull colored" egg. "But, Alas! when the eggs were hatched the raven came from the blue egg and the macaw from the other" (Stevenson 1904:40). A classic modern Zuni comment, on hearing this episode, is, "Well, the Zunis always do like something *tso'ya*." But what the *tso'ya* egg turns out to contain is the raven, and these birds taken by themselves are *attanni*. It would seem that the *tso'ya* aesthetic is indeed capable of containing all the complexities that make up the totality of Zuni culture; within its bright and sharply delineated domain, there can be allowed moments of the dark, fearful, and indistinct.

The *tso'ya* aesthetic, like the *attanni* aesthetic, also has at least one root in the broader Native American world, namely in cosmological systems that symbolize the cardinal points with a succession of different colors. Such systems are less widespread in North America than bear shamanism, but they do exist throughout the Southwest. The points of closest comparison are to be found among certain of the Pueblos, where the colors of the four cardinal directions are brought into direct juxtaposition by designating either the nadir (Hopi) or the zenith (Jemez, Tewa, and Zuni) as "multicolored." The problem as to what is finally distinctive about the Zuni sense of *tso'ya*, as opposed to the polychromatic qualities of the arts of some neighboring pueblos, reaches crisis proportions in the case of the Hopi. Outside observers would say that Zuni art and music are closer to the Hopi than to any other tradition, but the Zunis themselves, as if trying to maintain the boundaries of their own identity, are extremely critical of various aspects of Hopi aesthetics, all the way from Hopi song composition and voice quality, right down to Hopi cooking. Zunis specifically dislike Hopi mixed-meat stews, with many ingredients that have been cooked down into a single blended flavor; they prefer a meal composed of a large variety of relatively simple dishes.

Ruth Benedict, in her controversial study *Patterns of Culture* (1934:52-119), described the Zunis as modest, mild-mannered "Apollonians," while her critics have argued that such a description covers just one side of the Zuni character (Bennett 1946). The height of *tso¹ya* expression comes in the Kachina Society ceremony known as Sha¹lako, which features fabulous public displays of wealth, both in costume and in interior decoration; *attanni* expression reaches its greatest intensity in the private, bare, dimly lit rooms where medicine society members become possessed by the bear. As for Benedict's much repeated contention that Zunis are patient lovers of ritual monotony, I can only point out that neither the variety of *tso¹ya* ritual nor the fearfulness of *attanni* ritual fits her description.

The question as to whether the Zuni *tso¹ya* aesthetic, which is so closely tied to Zuni cultural and social identity, might have a counterpart in Zuni grammar is raised by the classic work of Benjamin Lee Whorf (1956:57-86) on the Hopi and the more recent work of Gary Witherspoon (1977) on the Navajo, in which they both attempt to correlate cultural patterns with the grammatical features of languages. There would seem to be a promising lead in the fact that in addition to simple pluralizing devices, Zuni has no fewer than seventeen different suffixes denoting the diverse ways in which objects may be assembled into larger entities: for example, -*li* "objects in a shallow container," -*limo* "a dispersed collectivity of," -*lhlhi* "objects in a pile on," -*palha* "a wrapped bundle of," -*ppo* "objects in a deep container," -*tta* "a growing collectivity of" (Newman 1958:132-43). But in fact, these suffixes correlate negatively with the *tso¹ya* aesthetic, since they designate assemblages in which all the objects are of the same sort, whereas only assemblages with variety would earn the *tso¹ya* designation. One might be tempted to argue that the *tso¹ya* aesthetic represents a sort of effort to push beyond the limitations implied by Zuni grammatical categories, but this idea will not survive a comparison with the Navajo situation. There, the grammar gives just as much attention to assemblages as does Zuni grammar (Witherspoon 1977:120-40), but polychromaticism does not emerge as a major feature in Navajo cosmology or art (although they have a four color directional system, they do not have the focal points — nadir or zenith — where all colors meet), and I might add that musical chromaticism is also not a feature of Navajo songs (McAllester 1954).

Figure 3. Zuni Sha¹lako House Wall Decoration, with Textiles Hung in Horizontal Rows and a Deer Trophy on a Rampant Buckskin. Photographer, Dennis Tedlock.

Another difference between the Navajo and Zuni aesthetics is that although overall

Zuni designs or compositions may contain symmetrical elements, as in the case of the swallowtail butterfly painted on pottery, that same composition will also contain elements that give a strongly asymmetrical thrust, diagonally or to one side. In the case of the butterfly, the deer beneath it is in side view, moving across the compositional field rather than facing stably forward. In Sha'lako house decorations, textiles hung in horizontal rows are topped with rampant buckskins, folded and placed so as to give a side view, with the deer rearing up on a diagonal and facing toward the altar (cf. Fig. 3). The individualist kachina dancers, as mentioned, are placed off-center in the line of kachinas. And, finally, the parts of the kachina songs are themselves arranged off-center, with the two B sections closer to the end than to the beginning—AABBA rather than ABABA. In other words, spatial asymmetry has its counterpart in temporal asymmetry.

I have offered only an outline of Zuni aesthetics, but I hope I have made it clear that the greatest rewards lie in an approach that crosses sensory domains. The Zunis do so constantly, applying the terms *tso'ya* and *attanni* across arts that academicians have divided among several departments.

References Cited

Armstrong, Robert Plant
  1971   *The Affecting Presence: An Essay in Humanistic Anthropology.* Urbana: University of Illinois Press.
  1975   *Wellspring: On the Myth and Source of Culture.* Berkeley: University of California Press.
  1981   *The Powers of Presence: Consciousness, Myth, and Affecting Presence.* Philadelphia: University of Pennsylvania Press.

Benedict, Ruth
  1934   *Patterns of Culture.* New York: Mentor Books.
  1935   *Zuni Mythology.* New York: Columbia University Press.

Bennett, John W.
  1946   "The Interpretation of Pueblo Culture: A Question of Values." *Southwestern Journal of Anthropology* 2:361-74.

Bohannan, Paul
  1961   "Artist and Critic in an African Society." *The Artist in Tribal Society*, ed. Marian W. Smith, pp. 85-94. London: Routledge and Kegan Paul.

Bunzel, Ruth L.
  1929   *The Pueblo Potter: A Study of Creative Imagination in Primitive Art.* Columbia University Contributions to Anthropology, no. 8. New York: Columbia University Press.
  1932   "Zuñi Katchinas." *47th Annual Report of the Bureau of American Ethnology*, pp. 611-946.

Chernoff, John Miller
  1979   *African Rhythm and African Sensibility: Aesthetics and Social Action in African Musical Idioms.* Chicago: University of Chicago Press.

Cushing, Frank H.
  1896   "Outlines of Zuñi Creation Myths." *13th Annual Report of the Bureau of American Ethnology*, pp. 321-447.

Dark, Philip J. C.
1967   "The Study of Ethno-Aesthetics: The Visual Arts." *Essays on the Verbal and Visual Arts*, ed. June Helm, pp. 131-48. Proceedings (1966) of the American Ethnological Society.

d'Azevedo, Warren L.
1958   "A Structural Approach to Esthetics: Toward a Definition of Art in Anthropology." *American Anthropologist* 60:702-14.

1973   *The Traditional Artist in African Societies.* Bloomington: Indiana University Press.

Farrer, Claire R.
1979a   "Aesthetics and Native North Americans." *Forms of Play of Native North Americans*, ed. Edward Norbeck and Claire R. Farrer, pp. 111-19. Proceedings (1977) of the American Ethnological Society.

1979b   "'It's the Same Thing': Aspects of Mescalero Apache Ethnoaesthetics." Paper presented at the First New Directions in Native American Art Conference, October 24-26, Albuquerque.

Fernandez, James
1971   "Principles of Opposition and Vitality in Fang Aesthetics." *Arts and Aesthetics in Primitive Societies*, ed. Carol Jopling, pp. 356-73. New York: Dutton.

Fewkes, Jesse Walter
1897   "Tusayan Katcinas." *15th Annual Report of the Bureau of American Ethnology*, pp. 245-313.

1903   "Hopi Katcinas." *21st Annual Report of the Bureau of American Ethnology*, pp. 3-126.

Frisbie, Charlotte J.
1967   *Kinaaldá: A Study of the Navaho Girl's Puberty Ceremony.* Middletown: Wesleyan University Press.

1980   *Southwestern Indian Ritual Drama.* A School of American Research Book. Albuquerque: University of New Mexico Press.

Graburn, Nelson H. H.
1972   "A Preliminary Analysis of Symbolism in Eskimo Art and Culture." *Proceedings of the XL International Congress of Americanists* (Rome) 2:165-70. Genoa: Tilgher.

1976   "Eskimo Art: The Eastern Canadian Arctic." *Ethnic and Tourist Arts*, ed. Nelson H. H. Graburn, pp. 39-55. Berkeley: University of California Press.

Hinton, Leanne
1980   "Vocables in Havasupai Song." *Southwestern Indian Ritual Drama*, ed. Charlotte J. Frisbie, pp. 275-305. A School of American Research Book. Albuquerque: University of New Mexico Press.

Holm, Bill
1965   *Northwest Coast Indian Art: An Analysis of Form.* Thomas Burke Memorial Washington State Museum Monograph, no. 1. Seattle: University of Washington Press.

Hsu, Francis L. K.
1979   "The Cultural Problem of the Cultural Anthropologist." *American Anthropologist* 81:517-32.

Kaeppler, Adrienne L.
1971   "Aesthetics of Tongan Dance." *Ethnomusicology* 15:175-85.

1978   "Melody, Drone and Decoration: Underlying Structures and Surface Manifestation in Tongan Art and Society." *Art in Society: Studies in Style, Culture, and Aesthetics*, ed. Michael Greenhalgh and Vincent Megaws, pp. 261-74. New York: St. Martin's Press.

Kealiinohomoku, Joann W.
1967   "Hopi and Polynesian Dance: A Study in Cross-Cultural Comparisons." *Ethnomusicology* 11:343-58.

Kenagy, Susan G.
1978   "Deer-and-Medallion Style Pottery at Zuni Pueblo: Iconography and Iconology." *New Mexico Studies in the Fine Arts* 3:46-52.

Ladd, Edmund J.
1963   "Zuni Ethno-ornithology." M.A. thesis, University of New Mexico, Department of Anthropology.

Liffman, Paul
1981   "Comment on Strong's Review of David P. McAllester's and Susan W. McAllester's *Hogans: Navajo Houses and House Songs*." *Chicago Anthropology Exchange* 14:182-88.

McAllester, David P.
1954   *Enemy Way Music: A Study of Social and Esthetic Values as Seen in Navaho Music*. Papers of the Peabody Museum of American Archaeology and Ethnology, Harvard University, 41/3.

1960   "The Role of Music in Western Apache Culture." *Selected Papers of the Fifth International Congress of Anthropological and Ethnological Sciences*, ed. Anthony F. C. Wallace, pp. 1-9. Philadelphia: University of Pennsylvania Press.

McAllester, David P., and Susan W. McAllester
1980   *Hogans: Navajo Houses and House Songs*. Middletown: Wesleyan University Press.

Memel-Fote, Harris
1968   *The Perception of Beauty in Negro-African Culture*. Colloquium on Negro Art. Paris: Presence Africaine.

Newman, Stanley
1958   *Zuni Dictionary*. Indiana University Research Center in Anthropology, Folklore and Linguistics, Publication 6.

O'Neale, Lila
1932   *Yurok-Karok Basket Weavers*. University of California Publications in American Archaeology and Ethnology, 32/1:1-184. Berkeley: University of California Press.

Parsons, Elsie Clews
1923   "The Origin Myth of Zuni." *Journal of American Folklore* 36:135-62.

Peterson, Roger Tory
1961   *A Field Guide to Western Birds*. 2nd ed. Boston: Houghton Mifflin.

Price, Sally, and Richard Price
1980   *Afro-American Arts of the Suriname Rain Forest*. Berkeley: University of California Press.

Schneider, H. K.
1956   "The Interpretation of Pakot Visual Art." *Man* 56:103-06.

1966   "Turu Esthetic Concepts." *American Anthropologist* 68:156-60.

Sherzer, Dina, and Joel Sherzer
1976   "Mormaknamaloe: The Cuna Mola." *Ritual and Symbol in Native Central America*, ed. Philip Young and James Howe, pp. 23-42. University of Oregon Anthropological Papers, no. 9.

Sieber, Roy
1971   "The Aesthetics of Traditional African Art." *Art and Aesthetics in Primitive Societies*, ed. Carol Jopling, pp. 121-31. New York: Dutton.

Silver, Harry R.
1979   "Ethnoart." *Annual Review of Anthropology*, ed. Bernard J. Siegel, Alan R. Beals, and Stephen A. Tyler, pp. 267-307. Palo Alto, Calif.: Annual Reviews.

Stevenson, Matilda Coxe
1904   *The Zuni Indians: Their Mythology, Esoteric Fraternities, and Ceremonies.* 23rd Annual Report of the Bureau of American Ethnology.

Tedlock, Barbara
1973   "Kachina Dance Songs in Zuni Society: The Role of Esthetics in Social Integration." M.A. thesis, Wesleyan University, Department of Anthropology.

1980   "Songs of the Zuni Kachina Society: Composition, Rehearsal, and Performance." *Southwestern Indian Ritual Drama,* ed. Charlotte J. Frisbie, pp. 7-35. A School of American Research Book. Albuquerque: University of New Mexico Press.

Tedlock, Dennis
1972   *Finding the Center: Narrative Poetry of the Zuni Indians.* New York: Dial Press.

Thompson, Robert Farris
1966   "An Aesthetic of the Cool: West African Dance." *African Forum* 2/2:85-102.

1973   "Yoruba Artistic Criticism." *The Traditional Artist in African Societies*, ed. Warren L. d'Azevedo, pp. 19-61. Bloomington: Indiana University Press.

1974   *African Art in Motion: Icon and Act.* Berkeley: University of California Press.

Vogel, Susan M.
1980   *Beauty in the Eyes of the Baule: Aesthetics and Cultural Values.* Working Papers in the Traditional Arts, no. 6. Philadelphia: Institute for the Study of Human Issues.

Warren, D. M., and J. Kweku Andrews
1977   *An Ethnoscientific Approach to Akan Arts and Aesthetics.* Working Papers in the Traditional Arts, no. 3. Philadelphia: Institute for the Study of Human Issues.

Wetmore, Alexander
1964   *Song and Garden Birds of North America.* Washington: National Geographic Society.

Whorf, Benjamin Lee
1956   "An American Indian Model of the Universe." *Language, Thought, and Reality*, ed. John Carroll, pp. 57-86. Cambridge: M.I.T. Press.

Wilson, Edmund
1956   *Red, Black, Blond, and Olive.* New York: Oxford University Press.

Witherspoon, Gary
1977   *Language and Art in the Navajo Universe.* Ann Arbor: University of Michigan Press.

VI AUTOBIOGRAPHICAL SKETCH
AND BIBLIOGRAPHY

Autobiographical Sketch

David P. McAllester

"How could you get lost in the woods? Where's your Indian blood?"

With such exhortations my mother, Maude Park McAllester, often reminded me and my three older siblings of our somewhat remote Narragansett heritage. We were frequent companions on her field research in natural history which included long family walks in the woods. Especially fascinating was following a fox track in the snow. We learned to read the record of mouse kills, rabbit misses, urinary defiance of squirrels from a tree above, and the wing sweeps of a mobbing by crows. Then there was the thrill of seeing it later in her weekly articles in the *Boston Sunday Herald*. We would be on the lookout for our own remarks that were sometimes included to liven up the column.

Though we grew up and went to the schools in Everett, Massachusetts, a suburb north of Boston, we also got our education in the woods of Saugus, Lynn, Stoneham, and other outlying towns. Our training in the woods was augmented by ocean lore during summers on Cape Cod. In 1923, when I was seven, we began going to the Adirondacks to my aunt's summer camp for her dance students. The natural history walks with my mother continued since she summered there with us and went on with her studies and writing in her own tent back in the woods. In addition there were long horseback excursions into the mountains over abandoned roads. It was a feast of learning about plants and wildlife and I remember sometimes singing our way home by moonlight.

So two dominant themes in my life were established early: nature and Indians. The latter interest was much encouraged by the collected works of Ernest Thompson Seton. I was given the five or six volume Birch Bark Library when I was about twelve, and the teachings of this gifted naturalist-ethnographer are still vivid in my mind. We were an "outdoors" family, and many of the authors we read and talked about reflected this: Bret Harte, James Oliver Curwood, Gene Stratton Porter, James Fenimore Cooper, and Henry David Thoreau. My grandmother and I were confederates in the reading of Edgar Rice Burroughs' Tarzan stories. I also read James Willard Schultz's biographical novels about the Blackfoot Indians and Derick Nussbaum's books about his boyhood at Mesa Verde National Park. S. E. White's *Magic Forest* was my dream for a while. I yearned to sleepwalk into a year of travel with the hunting Indians of the north. But other daydreams carried me into the treetops with Tarzan of the Apes, where I shed the thin veneer of civilization and followed the spoor of adventure and conquest.

My father, Ralph W. McAllester, was a small, somewhat remote man with a delightful streak of gentle humor. He was a doctor, Harvard 1900 and Harvard Medical School 1904.

Figure 1. David P. McAllester, about 1926. Photographer, Wilmot R. Evans.

His passion on our walks was birding; on his vacations, fishing; and in his reading, Russian novels. He engineered a great event in the family, a summerlong western camping trip in 1927. My next brother, Ralph, Jr. and I, thirteen and eleven respectively, were judged too young to go. However, we lived the trip intensely through the steady stream of letters and photographs that came to us from Yellowstone Park, the Grand Canyon, the Hopi Snake Dance, and from pack trips with Indian guides. We heard of adventures like the epic walk by my older brother, Robert, to the bottom of the Grand Canyon and back in one day. My mother sent stirring mementos such as a paper-thin skin from a sidewinder or the ears, preserved in salt, of a jackrabbit found dead in the road. And of course the family brought back pottery, Navajo rugs, and even, from Oraibi, a musical rasp carved in the shape of a snake.

All this intensified my interest in Indians. I had built my first tipi when I was eight and I was reading ethnographies in my early teens. When I was fifteen, a long mystical Indian poem by me appeared in the *Boston Globe* and attracted the attention of a kind reader who presented me with a dozen Bureau of American Ethnology reports that had been part of her husband's library.

When I was eight or nine I began a career as a boy soprano. I sang in the Trinity church choir in Boston and had regular voice lessons with a succession of teachers over the next five or six years. Seton's *Wisdom of the Red Man* contained a selection of songs from Densmore, Fletcher, and Curtis, and I included some of these in my concerts before I had any idea how they should sound. I was also singing the "Indian" songs of Thurlow Lieurance and Charles Wakefield Cadman. When I first heard Plains Indians singing, in a performance in Boston of the 101st Ranch Wild West Show, my reaction was appalled disbelief. I was convinced, though, when I met Chief Crazy Bull as a co-performer on Boston's first television broadcast in the early 1930s. I was in a warbonnet of turkey feathers from the farm of a family friend, and was wearing a velvet shirt with a chamois fringe my sister, Jean, had made for me. Crazy Bull was friendly and resplendant in eagle plumes, buckskin, and beads. He, like the Wild West Indians, sang in that strange, nasal, quavering way. There was only one television receiving set in Boston outside the studio at that time, so the public was spared the contrast between real and parlor Indian songs.

My voice never "broke," but a baritone range began to be available along with the soprano in my middle teens. I studied with William L. Whitney at the New England Conservatory while I was still in high school and the assumption was that I would pursue an adult musical career. I went on concertizing as a baritone but I dropped "By the Waters of Minnetonka" and "Indian Love Call" from my repertory. I was cautious about real Indian songs, too, since I had seen that I did not know how to do them.

My parents felt that a liberal arts education would provide a broader background for life than an early focus on music in a conservatory, and I had the good fortune to go to Harvard. There I found that I could foster my interest in Indian studies by taking anthropology. I already knew the Peabody Museum Indian exhibits by heart from many childhood visits, and now I began to see them anew in the context of courses on general ethnology and "primitive technology" with Carleton S. Coon, and southwestern ethnology and linguistics (with a Navajo informant) with Clyde Kluckhohn, who was also my tutor. I remember his amusement at my first tutorial when I had discovered the answer to everything in Ruth Benedict's *Patterns of Culture*. He gently suggested that those glorious congruencies might be less clear in other cultures, or to other scholars studying the same cultures.

That music and anthropology might have some connection was not perceived at Harvard in those days, though at Columbia, Boas and some of his students were already studying music as an integral part of human culture. Ironically, Fewkes' wax cylinders of Passamaquoddy and Zuni music, the first ethnomusicological recordings ever made, were stored in the attic of Peabody Museum, unknown to anybody. I began to take music theory and history with Donald Grout and Tillman Merritt, then young section men, and I became a soloist with the Harvard Glee Club. I had leading roles in House musicals such as Bach's *Coffee Cantata* and Purcell's *Dido and Aeneas*, and I was Peachum in an elegant production of *The Beggar's Opera* given by a girls' school in Boston. I was also learning about Western classical music through my continuing lessons with William Whitney and a season ticket to the Boston Symphony Orchestra. My own concerts took a "serious" turn with lieder and operatic arias, and the Glee Club sang Bach, Beethoven, and Brahms with the Boston Symphony Orchestra and the Radcliffe Choral Society.

I met Susan Watkins at rehearsals of the *St. Matthew Passion* and that work has ever since had connotations of romance to me as well as passion in the ecclesiastical sense. It was Coon who quipped that these endogamous engagements are not uncommon in the Harvard-Radcliffe community, and Ernest Albert Hooton observed that my academic record indicated a gradual withdrawal from anthropology in favor of music.

In 1936 I began a lifetime of making up for having had to stay behind on my family's great western trip. F. H. H. Roberts, Jr. was staffing his archaeological dig at the Lindenmeier Site in Colorado with anthropology students. Two of us from Harvard were allowed to share the hard work and scientific excitement at this 20,000-year-old campsite of early humans in America. The rest of the crew was largely made up of young people from Colorado and we were cordially received in their homes on our weekends off. The west took on reality for me at our dig in the foothills of the Rockies and on the trips with new friends to Denver, Pueblo, and Rocky Mountain National Park. I also had my own adventures with rattlesnakes, antelope, and deer on solitary weekend walks into the foothills. The following summer I was back at the Lindenmeier Site, but my classmate of the year before, Kenneth MacLeish, had gone to Harvard's Awatovi dig near First Mesa in Arizona, and I visited him there at the end of the summer. There were Hopi workmen as well as Harvard students on the dig, and I saw my first reservation Navajo. When we were going down to Holbrook he came dashing towards us through the sagebrush on a big white horse. "When you boys get into town will you go to the Chevy place and pick up my generator?" he cried.

In the summer of 1939 I was again at Lindenmeier after my first year at Juilliard. This time MacLeish was at Moenkopi doing linguistic fieldwork and I joined him there for another end-of-summer visit. On the way from Colorado I heard Navajo Ye'iibichei and Squaw Dance songs at Mesa Verde. Then at Moenkopi I notated by ear my first Indian recordings: Hopi children's songs. MacLeish and I went to a real Squaw Dance where a host of little girls swarmed after us as paying partners. I did dance with one attractive teenage girl and I asked her what the songs were about, wondering if she would understand English. "I don't have the least idea," she replied, and vouchsafed no further conversation.

The year at Juilliard raised doubts in my mind as to whether I had the call to be a professional singer. Also, I discovered that there was a course, "Primitive Music," offered at Columbia by George Herzog. As far as I know, it was the first ethnomusicology class in the United States. While still at Juilliard I began attending Herzog's course and I decided that spring that if there could be a musical anthropology I would stay with anthropology. And so, in 1940, with the continued understanding and support of my family, I began Ph.D. studies in anthropology with the focus on American Indian music. At Columbia I found myself squarely in the middle of the dawn of "personality and culture" theory with Ralph Linton and Abram Kardiner. Their seminar was a high point of intellectual ferment in the anthropology of that time.

That year was a lively one for me, intellectually and spiritually. World War II was underway and the involvement of the United States seemed inevitable. The spectacle of violence as the ultimate recourse in international relations raised my interest in the Quaker alternatives. Susan and I had participated in the Oxford Movement and in a widespread college spoof called "Veterans of Future Wars." I began further readings in pacifism and started attending the Fifteenth Street Meeting of the Society of Friends which I later joined.

In the summer I joined a linguistic field party among the Comanches in Oklahoma under the tutelage of George Herzog. My own assignments included the recording of Comanche music, and this quickly led to a focus on Peyote songs, the principal musical interest of most of our Comanche collaborators. At the same time, Susan and I, by mail, decided on an early marriage since the rumblings of war suggested the probability of dislocations unguessable in the near future. We were married on September 1, with the support of two families even though they had never before countenanced the idea of weddings before jobs.

In the academic year of 1940-41 the personality and culture furor at Columbia was in full swing, and an impressive group of faculty and fellow graduate students provided great stimulation in this and other theoretical pastures. I even manufactured excuses to seek out Franz Boas in his retirement, and once sat in on a linguistic session with him and the famed Ella Deloria, his Sioux collaborator. Willard Rhodes was both a graduate student in ethnomusicology and a professor in the Music Department. He was beginning his famous collection of Indian recordings for the Bureau of Indian Affairs.

I was writing up my Comanche field notes: a collection of riddles, a wonderful store of humorous stories, a natural history, and the Peyote songs. I wrote a paper on Margaret Mead for one of Ruth Benedict's courses and went down to the Museum of Natural History to interview the great lady. But, of course, *she* interviewed *me*, and in an hour set the direction of my future work. "It's all well and good to collect that music," she said, "but how does it *relate* to the rest of the culture?"

This inclusion of music within the "configurational framework" startled and delighted me. My first article, however, was psycho-ethnological in another area of expressive culture, mythology. I was struck by the water monsters in Blackfoot legends and did a Linton-Kardiner style connection with what seemed to be an unusual use of water in childhood disciplines. Linton published it in the *American Anthropologist*, and then I learned from some of the specialists in Blackfoot studies that not everybody was entranced with psycho-ethnological explanations.

During World War II, I engaged in "work of national importance" as a conscientious objector: two years in a forestry camp at Cooperstown, New York, and two at a variety of jobs in the state mental hospital in Middletown, Connecticut. Susan worked at a nursery school near Cooperstown and then on the wards of the hospital where we had an apartment in the married quarters. We became acquainted with Wesleyan University through the Friends Meeting there and through occasional lectures I was invited to give. We also made much use of its library and cafeteria. Susan had spotted Laura Boulton's record album *Indian Music of the Southwest*, first issued in 1941, and she gave me a copy. This was the first modern recording of American Indian music. I listened to it a great deal and the Navajo Ye'iibichei and Squaw Dance songs on it fixed my interest on Navajo music forever.

We returned to Columbia when the war ended in 1945. I began work on my dissertation based on the Peyote songs recorded among the Comanches, and I had a part-time job working in the Archive of Primitive Music for George Herzog. I met his friend Béla Bartók in the Archive one great day, and most of the other folk music scholars of the day found their way there as well. In 1946-47 I added to my small earnings by teaching introductory anthropology, evenings, at Brooklyn College.

As we began to consider where I might apply for a full-time teaching job, Susan and I decided against New York and big universities. I composed a letter to be sent to the presidents of several small New England colleges, but before it went out there came a phone call from Victor Butterfield of Wesleyan inviting me for an interview. It developed that I had found my academic home for the next 35-40 years.

At Wesleyan I taught psycho-ethnography in the Psychology Department and a general course on evolution with Hubert B. Goodrich in the Biology Department. It was Goodrich and David C. McClelland of Psychology who had proposed that Wesleyan hire an anthropologist for this inter-departmental function. But Wesleyan was also the scene of my long delayed liberal arts education. Butterfield had launched a pioneering program in the Humanities which included an emphasis on direct experience. While the entire freshman class read from Plato to T. S. Eliot, it also engaged in "laboratories" in the making of art, theater, music, writing, and dance. For my first ten years at Wesleyan I was privileged to teach ideas from Euripedes to Schrödinger. I also taught a music workshop, following the unfolding of *Otello* with the help of Verdi, and creating with the class a folk opera on Eliphaz, Bildad, and Zophar, as we read the Book of Job.

My teaching load was kept humanely light while I finished my dissertation on Peyote music. It was descriptive-historical in the Herzog style, but I was already eager to get on to another kind of ethnomusicology. The ferment of psychological interpretations was in my mind from my exposure to them at Columbia and also from the personality studies going on at Wesleyan under McClelland. I hoped to study music as ethnology and as a way of seeing into psychology, religion, and philosophy. And I wanted that music to be Navajo.

In the Columbia Archive I had been responsible for the housing and cataloging of the hundreds of wax cylinders of Navajo music recorded by Herzog, Hoijer, and others for the Museum of Navajo Ceremonial Art in Santa Fe. I thought a good apprenticeship in Navajo sacred music would be to transcribe and study this material, so I wrote to Mary Cabot Wheelwright, founder and director of the Museum, asking for her permission. She was eager to have the material studied and immediately set up a meeting at the Chilton Club where she stayed on her trips to Boston. Tall, imperious, witty, and elegant, she had cared for her invalid mother on Beacon Hill and had never married. "I never found a man strong enough for me!" she once declared to me. When her mother died she had walked out of her Boston house into a life dedicated to research in comparative religion. Over tea she gave me *carte blanche* to work with her collection, now removed to the Peabody Museum at Harvard, and I spent a good part of the next several years transferring the chants from cylinders to magnetic tape, transcribing the songs into musical notation, and studying the cosmic imagery of the epic-length texts. I was also recording the infant sound of our daughter, Bonner, who had joined the family in 1949.

The opportunity to engage in psycho-ethno-musical-Navajo fieldwork came in 1950 when Harvard started its Values Project, a study of comparative values in five cultures in the Ramah, New Mexico area of the Southwest. A large group of students and older scholars, including sociologists, psychologists, historians, physical anthropologists, linguists, and ethnologists, was to carry on a variety of studies. Clyde Kluckhohn, the originator of the project, had a background in classics, philosophy, and psychiatry, as well as in anthropology. He stated, in effect, that if we could not study human values scientifically, anthropology was missing the central meaning of culture. When I offered to add a musical wing to the study, the idea was accepted and the way was open for me to see if I could relate music to the other aspects of culture.

In September, Susan and I set sail for the Southwest in an old Pontiac station wagon we fixed up as a camper and named "The Prairie Schooner." Friends and relatives joined forces to look after Bonner and give Susan a month's vacation. Headquarters for the Values Project were in Gallup, New Mexico, and our first night there included a long drive into the desert to attend a Navajo Squaw Dance. This was the music I planned to study as the most accessible to a beginner and, I thought, the least associated with ceremonial restrictions. Above all I hoped to avoid any association with matters of exorcism and witchcraft. After hours of search we found the dance and I was greeted loudly by two Navajo youths from Ramah with: "Hello, anthropologist, are you here to study witches?" I soon learned that though Squaw Dance songs are, indeed, close to being "secular," the ceremonial itself, Enemyway, is one of those most deeply surrounded by restrictions of all kinds.

I worked with Kluckhohn in choosing a proper sample of the Ramah population for my study, and he gave me valuable advice on the psycho-musical questionnaire I had dutifully prepared in order to study values scientifically. It turned out that the conditions for administering a controlled questionnaire could not be found in a Navajo household. My "subject" could not be separated from the rest of the family. There would be a group conference on each of my questions and I would be presented with a consensus on each point. The ordering of questions in carefully graded levels of specificity fell in ruins because the discussions anticipated some of them out of order. And the sample turned out to have few women and no singers (ceremonial practitioners) in it! I interviewed my all-too-random sample for science's sake and then added a stratified sample out of my own head for the sake of common sense. The questionnaire did help me not to forget things I wanted to ask. Translating it into Navajo with the help of my interpreters, Robert Pino and Tom José, was my first real step in learning the language to the limited extent that I have been able to. The important thing was that Tom and Robert and their friends and relations recorded many Navajo songs, and the recording situations were rich occasions for long and sometimes deep discussions of the music and the culture.

A frequent occurrence when I arrived at some household was for a young man, back from World War II, to ask me to sing songs from Italy, Germany, or France where he had been in service. He would listen with a smile and say, "Yes, that's where I was." Then the word would spread that I was some kind of spy from Europe casing out Ramah, which of course would be the prime enemy target in the next World War. Tom had been wounded in Germany and invalided to Paris where he was appreciated as a *peau rouge* warrior hero. He spent weeks learning "Brave Marin" from me. Its tale of a sailor returned from the wars to find his wife remarried fitted Tom's case. He also said, "I want to be able to sing this when the next anthropologist comes along asking for songs."

Figure 2. David P. McAllester in 1953. Photographer unknown.

During my six months on the Values Project I also found time to carry on some work for Mary Wheelwright. She was hoping to publish an album of some of the Creation Songs that she had recorded from Hastiin Klah. Her wax cylinders had too many mechanical flaws to be usable, but I was able to find a singer who knew the songs well enough to reproduce them for a tape recording as soon as he heard the originals. After the Enemyway material was published in 1954, I edited Miss Wheelwright's manuscripts on the Great Star Chant and the Coyote Chant. From our first meeting in 1948 until her death in the late 1950s I admired and enjoyed her independent spirit, her peppery humor, and her dedication to the study of comparative religion. When she announced one day that she felt I was her spiritual son I felt honored and a bit overwhelmed.

In my early years at Wesleyan I became a founding member of the Middletown Friends Meeting when it became an independent constituent of the New England Yearly Meeting. In the 1950s the Quaker strand of my life joined with the ethnomusicological. The Society of Friends hoped to help heal the wounds of the war and take what measures they could to prevent the next one. They were involved in relief programs and were among the principal consultants in the organization of UNESCO and the United States Peace Corps. The Friends were convinced that financial and technological aid without cultural understanding could bring worse results than no aid at all. I was one of their researchers who prepared documentation on such programs that had failed. The Quakers also organized a number of International Service Seminars abroad and in this country to bring together college students from recently hostile countries to study international relations in an atmosphere of reconciliation. I was a resource person in a number of these. The situations were often dramatic: I remember a Polish girl with her concentration camp number tattooed on her arm undergoing the trauma of being in the seminar with a former member of the Wehrmacht.

In 1953 I was dean of such a seminar at the Verde Valley School in Arizona. Part of the plan was for us to visit nearby Indian reservations in order to study cultural differences and also to show that the United States had been no more successful than anyone else in trying to deal with them. One of my functions at the seminars was to use music as an instrument for mutual understanding and *Gemütlichkeit*. I often made recordings of our singing sessions to add to the fun and to help me learn the songs. One of the participants of the Verde Valley School seminar was a Navajo, Albert Smith. He warmed to my interest in Navajo music, and stayed on at the school after the seminar and helped me record the Blessingway ceremony of Hastiin Naat'áanii from Wupatki. The Apache trip of the seminar led to a summer's field trip two years later to Whiteriver where I obtained valuable comparative material to study along with my growing body of Navajo recordings and field notes.

World War II had done much to end the parochialism of the United States with respect to other cultures. The Peace Corps had sent thousands of young men and women all over the world, usually with careful preliminary training in, and appreciation for, languages and customs different from their own. Out of UNESCO came the International Folk Music

Council, which jogged European and American musicology into a general realization that music did not stop with Western Europe and its offshoots. Young people began returning to the United States after several years of work and study abroad, and those who were musical had often become fascinated by what they had encountered. Many of them were looking for some way to study such musics further.

At Wesleyan my senior colleague in the evolution course retired in 1956 and there was no one to take his place. I took advantage of the curricular flexibility and student interest to begin a course on "primitive music." Willard Rhodes was already teaching world music at Columbia, and Herzog, who had moved to Indiana, was giving his course there. Kolinski had started a course at Northwestern, and Mantle Hood had begun a program at UCLA which actually involved students in performing sophisticated Asian musics. The time was right for world music to take its place in the academy.

Willard and I customarily sought each other out at scholarly meetings, and we got together with a significant addition at the 51st annual meeting of the American Anthropological Association in Philadelphia in 1952. Willard introduced me to a student of Kolinski, an imposing young man named Alan Merriam, who proposed that we communicate with our anthro-musical colleagues everywhere and start a newsletter. Rhodes was familiar with the organizing genius and worldwide interests of Charles Seeger, and suggested that we journey to the American Musicological Society meetings then in session at New Haven and discuss the whole matter as a committee of four.

The first newsletter came out in December 1953. Merriam acted as secretary and editor, *pro tem*, and I typed up the copy and organized the mimeographing and address list at Wesleyan. Rhodes and Seeger provided liaison with their network of colleagues abroad and we split the cost of each issue four ways. When we moved to a pamphlet format in Newsletter No. 6, January 1956, I consulted Raymond Walsh, president of the recently established Wesleyan University Press, and asked him to be our publisher. Wesleyan was producing *My Weekly Reader*, *Current Events*, and other educational material, and Ray asked, "Will it be comprehensible at the third grade level?" But he intended to develop scholarly publications, and the Press undertook the cost of that issue of the Newsletter and provided much technical and design assistance. The Press also provided an annual subsidy thereafter, which helped greatly in keeping us solvent until we could stand on our own feet.

At the organizational meeting of the Society for Ethnomusicology in 1955 I became secretary-treasurer for the next four years, a job from which I resigned in June of 1957 to take my first full year's sabbatical with a Guggenheim grant to study the Blessingway of the Navajos. In 1959 I became editor for four years and in 1964-66 I took my turn as president.

It was Gladys Reichard, on a visit to the Verde Valley School seminar, who encouraged me to apply for the Guggenheim grant. My work with Naat'áanii and then with Sam Hubbell of Ganado, in 1955, on the way to visit the Apaches, had interested me in trying to do some definitive work on that most important of all Navajo ceremonies. When the application was successful, our whole family packed up for a year in Arizona and New Mexico. The party included our son Burling, who had been born in 1952. We bought the first of our long succession of Volkswagen buses, and fixed it up as a camper. Then we headed for the Navajo Reservation by a circuitous route that included the Colorado Rockies, friends on the West Coast, and Disneyland. In Arizona, through friends at the Verde Valley School, we had the good fortune to meet Margaret and Bill Leenhouts who had a vacant cottage on their beautiful ranch on Oak Creek, south of Flagstaff. Bonner went to school in Sedona, and I began many sorties to the nearby Navajo country. One of my first Navajo contacts was Albert G. ("Chic") Sandoval, the official tribal interpreter. He was interested in my project, but his time

Figure 3. Playing Back Navajo Children's Songs to Benjamin and Tom Wilson Yazzie, ages 6 and 7, at Tse Bonito, July 1955. Photographer, Francis Cancian.

was fully occupied. He recommended his son, Albert Jr., and I began the warm friendship with "Sandy" that continued until his death in 1984.

Sandy took me first to a relative, Jim Smith, of Ganado. After a few hours of talks with Jim, interrupted by visits of people coming to seek his help, we all agreed that we could work better if we removed to Sedona. Jim was willing to take a leave from his busy practice, and so I made my third recording of Blessingway. Jim's version was specifically for someone going away to war: he called it Enemy-Blessingway. It is an unusual combination of elements that some singers feel to be completely antithetical, and is a reminder to the outsider of the flexibility of use possible in Navajo ceremonialism.

During the work with Jim Smith, I began to wish it were possible to attend an actual ceremony. I remembered that Leland C. Wyman had done so in his work and so I wrote to him to inquire how he had obtained permission to attend and record, and whether I might hope to do the same thing. His immediate detailed and helpful response broadened my understanding of the circumstances of ceremonial performances and gave me the courage to think I might be able to see in actual practice the songs, prayers, and other ritual I was beginning to understand.

In November, Sandy and I stopped for the second time at the home of another relative, Frank Mitchell, a much respected Blessingway singer and leader in the Chinle community.

In a general family talk about recording ceremonies, Frank's daughter Augusta said, "Why not film my father's Blessingway?" Frank expressed his willingness, and suddenly my head was spinning with possibilities. I had met James Bosch, who was studying Navajo tribal law and was serving the Tribe as its official photographer, so I went and conferred with him on the logistics of a filming project. We returned to the Mitchells' and a long conference ensued. Frank wanted to give a Blessingway for his daughter Isabel, who was pregnant and needed the ceremony to ensure the safe delivery of the child. Frank also felt that it was imperative to preserve the ceremony for the Navajo people. As he put it, "Without the Blessingway there will be no Navajo people."

Next came much hurried preparation. I had visited Fr. Berard Haile at St. Vincent's Hospital in Santa Fe and he had given me permission to consult his Blessingway manuscripts at St. Michaels. As we began assembling equipment and crew I paid several visits to the hospitable Franciscan Fathers and studied the hundreds of pages of myth, song and prayer texts, and descriptions of procedure recorded by Fr. Berard. One of the contributors to this material had been Frank Mitchell himself, and his work with the well-loved priest-anthropologist was a key factor in disposing Frank to make the film.

During the shooting of the film and many subsequent visits, my acquaintance with the Mitchell family deepened into a closeness that precipitated the question in my own mind as to whether I was their friend and relative or their scientific observer. I began to see their private lives as their own business and I felt an increasing respect for, and emotional involvement in, the humanistic value of their art and philosophy. From early in our relationship, Frank considered me to be a replacement for his son David, who had died in 1938.

While the Blessingway film was being developed, Sandy introduced me to another of his relatives, Ray Winnie of Lukachukai. He was willing to record his principal ceremony, the House Chant. This is a nine-day version of Shootingway, one of the most elaborate of all the ceremonials. As we had done with Jim Smith, we retired to Sedona with Ray, his wife Fanny, and Sandy, and together we made the recording. Ray talked through the entire ceremony, describing the preparations and procedures and the sacred paraphernalia. He recited the prayers and sang the songs as he came to them. We then went through the whole remarkable corpus phrase by phrase, translating and discussing the texts and making sketches of the sandpaintings, body-painting, and costumes.

At one point Ray said, "It would take years to tell you everything there is to tell!" It was also evident that I would have to see the ceremony if I was ever to have a clear idea of its many events. Clyde Kluckhohn's analogy came to mind, that one of the large Navajo ceremonials is a musical drama equivalent to a Wagnerian opera in the extent of text, music, stage properties, and mythic content.

Later, when Sandy was back in Sedona helping me go over the Blessingway and Shootingway texts, he told me his father was interested in being the protagonist in a performance of the House Chant, and that I could make recordings if I could help with the considerable costs. The project became a reality later in the spring. The singers were Denet Tsosie and his brother Red Moustache, and Ray and Fanny were helpers. Now I was able to see how the complex structure of Shootingway all came together and I was able to participate in the gathering of sacred herbs and other properties and in the sweatbath and making of sandpaintings. My hope to study Navajo ceremonialism in its cultural context was being realized.

When we returned from the Southwest, the job as editor of *Ethnomusicology* was waiting for me. The expansion of the Wesleyan program also began that year with the addition of Robert E. Brown to the music faculty. He was trained at UCLA and with his guidance we began to put into practice Mantle Hood's doctrine of bimusicality. Groups of our students began enthusiastically learning, both in theory and performance, the musics of India, Japan, Africa, and Indonesia under the guidance of visiting artists from those countries. In 1960 we also had John Cage and Leonard Meyer as visiting fellows at Wesleyan. Both had a profound effect on the direction of our music program. Richard K. Winslow, chairman of the department, supported ethnomusicology from the first and firmly incorporated its perspectives into the music program as a whole.

Now came a memorable break in our Middletown-Southwest orbit: I was invited to be a Carnegie Visiting Professor in the Music Department of the University of Hawaii. In part the program was to acquaint mainlanders with what Hawaii is really like. Barbara Smith, our hostess, gave us an introduction to the islands that has fixed a large part of our interest and affection there ever since. Barbara found entrées for us into aspects of Hawaiian life that new visitors rarely experience. One of the most delightful was the ninetieth birthday party of Aunt Jennie Wilson, the last surviving dancer from the court of King Kalakaua. Though in a wheelchair, she did a naughty hula that outshone the many other dances performed in her honor.

My job at the university was to give a seminar and an introductory course in ethnomusicology. The latter was, in part, a demonstration for the growing world music program at Hawaii of how such a course had developed at Wesleyan. My whole family was so pleasantly involved in things Hawaiian that we stayed right through the summer when my teaching was over. The temptation was very great to forget all about the mainland and try to stay in the islands forever.

Navajo studies began to call, however, and the rapid growth of the Wesleyan ethnomusicology program needed direction. I spent the year of 1962-63 shepherding proposals for a Ph.D. program through Wesleyan's various planning committees. Mr. Butterfield was looking for innovative educational ventures, and a world music program seemed to be a valuable variation on the theme of area studies and other intra-cultural developments of those years.

The fall of 1962 brought Charlotte Frisbie (then Johnson) to Wesleyan. She was my first graduate student in Navajo studies and has been my colleague in the field ever since. I received a National Science Foundation grant for three years' study of the Blessingway complex of ceremonies in Navajo religion, and Charlotte was the first of a number of students to assist in this project. She spent the summer of 1963 gathering the material for her study of the girls' puberty ceremony, an important aspect of Blessingway. She also became a member of the Mitchell family at Chinle, and among her many projects began taping Frank's life story.

In the summer of 1966 another strand of activity became important in my life through the good offices of William Malm. I had been lecturing widely in the lower schools on Indian music and Indian life, trying to correct the Hollywood and TV image of American Indians, but the field of education in the lower schools was largely unknown to me. Bill arranged for me to be invited to the International Conference of Music Educators at Ann Arbor. My paper, "Teaching the Music Teacher To Use the Music of His Own Culture," was widely reprinted and led to my being invited to the Tanglewood Conference in 1967. The "Tanglewood Declaration," which I helped to compose, stressed the importance of popular music, world music, and contemporary music in a holistic music curriculum.

Wesleyan was also broadening its commitment to the earlier levels of education with a Master of Arts in Liberal Studies, and I taught in this program in evening and summer courses for teachers. In 1968 I taught an anthropology course in a summer program for gifted high school students at Mt. Hermon School, and the following summer I taught a course in ethnomusicology to music teachers at Boston University.

Figure 4.   David P. McAllester in 1959.
Photographer, Jeanne Davis.

In the 1960s I was also involved in preparing ethnomusicological articles and recordings for school children. Two music magazines, *Keyboard, Jr.* and *Young Keyboard, Jr.*, were being issued in New Haven by Dr. Ian Minenberg, an independent music educator. He saw the importance of World Music and asked me to write several articles with accompanying records, which he published and then issued as boxed sets on a continuing basis. Though he retired from this enterprise in 1978, the records are still issued by Litton Educational Publishing.

My Navajo father and teacher, Frank Mitchell, died in 1967. Charlotte Frisbie and I attended his funeral and we discussed his wish that the story of his life be preserved for his family. It seemed to us that the account Charlotte had taped and the additional material in my notes could be combined in an autobiography that would give an impression of that extraordinary man. In the summer of 1971 Charlotte received a grant from the American Philosophical Society to do archival work for the project, and Susan and I joined her at the ever-hospitable Verde Valley School for an organizing and preliminary writing conference. By that time we had both transcribed our many hours of interviews with Frank and we could see that we had an unusually valuable document. Augusta joined us, adding material on Frank's last days of illness. Then we all went to Chinle to consult the family's wishes about such an autobiography. We also discussed questions of publication and the allocation of royalties, if there were to be any. With the family's consent we then went ahead with the book except for a break in 1972-73 when Susan, Bonner, and I took a sabbatical trip around the world.

This nine-month journey was partly vacation, but it was inevitably ethnomusicological as well. There were Wesleyan students doing field studies in the musics of Japan, Indonesia, and India. It was helpful to bring them word from home and discuss their work with them. There were also a good many former visiting artists and professors for whom a live visit was a welcome change after communications by other means. The Wesleyan Music Department had become an international institution. There was, for instance, a party in Tokyo in which nineteen of the participants were or had been Wesleyan people. I gave a six weeks' course in ethnomusicology in Surakarta and lectures in Hawaii, Japan, India, and even Finland.

In these years several members of the Mitchell family came to Middletown, either to contribute to the Navajo studies program in various ways or just to visit. The first of these was Frank's grandson, Douglas Mitchell. He was a gifted singer and linguist and was a visiting artist in American Indian music at Wesleyan from 1969 until his untimely death in 1972.

In 1971 he was co-author, with me, of an article on Navajo music for the Smithsonian Institution's new *Handbook of North American Indians* and he sang a leading role in an opera by Richard Winslow. Faculty and students of that time remember his prodigious talents and sometimes still speak of "the Doogie era."

Figure 5. Founders of the Society for Ethnomusicology
at the Annual Meeting in Chapel Hill, North Carolina, November 1971.
Left to Right: Charles Seeger, Alan P. Merriam, Willard Rhodes, and David P. McAllester.
Photographer, William P. Malm.

In 1974 and 1975 Charlotte and I finished Frank's life story by mail and with the help of occasional conferences. In June of 1975 we went to see the Mitchells for a final discussion on whether the book was acceptable to the family. We had sent copies to Agnes and Augusta, the two daughters who could most readily read their way through the 800-page manuscript. After a day-long conference we made certain deletions and revisions on the spot. A month or so later we sent the manuscript to the University of Arizona Press and it was published in January 1978.

I was becoming increasingly aware that the ceremonial music I was studying was known primarily to the Navajo intellectuals and philosophers and that even the popular songs of the Squaw Dance were no longer the dominant music in Navajo culture. I decided to look into the interesting question of contemporary musical change among the Native Americans in general, and I spent the summer of 1976 listening to radio broadcasts beamed to Indian reservations, getting a sense of the records Indians were publishing and buying, and talking to radio program directors about the requests for music coming from Indian audiences. I was especially helped by Tony Isaacs of Indian House Records and by Robert Nuss and Ray Boley of Canyon Records. I attended the Fourth of July Powwow at Flagstaff where I was impressed to hear Navajo and Hopi singers' excellent Plains singing, even to the very difficult drumming techniques. I found that Country and Western music was the great favorite with radio listeners and that Indian Rock and Gospel were well established. Indian protest music was another element that had grown up, especially among urban Indians. There was also a genre of music conveying a message to the Indian world, and the world in general, concerning the special values in Indian perspectives.

In the spring of 1977 I began another collaboration, this time with Susan, to do a book on Navajo hogans. We planned to put together her photographs of all kinds of Navajo dwellings with my translations of a selection from the hundreds of Navajo house songs. In April and May we traveled widely on the reservation, including a long visit with our Navajo family in Chinle and with Sandy at Lukachukai.

1977-78 was my last year of full-time teaching. I then began what I call my "new thirty-year plan," which includes one semester a year of full-time teaching and then eight months at our new home in the Berkshires. We inaugurated the plan with a summer's visit to Australia in 1978 where I taught at the Universities of Sydney and Queensland and lectured across the country on ethnomusicology and American Indian music, philosophy, and culture in general. I also did a small study of the Aborigines' lively interest in Country and Western music.

On our return from Australia we attended an Enemyway for my Navajo nephew, A. C. Davis, in Arizona and then came on to the Berkshires in a blaze of fall color. We were visiting Bonner and her husband Joe Baker, who now live on our family land there, when we got the news that *Hogans* was to be published by Wesleyan University Press. We had now made the decision to build a home in the Berkshires ourselves, and we spent the year working on *Hogans* and getting ready to move. Susan designed our new house that winter. We were so attached to the eighteenth-century house we had lived in for twenty-one years in Portland, Connecticut that I spent a good part of 1979 researching and writing up its history. We were surprised to discover that the Ranney family who had built it were distant relatives. We broke ground for our new house that summer, with Joe as contractor, and in October 1980 we moved.

My interest in education at the earlier levels continues. In March 1981 I visited the Red Rock School on the Navajo Reservation to consult on the question of introducing Navajo music into the curriculum, and had a similar assignment at the Menominee High School in Keshena, Wisconsin in 1983. I have been teaching American Indian literature and philosophy to Middletown high school seniors in High School Humanities seminars since 1982. In the summer of 1984 I organized the Wesleyan Symposium, a week-long conference on the application of anthropological and ethnomusicological perspectives to the teaching and learning of music and dance. Ten of my colleagues from the United Kingdom, Germany, Canada, and the United States came to present the insights gained from their fieldwork around the world. The Music Educators National Conference, which cosponsored the symposium with Wesleyan, published the proceedings in the summer of 1985.

What I hope, as I proceed deeper into my new thirty-year plan, is to continue to enjoy the stimulus I have always felt in the Wesleyan community with my one-semester teaching load and consultations with advisees, both graduate and undergraduate. With full retirement in the spring of 1986, I anticipate other kinds of teaching opportunities. Continuing research in ceremonial and new Navajo music is a large part of the plan. My Quaker activities continue: I helped found the South Berkshire Monthly Meeting in 1984 and am serving as its first recording clerk.

Still another strand is now also woven into the mix: in 1977, on the plane to a proofreading conference on Frank Mitchell's autobiography, I began to write a utopian, science fiction novel about an Indian community that finds a way to meet the challenge of the European invasion by inventing a new culture. I am halfway into it now and my characters are turning out to be rather Quakerly people with a great deal of music and folklore and a tendency to celebrate life as they live it. The novel might turn out to be my letter to the world.

Figure 6. David P. McAllester in 1982.
Photographer, Susan McAllester.

Bibliography

Books and Articles

1934   "Chippewa War Dance." "Everett High Boy Writes His Own 'Piece' for Prize-Speaking Contest," by Dorothy C. Wayman. *Boston Globe* 125/27 (February 16, evening ed.): 15.

1941   "Transcriptions and Analyses." "A Few Hopi Songs from Moenkopi," by Kenneth MacLeish. *Masterkey* 15:178-84.

      "Water as a Disciplinary Agent among the Crow and Blackfoot." *American Anthropologist* 43:593-604.

1946   "The Camel in Media." *Worldover: A Magazine for Jewish Boys and Girls* 8:8-9. New York: Jewish Education Committee.

1947   "The Fox and the Beetle." *Worldover: A Magazine for Jewish Boys and Girls* 8/12:8-9. New York: Jewish Education Committee.

1949   "Anthropology and Ethnology." *American Yearbook*, ed. William A. Schuyler, pp. 682-87. New York: Thomas Nelson and Sons.

      Peyote Music. Viking Fund Publications in Anthropology, 13. New York: Viking Fund.

1951   "Statement on Peyote" (with four other anthropologists). *Science* 114/2970:582-83.

1952   "Menomini Peyote Music." "Menomini Peyotism," by J. S. Slotkin. *Transactions of the American Philosophical Society* (n.s.) 42:681-700.

      "Navajo Creation Chants," album of five 10″ 78 rpm records, and pamphlet. Peabody Museum, Harvard University.

1954   *Enemy Way Music: A Study of Social and Esthetic Values as Seen in Navaho Music.* Papers of the Peabody Museum of American Archaeology and Ethnology, Harvard University, 41/3.

1955   "American Indian Songs and Pan-Tribalism." *Midwest Folklore* 5:132-36.

      Race: Its Bearing on Intelligence, Health, and Culture: A Seminar in Anthropology. Middletown, Conn.: Wesleyan University Press.

1956   "An Apache Fiddle." *Ethno-Musicology Newsletter* 8:1-5.

Editor and author of commentaries on *The Myth and Prayers of the Great Star Chant and the Myth of the Coyote Chant* recorded by Mary C. Wheelwright, Navajo Religion Series, 4. Santa Fe: Museum of Navajo Ceremonial Art.

1959   "Memorial to Edwin Grant Burrows." *Ethnomusicology* 3:14-17.

"Whither Ethnomusicology?" Report on two panels. *Ethnomusicology* 3:99-105.

1960   "Culture and Psychosis," with Kai Hirano Howes. *Review and Newsletter, Transcultural Research in Mental Health Problems* (McGill University), 9:51-57.

"Inexorable Malthus and Irrational Man." *Wesleyan University Alumnus* 45:22-24.

"The Role of Music in Western Apache Culture." *Men and Cultures: Selected Papers of the Fifth International Congress of Anthropological and Ethnological Sciences,* September 1-9, 1956, ed. Anthony F. Wallace, pp. 468-72. Philadelphia: University of Pennsylvania Press.

"What Can We Learn from the Indians?" *Read Magazine* 9:3.

1961   *Indian Music in the Southwest.* Colorado Springs: Taylor Museum of the Colorado Springs Fine Arts Center.

1962   "Alan Lomax and American Folk Song." *Ethnomusicology* 6:233-38.

Blessingway. 16 mm. color film, 70 min. Workprint only, because of religious restrictions.

Music of the Pueblos, Apache and Navaho, with Don N. Brown. 12″ LP record and pamphlet. Colorado Springs: Taylor Museum of the Colorado Springs Fine Arts Center.

1963   "Ethnomusicology, the Field and the Society." *Ethnomusicology* 7:182-86.

"Indian Music." *Encyclopedia Americana* 15:30. New York: Americana Corp.

1964   "Hunters of the Plains." *Young Keyboard, Jr.* 17:2-3.

"Skilton's War Dance of the Cheyennes" (with Eleanore Milmore). *Young Keyboard, Jr.* 17:4-5.

"Artists of the Desert." *Young Keyboard, Jr.* 17:8.

"Riddles and Other Verbal Play among the Comanches." *Journal of American Folklore* 77:251-57.

"The Companion Program in its Educational Context." *Contributions to the Social Rehabilitation of the Mentally Ill.* Proceedings of the College Student Program Conference (1962): 49-53. Hartford: Connecticut State Department of Mental Health and the National Institute of Mental Health.

1966   *Music of the American Indian; Drum Beats around the World; Music of India; Music of Hawaii; Japanese Music; Music of Japan.* Six 12″ LP records with pamphlets. New Haven: Keyboard, Jr., and since 1978 by Litton Educational Publishing, New York.

"Ritual Communication and the Navaho Song of Protection." *Io* 3:45-51. Ann Arbor: Richard Grossinger and Lindy Hough.

1967   "Growing Up Prayer: From a Navaho Protection Rite." *Reflection: Wesleyan Quarterly* 4:26-31.

"Teaching the Music Teacher To Use the Music of His Own Culture." *International Seminar on the Teaching of Music*, Aug. 8-18, 1966, pp. 205-12. Ann Arbor: University of Michigan Press. Reprinted in *International Music Educator*, Paris, Sept. 1967; *Australian Journal of Education* 10 (1972): 17-20; and also in the following forms and places: "Hvad er Musikpaedagogikkens Genstand?" *Dansk Musiktidsskrift* (1966): 198-200; "Da Razirate Nashite Detsa," *Bulgarian Cultural Bulletin* 61 (1968): 1-7, American Embassy, Sofia; "Aby Zrozumiec Nasze Dzieci," *Polish Cultural Bulletin* 62 (1969): 15-21, American Embassy, Warsaw; "To Understand Our Children," *New York Times*, Oct. 1, 1967; "Abychom Chápali Své Děti," *Czechoslovakian Cultural Bulletin* 6 (1970): 17-22, American Embassy, Prague.

"Comments on Kolinski's 'Recent Trends in Ethnomusicology.'" *Ethnomusicology* 11/1:iv. (Reply by Kolinski in *Ethnomusicology* 11/2:238-39.)

"The Tanglewood Declaration" (one of multiple authors). *Music Educators Journal* 54/3:51.

1968 "The Substance of Things Hoped For." *Music Educators Journal* 54/6:48-52.

"The Present State of Musical Studies: Ethnomusicology." *Studies in Music* 2:15-20. Nedlands: University of Western Australia Press.

"War God's Horse Song II." *Technicians of the Sacred: A Range of Poetries from Africa, America, Asia & Oceania*, by Jerome Rothenberg, pp. 41-43. New York: Doubleday.

1969 "American Indian Music, Part II: Central and South America." *Harvard Dictionary of Music*, by Willi Apel, pp. 35-36. Cambridge: Harvard University Press.

"Willard Rhodes." *Ethnomusicology* 13/2: iv.

"The Tenth Horse Song." *Stony Brook* 3/4:306-15.

1970 "The Many Faces of the American Indian," pp. 4-8; and "A Man for These Times," pp. 14-18. *American Indians Today: A Search for Identity*, ed. Charles L. Cutler. Middletown, Conn.: American Educational Press. (Also consultant for the volume.)

"Songs of the Talking God: A Navajo Transposition." *Alcheringa, Ethnopoetics* 1:47-48.

Translations of Blessingway Songs. *Blessingway*, by Leland C. Wyman, pp. 177-94. Tucson: University of Arizona Press.

"Ethnomusicology." *Kord* 1:15. Northampton, Mass.

1971 *Readings in Ethnomusicology*, ed. David P. McAllester. New York: Johnson Reprint Corporation.

"Indian Music in the Southwest." *Readings in Ethnomusicology*, ed. David P. McAllester, pp. 215-26. New York: Johnson Reprint Corporation.

"Some Thoughts on 'Universals' in World Music." *Ethnomusicology* 15/3:379-80.

1972 "American Indian Music." *Growing with Music*, by Harry R. Wilson et al, p. 39. New York: Prentice-Hall.

"Music of the Americas." *Music in World Cultures*, special issue of *Music Educators Journal* 59/2:54-58.

Transcriptions and Notes on Yakutat Songs. *Under Mount Saint Elias: The History and Culture of the Yakutat Tlingit*, Part 3, by Frederica de Laguna. *Smithsonian Contributions to Anthropology* 7:1149-367. Washington, D.C.

1973   "Cerebration or Celebration?" *Current Musicology* 15:95-97.

"The Role of Music in Western Apache Culture" (1960). Reprinted in *Explorations in Anthropology*, ed. Morton H. Fried, pp. 436-40. New York: Thomas Y. Crowell Company.

1974   "Foreword" for *An Introduction to Japanese Folk Song*, by Patia Isaku. Ann Arbor: University Microfilms.

1975   "Music of the First Americans." *Current Events*, Teachers Edition, 75:1.

1976   Consultant for *Our Indian Heritage*, ed. Charles L. Cutler, G. Pollock, and C. Munat. Middletown, Conn.: Xerox Education Publications.

1977   "Analysis of the First Snake Song." Quoted in *Language and Art in the Navajo Universe*, by Gary Witherspoon, pp. 155-60. Ann Arbor: University of Michigan Press.

"A Different Drum: A Consideration of Music in Native American Humanities." *The Religious Character of Native American Humanities*, ed. Sam D. Gill, pp. 155-83b. Tempe: Arizona State University, Department of Humanities and Religious Studies.

1978   "Culture, the Contagious Commodity." *The Tanglewood Symposium Revisited: Music in American Society Ten Years Later*, ed. Gerard McKenna and William Schmid, pp. 18-26. Milwaukee: University of Wisconsin Press.

Navajo Blessingway Singer: The Autobiography of Frank Mitchell 1881-1967. Co-edited with Charlotte J. Frisbie. Tucson: University of Arizona Press.

1979   "The Astonished Ethno-muse." *Ethnomusicology* 23/2:179-89.

"A Paradigm of Navajo Dance." *Parabola: The Quarterly of Myth and Meaning* 4:28-35.

1980   "Coyote's Song." *Parabola: The Quarterly of Myth and Meaning* 5:47-54.

"The First Snake Song." *Theory and Practice: Essays Presented to Gene Weltfish*, ed. Stanley Diamond, pp. 1-27. The Hague: Mouton.

Hogans, Navajo Houses and House Songs, with Susan W. McAllester. Middletown: Wesleyan University Press.

"Native Americans—Who Are They?" *Native Americans: Their Struggle for a Better Life*, ed. Richard Uhlich, pp. 3-8. Middletown, Conn: Xerox Education Publications. (Also consultant for volume.)

"North American Native Music." *Music of Many Cultures,* ed. Elizabeth May, pp. 307-31. Berkeley: University of California Press.

"Shootingway, An Epic Drama of the Navajos." *Southwestern Indian Ritual Drama*, ed. Charlotte J. Frisbie, pp. 199-237. A School of American Research Book. Albuquerque: University of New Mexico Press.

"'The War God's Horse Song,' an Exegesis in Native American Humanities." *Music of the North American Indians*, ed. Charlotte Heth. *Selected Reports in Ethnomusicology* 3/2:1-21. Los Angeles: University of California Press.

1981   "The Complexity of Cultural Process." *International Symposium on the Conservation and Restoration of Cultural Property: Preservation and Development of the Traditional Performing Arts*, pp. 1-15. Tokyo: Tokyo National Research Institute of Cultural Properties.

1981-   "History and Culture of the Mahican Indians." Monthly column from December 1981- in *Monterey News*, Monterey, Mass.

1982   "Leland C. Wyman: A Biography and Bibliography." *Navajo Religion and Culture: Selected Views. Papers in Honor of Leland C. Wyman*, ed. David M. Brugge and Charlotte J. Frisbie. *Museum of New Mexico Papers in Anthropology* 17:1-20. Santa Fe: Museum of New Mexico Press.

"Foreword" for *Roots of Black Music: The Vocal, Instrumental and Dance Heritage of Africa and Black America*, by Ashenafi Kebede, pp. ix-x. Englewood Cliffs, N.J.: Prentice-Hall.

"New Perspectives in Native American Music." *Perspectives of New Music* 20/1-2:434-46.

1983   "Foreword" for *Southwestern Indian Drypainting*, by Leland C. Wyman, pp. xix-xx. School of American Research Southwest Indian Art Series. Santa Fe: School of American Research, and Albuquerque: University of New Mexico Press.

"Navajo Music" (co-authored with Douglas F. Mitchell). *Handbook of North American Indians* 10/2, *The Southwest*, ed. Alfonso Ortiz, pp. 605-23. Washington, D.C.: Smithsonian Institution.

Worlds of Music: An Introduction to the Music of the World's Peoples, by Jeff Todd Titon, James T. Koetting, David P. McAllester, David Reck, and Mark Slobin. Jeff Todd Titon, general ed. New York: Macmillan and Co., Schirmer Books.

"North America/Native America." *Worlds of Music: An Introduction to the Music of the World's Peoples*, by Jeff Todd Titon, James T. Koetting, David P. McAllester, David Reck, and Mark Slobin. Jeff Todd Titon, general ed., pp. 12-63. New York: Macmillan and Co., Schirmer Books.

"The Tenth Horse Song of Frank Mitchell." *Symposium of the Whole: A Range of Discourse Toward an Ethnopoetics*, ed. Jerome Rothenberg and Diane Rothenberg (also authors of commentaries), pp. 393-98. Berkeley: University of California Press. (Reprinted from *Stony Brook* 3/4, 1969.)

"Foreword" for *Anthology of Sōkyoku and Jiuta Texts*, compiled and translated by Gen'ichi Tsuge et al, pp. vii-viii. Tokyo: Academia Music.

1984   "A Problem in Ethics." *Problems and Solutions: Occasional Essays in Musicology Presented to Alice M. Moyle*, ed. Jamie C. Kassler and Jill Stubington, pp. 279-89. Sydney, Autralia: Hale and Iremonger.

"American Indian Storytelling." *National Storytelling Journal* 1/1:7.

"The Mahicans of Stockbridge." *Berkshires Week*, September 14-21, pp. 8-9, 12, ed. Martha Nordstrom. (Supplement to *Berkshire Eagle*.) Pittsfield, Mass.: Berkshire Eagle Publishing Co.

"Navajo Musical Instruments." (Eleven entries, from *'Adee' agháář* to *Ts'its'óós.*) *The New Grove Dictionary of Musical Instruments*, ed. Stanley Sadie. London: Macmillan.

1985   "A Navajo Horse Song." *National Storytelling Journal* 2/1 (Winter): 3-6.

Becoming Human through Music: The Wesleyan Symposium on the Perspectives of Social Anthropology in the Teaching and Learning of Music, August 6-10, 1984, Wesleyan University, Middletown, Connecticut. Ed. and project director David P. McAllester. Reston, Virginia: Music Educators National Conference.

"The Wesleyan Symposium." *Becoming Human through Music: The Wesleyan Symposium on the Perspectives of Social Anthropology in the Teaching and Learning of Music*, ed. David P. McAllester, pp. 1-4. Reston, Virginia: Music Educators National Conference.

"Performances and Workshops." *Becoming Human through Music: The Wesleyan Symposium on the Perspectives of Social Anthropology in the Teaching and Learning of Music*, ed. David P. McAllester, pp. 123-28. Reston, Virginia: Music Educators National Conference.

In Press

"Native American Music." *Handbook of North American Indians*, general vol., ed. William Sturtevant. Washington, D.C.: Smithsonian Institution.

"Willard Rhodes and the Department of the Interior-Library of Congress American Indian Music Collection." "Foreword" for Rhodes' large pamphlet on his ten records made for the Library of Congress. Rhodes' part currently in preparation.

"Sacred Music of Indians of North and South America." *The Encyclopedia of Religion*, ed. Mircea Eliade. New York: The Free Press, Macmillan Publishing Co.

"Apache Music," "Flathead Music," "Navajo Music." *The New Grove Dictionary of American Music*, ed. H. Wiley Hitchcock and Stanley Sadie. London: Macmillan.

"Native American Music – A Hopi Cat Song." *Eagle Wing Press, Inc.* (newspaper), ed. Jim Roaix. Naugatuck, Connecticut.

Navajo Songs of the 1930s and 1940s, recorded by Laura Boulton. Notes by Charlotte J. Frisbie and David P. McAllester. New York: Laura Boulton Foundation and Folkways Records. One LP and pamphlet.

"Navajo Music: A Lecture Recital" (with Margaret Tsosie and Sam Yazzie, Sr.). The First Annual Laura Boulton Ethnomusicology Lecture, Arizona State University, Tempe, Arizona, March 22, 1984. Ed. J. Richard Haefer. Tempe: Laura Boulton Collection of World Music and Musical Instruments and the Laura Boulton Foundation, New York, N.Y.

Reviews

1941   *Inuit sange og danse fra Grönland*, by William Thalbitzer. *American Anthropologist* 43:461.

1950   *Navaho Religion*, by Gladys A. Reichard. *Hartford Courant* 114, June 23, p. 18.

1953   *Old World Overtones in the New World*, by Theodore Seder. *American Anthropologist* 55:272.

    Les Kissi: Une Societé noire et ses instruments de musique, by André Schaeffner. *American Anthropologist* 55:273.

1954   *Los instrumentos de las música afrocubana*, vols. 1 and 2, by Fernando Ortiz. *American Anthropologist* 56:927-28.

1955   *Drums of the Yoruba of Nigeria* (recordings and notes), by William Bascom. *American Anthropologist* 57:381.

   Beating the Tupan in the Central Balkans, by Yury Arbatsky. *American Anthropologist* 57:918.

1956   *Instrumentos musicales precortesianos*, by Samuel Marti. *Ethnomusicology Newsletter* 8:27-28.

   The Pueblo Indians in Song, Story and Dance (record). *Midwest Folklore* 6:186-87.

1957   *Songs of the Nootka Indians of Western Vancouver Island*, by Helen Roberts and Morris Swadesh. *Journal of the American Musicological Society* 10:44-47.

   Ethnomusicology: A Study of Its Nature, Its Problems, Methods, and Representative Personalities to Which Is Added a Bibliography, by Jaap Kunst. *Journal of American Folklore* 70:94-95.

   Festival in Haiti (record), by Jean Destiné. *Midwest Folklore* 7:191-92.

   Music of the American Indian: Northwest (Puget Sound) (record and notes), by Willard Rhodes. *Midwest Folklore* 7:55-57.

1958   *Beautyway, A Navaho Ceremonial*, ed., with commentaries, by Leland C. Wyman. *Midwest Folklore* 8:59-60.

1959   *Mythology and Values: An Analysis of Navaho Chantway Myths*, by Katherine Spencer. *Journal of American Folklore* 72/283:68-70.

   The Collecting of Folk Music and Other Ethnomusicological Material: A Manual for Fieldworkers, by Maude Karpeles. *Journal of American Folklore* 72:350-51.

1960   *Ethnomusicology: A Study of Its Nature, Its Problems* . . . (1960 ed.), by Jaap Kunst. *Journal of American Folklore* 78:69-70.

1961   *An Introduction to Folk Music in the United States*, by Bruno Nettl. *Midwest Folklore* 11:172-73.

1963   *An Introduction to Folk Music in the United States* (rev. ed.), by Bruno Nettl. *Midwest Folklore* 13:124.

   Sociopsychological Analysis of Folklore, by J. L. Fischer. *Current Anthropology* 4/3:279-80.

1965   *Music the Unknown*, by Mantle Hood. *Yearbook: Interamerican Institute for Musical Research* 1:116-18.

   Tapestries in Sand: The Spirit of Indian Sandpainting, by David V. Villaseñor. *Western Folklore* 24:54-55.

   Theory and Method in Ethnomusicology, by Bruno Nettl. *Musical Quarterly* 51:425-28.

1966   *Iroquois Music and Dance*, by Gertrude P. Kurath. *Ethnomusicology* 10/1:121-23.

1967   *The Red Antway of the Navaho*, by Leland C. Wyman. *American Anthropologist* 69:237-38.

1968   *Amerika: Eskimo und Indianische Bevölkerung*, ed. Paul Collaer. *Ethnomusicology* 12/2:284-85.

Navajo: Songs of the Diné; Apache: Songs by Philip and Patsy Cassadore of the San Carlos Tribe (2 records). *Ethnomusicology* 12/3:470-73.

Studies in Ethnomusicology, vol. 2, ed. Mieczyslaw Kolinski. *Western Folklore* 27:134-35.

The Anthropology of Music, by Alan P. Merriam. *Journal of Aesthetic Education* 2:139-42.

The Savage Mind, by Claude Lévi-Strauss. *National Elementary Principal* 47:93-95.

1969   *Ethnomusicology of the Flathead Indians*, by Alan P. Merriam. *Choice* 6/1:64.

Music in Aztec and Inca Territory, by Robert Stevenson. *Music Educators Journal* 55:79-80.

Music in Aztec and Inca Territory, by Robert Stevenson. *Choice* 6/2:286.

Dance and Song Rituals of Six Nations Reserve, Ontario, by Gertrude Prokosch Kurath. *Ethnomusicology* 13/2:380-82.

Navajo Sway Songs (record). *Ethnomusicology* 13/2:401-03.

My Music, My Life, by Ravi Shankar. *Choice* 6/4:520.

The Enduring Navaho, by Laura Gilpin. *Choice* 6/5-6:710-11.

Western Apache Witchcraft, by Keith Basso. *Choice* 6/10:1490.

The Albuquerque Navahos, by William H. Hodge. *Choice* 6/10:1492.

The Music Hunter: The Autobiography of a Career, by Laura Boulton. *American Anthropologist* 71:1005-08.

1970   *Blessingway: With Three Versions of the Myth, Recorded and Translated from the Navajo by Berard Haile*, ed. Leland C. Wyman. *Choice* 7/7:953.

The Navajo Mountain Community: Social Organization and Kinship Terminology, by Mary Shepardson and Blodwen Hammond. *Choice* 7/8:1149.

Indian Masks and Myths of the West, by Joseph H. Wherry. *Choice* 7/11:1672.

1971   *The American Rhythm*, by Mary Austin. *Choice* 8/5-6:842.

Memories of Navajoland (record), by Ed Lee Natay. *Ethnomusicology* 15/1:164-65.

Philip Cassadore Sings Apache Songs (record), by Philip Cassadore. *Ethnomusicology* 15/1:165-66.

Night and Daylight Yeibichei (record), by Klagetoh Navajo Singers. *Ethnomusicology* 15/1:167-70.

Navajo Skip Dance and Two-Step Songs (record). *Ethnomusicology* 15/2:296-97.

1972   *The Ethnomusicologist*, by Mantle Hood. *Choice* 9/4:1517.

Music and Dance of the Tewa Pueblos, by Gertrude P. Kurath with Antonio Garcia. *Ethnomusicology* 16/3:546-47.

Songs of the Teton Sioux, by Harry W. Paige. *South Dakota History* 2:181-83.

1973   *The Ethnomusicologist*, by Mantle Hood. *Journal of Research in Music Education* 21:187-88.

1975 *American Indian Music for the Classroom* (records and teaching guides), by Louis W. Ballard. *Music Educators Journal* 61:82, 85-86.

Pueblo Animals and Myths, by Hamilton A. Tyler. *Choice* 12/10:1298.

Peyote Hunt, by Barbara Meyerhoff. *Journal of Ethnic Studies* 3:106-08.

1977 *Cheyenne Peyote Songs*, vols. 1 and 2 (records), recorded by Tony Isaacs. *Ethnomusicology* 21/1:161-62.

Indian Artists at Work, by Ulli Steltzer, and *Walk in Beauty: The Navajo and Their Blankets*, by Anthony Berlant and Mary Hunt. *Parabola* 2:116, 118.

Songs of Earth, Water, Fire, Sky: Music of the American Indians (record), ed. Charlotte Heth. *Ethnomusicology* 21/3:523-24.

1978 *Giving Birth to Thunder, Sleeping with His Daughter, Coyote Builds North America*, ed. Barry H. Lopez. *Parabola* 3:105-06.

Hard Core Ethnography (Symposium on Form in Performance), ed. Marcia Herndon and Roger Brunyate. *Ethnomusicology* 22/2:354-55.

Oglala Religion, by William K. Powers. *South Dakota History* 8:161-63.

Language and Art in the Navajo Universe, by Gary Witherspoon. *Choice* 15/1:117.

1979 *Native North American Music and Oral Data: A Catalogue of Sound Recordings, 1893-1976*, by Dorothy Sara Lee. *Choice* 16/7:802.

A Cry From the Earth: Music of the North American Indian (book and record), by John Bierhorst. *Choice* 16/9:1209.

Sundancing at Rosebud and Pine Ridge, by Thomas E. Mails. *South Dakota History* 9:262-64.

1980 *Music as Culture*, by Marcia Herndon and Norma McLeod. *Ethnomusicology* 24/2:305-07.

Indian New England before the Mayflower, by Howard S. Russell. *Choice* 18/4:562.

1981 *Native American Music*, by Marcia Herndon. *Choice* 18/8:1134.

Cantometrics: An Approach to the Anthropology of Music, by Alan Lomax et al. *World of Music* 23:52-54.

Hand Me Doon de Fiddle: Shetland Fiddle Tunes for Bairns of Aa' Ages, by Tom Anderson and Pam Swing. *Wesleyan University Alumnus* 54/4:32.

1982 *Holy Wind in Navajo Philosophy*, by James Kale McNeley. *American Anthropologist* 84/2:467-68.

Navajo Symbols of Healing, by Donald Sandner. *Journal of American Folklore* 95:214-15.

Yuwipi: Vision and Experience in Oglala Ritual, by William K. Powers. *South Dakota History* 12/4:255-56.

1983 *Left Handed: A Navajo Autobiography*, ed. Walter Dyk and Ruth Dyk. *American Ethnologist* 10/1:207-08.

Music as Culture (rev. ed.), by Marcia Herndon and Norma McLeod. *Ethnomusicology* 27/1:123-24.

Now That the Buffalo's Gone: A Study of Today's American Indians, by Alvin M. Josephy, Jr., and *In the Spirit of Crazy Horse*, by Peter Matthiessen. *Parabola: Myth and the Quest for Meaning* 8/3:106-11.

1984   *The Musical Life of the Blood Indians*, by Robert Witmer. *Plains Anthropologist* 29/105:261-62.

Night Flying Woman: An Ojibway Narrative, by Ignatia Broker. *South Dakota History* 14/2:174.

In Press

The Main Stalk: A Synthesis of Navajo Philosophy, by John R. Farella. *American Anthropologist.*

Errata

Due to a realignment in the text by the publisher, please note the following:

Index / Subject

Index

Index

237

Index

Charlotte J. Frisbie, cultural anthropologist, is professor of anthropology at Southern Illinois University at Edwardsville. She earned a B.A. in music (cum laude) at Smith College, M.A. in ethnomusicology from Wesleyan University, and the Ph.D. in anthropology from the University of New Mexico. Other books she has written or edited are Kinaaldá: A Study of the Navajo Girl's Puberty Ceremony *(1967),* Music and Dance Research of Southwestern United States Indians *(Detroit Studies in Music Bibliography no. 36, 1977),* Navajo Blessingway Singer: The Autobiography of Frank Mitchell (1881-1967) *(with David P. McAllester, 1978),* Southwestern Indian Ritual Drama *(1980), and* Navajo Religion and Culture: Selected Views — Papers in Honor of Leland C. Wyman *(with David M. Brugge, 1982).* Navajo Medicine Bundles or Jish: Acquisition, Transmission and Disposition in the Past and Present *will be published by the University of New Mexico Press in 1987. She is active in the Society for Ethnomusicology and the American Anthropological Association. She and her husband Ted live on a farm, raising sheep and restoring their home with daughters Elizabeth and Jennifer. Her musical activities include singing, playing handbells, and being a church organist.*